Tracing Mobility and Identity

Bioarchaeology and bone chemistry
of the Bronze Age Sant'Abbondio cemetery
(Pompeii, Italy)

Mary Anne Tafuri

BAR International Series 1359
2005

Published in 2016 by
BAR Publishing, Oxford

BAR International Series 1359

Tracing Mobility and Identity

ISBN 978 1 84171 804 0

© M A Tafuri and the Publisher 2005

The author's moral rights under the 1988 UK Copyright,
Designs and Patents Act are hereby expressly asserted.

All rights reserved. No part of this work may be copied, reproduced, stored,
sold, distributed, scanned, saved in any form of digital format or transmitted
in any form digitally, without the written permission of the Publisher.

BAR Publishing is the trading name of British Archaeological Reports (Oxford) Ltd.
British Archaeological Reports was first incorporated in 1974 to publish the BAR
Series, International and British. In 1992 Hadrian Books Ltd became part of the BAR
group. This volume was originally published by Archaeopress in conjunction with
British Archaeological Reports (Oxford) Ltd / Hadrian Books Ltd, the Series principal
publisher, in 2005. This present volume is published by BAR Publishing, 2016.

Printed in England

BAR titles are available from:

        BAR Publishing
        122 Banbury Rd, Oxford, OX2 7BP, UK
EMAIL   info@barpublishing.com
PHONE +44 (0)1865 310431
FAX   +44 (0)1865 316916
        www.barpublishing.com

TABLE OF CONTENTS

CHAPTER ONE

MOBILITY AND SOCIAL DYNAMICS. THE ROLE OF DIET IN EXPLORING PAST BEHAVIOUR..................1
- INTRODUCTION 1
- MOBILITY BEYOND MIGRATION 1
- MOBILITY AND ITALIAN PREHISTORY 2
- THE CLASSICAL PROBLEM I. MOBILITY IN PASTORAL SOCIETIES OF THE ITALIAN BRONZE AGE 3
- THE CLASSICAL PROBLEM II. SOCIAL DYNAMICS AND GENDER ROLES IN THE BRONZE AGE OF ITALY 3
- GENDER AND MOBILITY 3
- FOOD AND IDENTITY 4
- DIET IN ECONOMY, SOCIETY AND IDENTITY 5
- TRACING MOBILITY ARCHAEOLOGICALLY. FOOD TO GO 6
  - *Trace element analysis, diet, and mobility: are we what we eat or are we where we eat?* 6
- THE CASE STUDY: SANT'ABBONDIO 7
- SUMMARY 7
- LINKING THE THEORETICAL BACKGROUND TO DATA EXPECTATIONS... 8

CHAPTER TWO

SANT'ABBONDIO. ARCHAEOLOGICAL DATA AND ANTHROPOLOGICAL ANALYSIS 10
- INTRODUCTION 10
- SOME DATA FROM THE EXCAVATIONS 10
- GEOGRAPHICAL, GEOLOGICAL AND PALEOENVIRONMENTAL DATA 12
- SANT'ABBONDIO SKELETAL SAMPLE 14
- THE BIOARCHAEOLOGICAL ANALYSIS 15
- OSTEOMETRIC ANALYSIS 15
- PALEOPATHOLOGIES 15
- DENTAL ANALYSIS 16
  - *Occlusal surface wear* 16
  - *Dental caries* 16
  - *Dental calculus and periodontal disease* 17
  - *Enamel defects* 17
  - *Dental non-metric traits* 18
  - *Discussion and comparisons* 18
  - *Archaeological and anthropological data* 20
- SUMMARY 22

CHAPTER THREE

ARCHAEOLOGICAL BONE CHEMISTRY. METHODOLOGICAL FRAMEWORK 23
- THE CHEMISTRY OF ANCIENT HUMAN BONE 23
  - *The chemical composition of human bone* 23
  - *The chemical composition of teeth* 23
- HUMAN METABOLISM AND TRACE ELEMENTS 24
  - *Elemental homeostasis, biochemical function and bioavailability* 25
  - *Vanadium (V)* 25
  - *Chromium (Cr)* 26
  - *Manganese (Mn)* 26
  - *Cobalt (Co)* 26
  - *Copper (Cu)* 26
  - *Zinc (Zn)* 27
  - *Arsenic (As)* 27
  - *Rubidium (Rb)* 27
  - *Strontium (Sr)* 27
  - *Nickel (Ni)* 27

    Zirconium (Zr) *27*
    Tin (Sn) *28*
    Lead (Pb) *28*
  The use of trace element data. Problems of diagenesis and 'elemental models' 28
  Single-element investigations and strontium studies 29
  Multi-elemental studies 29
  Previous multi-elemental investigations and methods for data analysis 30
  Inductively Coupled Plasma-Mass Spectrometry 30
  Sample preparation methods in this study 31
  Sample collection 31
  Sample preparation for ICP-MS analysis 33
  Assessing the reliability of the analysis 35
  Data preparation and analysis 35
  Summary 35

CHAPTER FOUR

SANT'ABBONDIO ICP-MS TRACE ELEMENT DATA ANALYSIS. ASSESSING DIAGENESIS 36

  Introduction 36
  Methods for assessing diagenesis 36
    Procedural criteria *36*
    Comparison with reference values *37*
    Comparison with soil *37*
    Comparison with fauna *38*
    Comparison between tissues *38*
    Observation of expected chemical behaviour *38*
    Observation of expected biological behaviour *39*
    Comparison with samples from other sites *39*
    Intra-site comparison *39*
  Assessing diagenesis at Sant'Abbondio 39
    Procedural criteria *40*
    Comparison with reference values *40*
    Comparison with soil samples from Sant'Abbondio and the Sarno area *43*
    Comparison between human and animal samples *46*
    Comparison between tissues *46*
    Testing expected chemical behaviour *47*
    Testing expected biological behaviour *48*
    Comparison with other humans *49*
    Intra-site comparison of individuals from Sant'Abbondio *50*
  Discussion 52

CHAPTER FIVE

SANT'ABBONDIO ICP-MS TRACE ELEMENT DATA ANALYSIS AND INTERPRETATION 55

  Introduction 55
  Data preparation and exploration – preliminary analysis 55
  Bivariate analysis 56
    Biogenic processes and biological factors *56*
    Subadult metabolism *56*
    Elemental variation in accordance with pathological conditions *57*
    Adult metabolism – sex and age differences *58*
  Non-biological factors 59
    Sex and differentiated diet *60*
    Geochemistry and mobility. Marrying in and eating out *61*
    Bone variation and male mobility in life *61*
    Enamel outliers and female exogamy *61*
    Organisation within the group: the eastern half of the cemetery vs. the western. *63*

SUMMARY 66

CHAPTER SIX

MOBILITY FOOD AND PRAXIS 67
    INTRODUCTION 67
    SANT'ABBONDIO TRACE ELEMENT DATA EXPLAINED THROUGH A CULTURAL PERSPECTIVE 67
    MOBILITY FOOD AND PRAXIS 70

REFERENCES CITED I

LIST OF FIGURES

CHAPTER TWO

FIG. 2.1 LOCATION OF SANT'ABBONDIO. 10

FIG. 2.2 LOCATION OF THE CEMETERY WITHIN POMPEII'S AREA. THE RIVER SARNO IS VISIBLE SOUTH OF THE SITE (IGM 1:25.000) (AFTER MASTROROBERTO 1998). 10

FIG. 2.3 SANT'ABBONDIO. PLAN OF THE MIDDLE BRONZE AGE CEMETERY. EAST AND WEST AREAS (RESPECTIVELY THE LONG STRETCH AND THE WIDER SECTION) RELATE TO THE TWO DIFFERENT SEASONS OF EXCAVATION. THE TWO SECTIONS ALSO CORRESPOND TO THE HILLTOP (EAST) AND ITS E-W SLOPE (WEST) TOWARDS THE RIVER (AFTER MASTROROBERTO 1998 MODIFIED AND INTEGRATED). 11

FIG. 2.4 THE SOMMA-VESUVIO VOLCANIC COMPLEX (AFTER CIVETTA *ET AL.* 1998). 13

FIG. 2.5 PALEODEMOGRAPHIC SUMMARY OF THE SANT'ABBONDIO SAMPLE. 15

FIG. 2.6 INDIVIDUAL 2/96, ROOF OF THE LEFT ORBIT- CRIBRA ORBITALIA. 16

FIG. 2.7 DISTRIBUTION OF DENTAL CARIES ACCORDING TO TEETH AFFECTED. THE TOTAL OF TEETH AFFECTED IS COMPARED TO THE TOTAL OF TEETH OBSERVED. 17

FIG. 2.8 FREQUENCY (IN % OF INDIVIDUAL AFFECTED/INDIVIDUAL OBSERVED) OF CARIES DISTRIBUTED BY SEX AND AGE AT DEATH. N=25. 17

FIG. 2.9 FREQUENCY (IN % OF INDIVIDUALS AFFECTED/INDIVIDUAL OBSERVED) OF CALCULUS DISTRIBUTED BY SEX AND AGE AT DEATH. N=20. 17

FIG. 2.10 FREQUENCY (IN % INDIVIDUAL AFFECTED/INDIVIDUAL OBSERVED) OF ENAMEL HYPOPLASIA DISTRIBUTED BY SEX. N=25. 18

FIG. 2.11 FREQUENCIES (%) OF NON-METRIC TRAITS (ASU METHODS) FOR UPPER AND LOWER TEETH. VALUES EXPRESS INDIVIDUALS SHOWING THE TRAIT/INDIVIDUALS OBSERVED. 19

FIG. 2.12 FREQUENCIES (IN % OF INDIVIDUALS AFFECTED/INDIVIDUALS OBSERVED) OF POST-CRANIAL PATHOLOGICAL CONDITIONS (PERIOSTITIS) AT SANT'ABBONDIO AND OTHER COMPARATIVE SAMPLES. SAB=SANT'ABBONDIO; GRV= GROTTA VECCHI; ML= MADONNA DI LORETO; CNV= COPPA NEVIGATA; TD= TOPPO DAGUZZO; MAR= MARCITA; GRS= GROTTA DELLO SCOGLIETTO. 19

FIG. 2.13 FREQUENCIES (IN % OF INDIVIDUALS AFFECTED/INDIVIDUALS OBSERVED) OF DENTAL PATHOLOGIES AT SANT'ABBONDIO AND OTHER COMPARATIVE SITES. SAB=SANT'ABBONDIO; ML= MADONNA DI LORETO; TD= TOPPO DAGUZZO; GRS= GROTTA DELLO SCOGLIETTO. 20

FIG. 2.14 FREQUENCIES (IN % OF INDIVIDUALS AFFECTED/INDIVIDUALS OBSERVED) OF ENAMEL HYPOPLASIA AND POROTIC HYPEROSTOSIS AT SANT'ABBONDIO AND OTHER COMPARATIVE SITES. SAB=SANT'ABBONDIO; GRV= GROTTA VECCHI; ML= MADONNA DI LORETO; TD= TOPPO DAGUZZO; GROTTA DELLO SCOGLIETTO. 20

FIG. 2.15 FREQUENCY (% OF TEETH AFFECTED/OBSERVED) OF DENTAL PATHOLOGIES FOR INDIVIDUALS BURIED IN THE TWO HALVES OF THE CEMETERY. 22

CHAPTER THREE

FIG. 3.1 MICROSCOPIC STRUCTURE OF CORTICAL BONE (AFTER MAYS 1998). 23

FIG. 3.2 SECTION OF A HUMAN TOOTH (FROM MAYS 1998 WITH MODIFICATIONS AFTER HILLSON 1996). 24

FIG. 3.3 INDUCTIVELY COUPLED PLASMA-MASS SPECTROMETER (AFTER JARVIS 1997 MODIFIED). 31

FIG. 3.4 AREA OF COLLECTION OF ENAMEL FROM THE CANINE (AFTER MALLEGNI AND RUBINI 1992 MODIFIED). 33

CHAPTER FOUR

FIG. 4.1. SANT'ABBONDIO. COMPARISON OF MEAN VALUES (EXPRESSED ON A LOGARITHMIC SCALE) OF ALL THE ELEMENTS FOR SOIL, BONE AND ENAMEL. MANGANESE (CIRCLED), CONSIDERED TO BE A HIGHLY MOBILE ELEMENT THEREFORE INDICATIVE OF DIAGENESIS, SHOWS HETEROGENEOUS CONCENTRATION IN THE VARIOUS SAMPLES. 45

FIG. 4.2 SANT'ABBONDIO. INDIVIDUAL 4(B)/96 – EASTERN HALF OF THE CEMETERY. COMPARISON OF ABSOLUTE CONCENTRATIONS (ON A LOGARITHMIC SCALE) OF ALL THE ELEMENTS FOR SOIL, BONE AND ENAMEL. THE DOTTED AREA SHOWS THE SPECTRUM OF ELEMENTS MORE SUBJECT TO DIAGENESIS. 45

FIG. 4.3 VANADIUM CONCENTRATION (PPM) IN HUMAN AND ANIMAL BONE SAMPLE FOR SANT'ABBONDIO AND COMPARATIVE SITES. AS= ANGLO-SAXON; POMPEII = ROMAN POMPEII; SAB= SANT'ABBONDIO. 46

FIG. 4.4 NICKEL CONCENTRATION (PPM) IN HUMAN AND ANIMAL BONE SAMPLES FOR SANT'ABBONDIO AND COMPARATIVE SITES. AS = ANGLO-SAXON; SAB = SANT'ABBONDIO. 46

FIG. 4.5 STRONTIUM CONCENTRATION (PPM) IN HUMAN AND ANIMAL BONE SAMPLES FOR SANT'ABBONDIO AND COMPARATIVE SITES (VALUES ARE EXPRESSED ON A LOGARITHMIC SCALE). AS = ANGLO-SAXON; POMPEII = ROMAN POMPEII; SAB = SANT'ABBONDIO. 47

FIG. 4.6 MANGANESE CONCENTRATION (PPM) IN HUMAN AND ANIMAL BONE SAMPLES FOR SANT'ABBONDIO AND COMPARATIVE SITES. AS= ANGLO-SAXON; POMPEII= ROMAN POMPEII; SAB= SANT'ABBONDIO. 47

FIG. 4.7 LINEAR REGRESSION ANALYSIS FOR CHROMIUM AND NICKEL CONCENTRATION IN ENAMEL SAMPLES. REGRESSION LINE IS DISPLAYED TOGETHER WITH CONFIDENCE INTERVAL BANDS (95%). INDIVIDUALS ARE DIVIDED BY SEX. A SLIGHT CORRELATION IS OBSERVABLE (RSQ = 0.6406). 47

FIG. 4.8 MANGANESE MEAN CONCENTRATION IN THE BONE ACCORDING TO AGE CLASSES (0= 0-10 YRS; 1=11-20 YRS; 2=21-30 YRS; 3=31-40 YRS; 4=40+ YRS), DIVIDED BY SEX. 48

FIG. 4.9 CHROMIUM MEAN CONCENTRATION IN THE BONE ACCORDING TO AGE CLASSES (0= 0-10 YRS; 1=11-20 YRS; 2=21-30 YRS; 3=31-40 YRS; 4=40+ YRS), POOLED BY SEX. 48

FIG. 4.10 STRONTIUM MEAN CONCENTRATION IN SANT'ABBONDIO FEMALES IN ACCORDANCE WITH AGE CLASSES. .48

CHAPTER FIVE

FIG. 5.1 SCATTERPLOT OF LEAD CONCENTRATION IN BONE AND ENAMEL. U= INDETERMINATE; M= MALES; J= JUVENILES; F= FEMALES. 57

FIG. 5.2 SCATTERPLOT OF COPPER CONCENTRATION IN BONE AND ENAMEL (VALUES ON THE X AXIS ARE EXPRESSED ON A LOGARITHMIC SCALE). U= INDETERMINATE; M= MALES; J= JUVENILES; F= FEMALES. 57

FIG. 5.3 SCATTERPLOT OF MANGANESE CONCENTRATION IN BONE AND ENAMEL (VALUES FOR BOTH AXES ARE EXPRESSED ON A LOGARITHMIC SCALE). U= INDETERMINATE; M= MALES; J= JUVENILES; F= FEMALES. 57

FIG. 5.4 SCATTERPLOT OF COBALT CONCENTRATION IN BONE AND ENAMEL. U= INDETERMINATE; M= MALES; J= JUVENILES; F= FEMALES. 58

FIG. 5.5 SCATTERPLOT OF CHROMIUM CONCENTRATION IN BONE AND IN ENAMEL (VALUES ON THE X AXIS ARE EXPRESSED ON A LOGARITHMIC SCALE). U= INDETERMINATE; M= MALES; J= JUVENILES; F= FEMALES. 58

FIG. 5.6 SCATTERPLOT OF NICKEL CONCENTRATION IN BONE AND ENAMEL (VALUES ON THE X AXIS ARE EXPRESSED ON A LOGARITHMIC SCALE). U= INDETERMINATE; M= MALES; J= JUVENILES; F= FEMALES. 58

FIG. 5.7 BAR CHART DEPICTING MEAN CONCENTRATIONS OF VANADIUM, MANGANESE, NICKEL AND STRONTIUM IN ENAMEL IN RELATION TO PRESENCE OR ABSENCE OF ENAMEL HYPOPLASIA. 59

FIG. 5.8 BAR CHART DEPICTING MEAN CONCENTRATIONS OF VANADIUM, MANGANESE, NICKEL AND STRONTIUM IN BONE IN RELATION TO PRESENCE OR ABSENCE OF ENAMEL HYPOPLASIA. 59

FIG. 5.9 SCATTERPLOT OF STRONTIUM CONCENTRATION IN BONE AND ENAMEL. U= INDETERMINATE; M= MALES; J= JUVENILES; F= FEMALES. 59

FIGURE 5.10 SCATTERPLOT OF RUBIDIUM CONCENTRATION IN BONE AND ENAMEL. U= INDETERMINATE; M= MALES; J= JUVENILES; F= FEMALES. 60

FIGURE 5.11 SCATTERPLOT OF VANADIUM CONCENTRATION IN BONE AND ENAMEL. U= INDETERMINATE; M= MALES; J= JUVENILES; F= FEMALES. THE ELLIPSES SHOW THE MALE/FEMALE CLUSTERING 60

FIGURE 5.12 BAR CHART DEPICTING THE MEAN CONCENTRATION OF VANADIUM, MANGANESE AND STRONTIUM IN BONE IN RELATION TO PRESENCE/ABSENCE OF CARIES. 60

FIGURE 5.13 SCATTERPLOT OF NIOBIUM CONCENTRATION IN THE BONE AND THE ENAMEL. U= INDETERMINATE; M= MALES; J= JUVENILES; F= FEMALES. 61

FIGURE 5.14 SCATTERPLOT OF TIN CONCENTRATION IN BONE AND ENAMEL. U= INDETERMINATE; M= MALES; J= JUVENILES; F= FEMALES. 62

FIGURE 5.15 SCATTERPLOT OF THORIUM CONCENTRATION IN BONE AND ENAMEL. U= INDETERMINATE; M= MALES; J= JUVENILES; F= FEMALES. 62

FIGURE 5.16 MEAN VALUES OF EACH ELEMENT CONSIDERED FOR ICP-MS ANALYSIS IN THE SOIL SAMPLES IN ACCORDANCE WITH THE TWO SECTIONS OF THE CEMETERY. 64

FIGURE 5.17 COBALT – CLUSTERS OF WESTERN FEMALES ALONG THE BONE AXIS. 64

FIGURE 5.18 VANADIUM – CLUSTERS OF WESTERN FEMALES ALONG THE BONE AXIS. THE ELLIPSE SHOWS THE WESTERN FEMALES. 64

FIGURE 5.19 STRONTIUM – CLUSTERS OF WESTERN FEMALES ALONG THE BONE AXIS. THE ELLIPSE SHOWS THE WESTERN FEMALES. 65

FIGURE 5.20 NIOBIUM – CLUSTER OF WESTERN FEMALES ALONG THE BONE AXIS. THE ELLIPSE SHOWS THE WESTERN FEMALES. 65

FIGURE 5.21 VANADIUM – DISTRIBUTION OF THE INDIVIDUALS ACCORDING TO AGE CATEGORIES. AGE CLASSES ARE EXPRESS IN YEARS. 65

FIGURE 5.22 STRONTIUM – DISTRIBUTION OF THE INDIVIDUALS ACCORDING TO AGE CATEGORIES. AGE CLASSES ARE EXPRESSED IN YEARS. THE ELLIPSE SHOWS THE WESTERN FEMALES. 65

FIGURE 5.23 NIOBIUM – DISTRIBUTION OF THE INDIVIDUALS ACCORDING TO AGE CATEGORIES. AGE CLASSES ARE EXPRESSED IN YEARS. 65

CHAPTER SIX

FIG. 6.1 SCHEME OF THE INTERPRETATION OF TRACE ELEMENT DATA FROM SANT'ABBONDIO. 69

LIST OF TABLES

CHAPTER ONE

TABLE 1.1 METHODOLOGICAL FRAMEWORK AND ICP-MS DATA EXPECTATION. 9

CHAPTER TWO

TABLE 2.1 SEX DIFFERENCES IN FEMORAL AND TIBIAL CROSS-SECTION. 15

TABLE 2.2 RESULTS OF THE KOLGOMOROV-SMIRNOV TEST FOR OCCLUSAL WEAR ON M1 AND M2 USING THE SCORING SYSTEM OF SCOTT (1979). 16

TABLE 2.3 FISHER'S EXACT TEST MEASURING THE DIFFERENCE IN OCCURRENCE OF NON-METRIC TRAITS ON THE MAXILLA ACCORDING TO AREA OF DEPOSITION IN THE CEMETERY (EAST VS. WEST). 18

TABLE 2.4 FISHER'S EXACT TEST MEASURING THE DIFFERENCE IN OCCURRENCE OF NON-METRIC TRAITS ON THE MANDIBLE ACCORDING TO AREA OF DEPOSITION IN THE CEMETERY (EAST VS. WEST) 18

TABLE 2.5 CROSSTABULATION FOR CATEGORIES OF INDIVIDUALS AND GRAVE GOODS. 21

TABLE 2.6 RESULTS OF THE FISHER'S EXACT TEST FOR CATEGORIES OF GRAVE GOODS IN ACCORDANCE WITH SEX OF THE INDIVIDUALS. 21

TABLE 2.7 CROSSTABULATION FOR CATEGORIES OF INDIVIDUALS AND GRAVE GOODS ACCORDING TO AREA OF DEPOSITION (EAST VS. WEST). 22

TABLE 2.8 FISHER'S EXACT TEST FOR MALES AND FEMALES AND JUVENILES TO MEASURE DIFFERENCES IN THE COMPOSITION OF GRAVE GOODS IN ACCORDANCE WITH THE AREA OF DEPOSITION. 22

CHAPTER THREE

TABLE 3.1 CHEMICAL COMPOSITION OF HUMAN ENAMEL AND BONE. 23

TABLE 3.2 LIST OF THE ELEMENTS CONSIDERED FOR ICP-MS ANALYSIS. 25

TABLE 3.3 RECORD OF SANT'ABBONDIO BONE, ENAMEL AND SOIL COLLECTION. 32

TABLE 3.4 SCHEME OF ICP-MS ANALYTICAL METHOD FOR BONE AND ENAMEL SAMPLES. 34

TABLE 3.5 SCHEME OF ICP-MS ANALYTICAL METHOD FOR SOIL SAMPLES. 34

CHAPTER FOUR

TABLE 4.1 SANT'ABBONDIO DATA CLASSIFICATION 40

TABLE 4.2 SANT'ABBONDIO MEAN VALUES (PPM) AND STANDARD DEVIATION FOR BONE SAMPLES WITH REFERENCE VALUES. 41

TABLE 4.3 SANT'ABBONDIO MEAN VALUES AND STANDARD DEVIATION FOR ENAMEL SAMPLES (IN PPM) WITH REFERENCE VALUES. 42

TABLE 4.4 MEAN AND STANDARD DEVIATION OF ELEMENTAL CONCENTRATION FOR SANT'ABBONDIO, AGEROLA, AND CASTELLAMMARE SOIL SAMPLES. 44

TABLE 4.5 MEAN AND STANDARD DEVIATION (PPM) OF THE ELEMENTAL CONCENTRATION (BONE ONLY) FOR SANT'ABBONDIO AND ROMAN POMPEII AND ANGLO-SAXON SITES. 49

TABLE 4.6 MEAN, STANDARD DEVIATION (IN PPM) AND COEFFICIENT OF VARIATION (IN %) OF THE ELEMENT CONCENTRATION OF BONE AND ENAMEL SAMPLES FROM SANT'ABBONDIO. 50

TABLE 4.7 SANT'ABBONDIO MEAN AND STANDARD DEVIATION (PPM) OF BONE AND ENAMEL ELEMENTAL CONCENTRATION FOR ADULTS DIVIDED BY SEX. 51

TABLE 4.8 SANT'ABBONDIO, MEAN AND STANDARD DEVIATION (PPM) OF BONE AND ENAMEL ELEMENTAL CONCENTRATION FOR JUVENILES (0-12 YEARS). 52

TABLE 4.9 SUMMARY OF THE RESULTS FROM THE DIFFERENT CRITERIA USED TO ASSESS DIAGENESIS AND DATA RELIABILITY AT SANT'ABBONDIO. 54

CHAPTER FIVE

TABLE 5.1 T-TEST OF THE Z-SCORES OF BONE AND ENAMEL VALUES DIVIDED BY SEX. RARE EARTH ELEMENTS ARE EXCLUDED. 55

TABLE 5.2 T-TEST ON THE CONCENTRATION OF RUBIDIUM IN THE BONE DIVIDED BY SEX. 60

TABLE 5.3 ABSOLUTE CONCENTRATIONS (IN PPM) OF RELEVANT ELEMENTS FOR THE GROUP OF OUTLYING FEMALES WITH INDICATION OF THE CUT-OFF LIMIT IN ACCORDANCE WITH PRICE *ET AL.*'S (1998) METHOD. 63

TABLE 5.4 T-TESTS FOR ELEMENTS SHOWING EAST/WEST PATTERNING. ONLY FEMALES ARE CONSIDERED. 64

ACKNOWLEDGEMENTS

I am particularly grateful to my supervisor Dr. John Robb (University of Cambridge, UK) and my co-supervisor Dr. Johanna Sofaer (University of Southampton, UK) for their help and guidance. To Prof. Giorgio Manzi (University of Rome, "La Sapienza", IT) and Loretana Salvadei (Museo Preistorico Etnografico "L. Pigorini", Rome, IT) for granting permission to use the skeletal material. I also wish to thank Dr. Marisa Mastroroberto (Soprintendenza Archeologica di Pompei, IT) for the authorization to use archaeological and anthropological data from the Sant'Abbondio site. Further thanks go to Rob Tykot (South Florida University, USA) for carrying out stable isotope analysis on a selection of samples. The following have made precious suggestions and significantly contributed to my work, Ruth Whitehouse, James Steele, Andrew Millard, Holger Schutkowski, Sonia Zakrezewski, Claude Albore Livadie, Kym Jarvis, Jo Greenwood, John Williams, Savino di Lernia, Anna Maria Mercuri; any mistake or omission is entirely my fault. Finally, very special thanks go to my partner for his inspiring perspective and his belief.

CHAPTER ONE
MOBILITY AND SOCIAL DYNAMICS. THE ROLE OF DIET IN EXPLORING PAST BEHAVIOUR

INTRODUCTION

The theoretical framework of this work places the emphasis on mobility as indicative of past dynamics, in social, economic or more general cultural terms. The means through which movement is to be identified is food consumption in its ability to define physical phenomena, i.e. mobility, as well as social ones, i.e. age, sex, gender, individual or collective identity. Two main aspects are in agenda, the archaeological use of bone chemistry in the reconstruction of past social dynamics and the use of these dynamics as new way of reading Italian prehistory. As a case study, the Middle Bronze Age cemetery of Sant'Abbondio (Pompeii, Naples) will be used. ICP-MS trace element analysis on human skeletal remains will be applied. The results will be used to explore theoretical hypotheses about social and economic structure of prehistoric groups of Central and Southern Italy.

Food is a material and therefore 'measurable' aspect of human life, although it carries immaterial meaning and offers a suitable ground to explore ideological as well as ontological concepts. The link between mobility and food resides in the idea of locality and in the assumption that nomadic or sedentary life would have implied, for prehistoric groups, a local-specific diet. It is in fact likely that on a general level, these groups gathered or grew their food within their surrounding environment. Hence reconstructing dietary habits informs us not only of past economy but also of past residence. It tells us where past people lived and how they engaged with their environment and with others. Overall it reflects human dynamics and these are unlikely to be exclusively economically driven. Food can offer the chance to infer ontological aspects of individual and social expression. Consumption can be related to age, sex and gender categories (Lupton, 1996; Counihan, 1999). After all, we are what we eat but, mostly, we eat according to what and how we are or believe to be.

The methodological use of human bone chemistry and more specifically ICP-MS trace element analysis on bone and dental enamel can help define paleonutrition in the study of locality. As will be discussed later in this work, the comparison between the two tissues will reveal the temporal and spatial dynamics of food consumption and allow us to examine social dynamics during the Bronze Age.

The traditional interpretation offered of Bronze Age society, as founded on patrilineal group based on a pastoral economy (Puglisi, 1959), represents the primary theoretical questions that underlies this research, however additional levels of complexity relating to this scenario are also investigated. The period of prehistory under study involves a specific conflation of economic and social dynamics. For Bronze Age people, moving equated to living, either in terms of the survival of the herd (through transhumance) or (in the case of exogamic exchanges) for the maintenance of the group. The patterns of mobility deriving from these dynamics are examined in this work as indicative of locality rather than of movement *per se*. Locality is traced via food consumption by virtue of its link with the environment.

If food consumption has the ability to track differentiated subsistence in relation to economic (transhumant pastoralism) or social (patrilineality) phenomena, within pastoral and patrilocal communities mobility may not only be restricted to a monolithic male-the-herder/female-the-bride pattern, but be rather more fluid. Diet, in fact, could reflect age-, sex- or gender-specific identities that fall beyond such a model.

Mobility is specifically the main subject of interest of this work, as it is conceived not as the mere consequence of past socio-economic choices but rather as the means through which such assumed choices could be explored in archaeology. What we need to consider is how mobility affected past *habitus* (*sensu* Bordieu 1977), where and how it influenced everyday life.

Social dynamics and identity have been reconstructed through material culture and burial practices (*e.g.* Sofaer Derevenski, 2000b), and, in a few cases, iconography (*e.g.* Barfield, 1998), although few works have relied on diet to investigate similar issues. The relationship with food becomes essential in this perspective. Animal as well as plant resources are linked to the environment and hence can be informative of locality. Furthermore, food and diet can be traced archaeologically and anthropologically through material culture and skeletal studies. Major support, for this perspective, is offered by ethnographical studies, used in the redefinition of traditional positions

MOBILITY BEYOND MIGRATION

Mobility is a universal aspect of social life. People move for economic interests, social relationships, political contacts, or following natural events. In archaeology, the concept of mobility is, or at least has been, normally associated with migration. The mass-movement of people has been approached by geographers and sociologists in the study of human behaviour while archaeologists have experienced a rather contradictory relationship with the issue, first relying on it to construct the basis of the evolution of culture (Childe, 1957), and then disregarding its importance as a result of the danger implied in earlier approaches and its inevitable association with diffusionism. This raises the fundamental question of why migration is seen as a mass movement of people. Why it is associated with a large group of persons and, nearly systematically, related to population pressure when it need not necessarily so? Migration is in fact mobility in its fundamental sense. To migrate is to move from place to place, and this can involve several levels of complexity in terms of space and time that would not alter the principle of the movement itself. To overcome linguistic misunderstandings and avoid ambiguous associations, the use of *mobility* will be preferred to the concept of *migration* in this work.

The first reconsideration of the study of mobility – in a non-migratory perspective – as a constructive contribution to archaeological discourse has been offered on an ecological basis. Scholars (see for example Binford, 1982; Gamble and Boismier, 1991) have focused on mobility mainly as an essential aspect of hunter-gatherer societies. In this viewpoint movement and economic strategies have often been portrayed as inter-dependent. Close (2000) stresses the limitation this kind of approach normally entails, as 'strategies' as opposed to 'dynamics' (Close 1991: 50) are examined. Moreover, mobility is normally perceived as the natural consequence of economic interest in its twofold nature of short-term or long-term occupation, and investigated through 'what is left behind' (Gamble 1991:1). Despite their essential contribution to archaeology, some of these approaches present a major limitation. They are confined to studies on early prehistory, and they understand mobility in typological terms (*sensu* Kelly, 1992) considering it as a monolithic issue to be investigated through a single perspective, which sometimes produces a simplistic picture of past societies, which inevitably results in a limited perception of their complexity.

Mobility is the bodily expression of several immaterial aspects of material life. It carries a meaning that goes beyond economic interests or social and demographic pressure, in other words is multidimensional, not least it can have a role in the definition of individual or social identity.

A great number of archaeological investigations focussed on mobility have dealt with the concept of space, particularly using a phenomenological approach, as opposed to that of residence, in an equation that opposes the concept of movement to that of location.

For phenomenologists, the stress is normally placed on the importance of moving as a way of experiencing the landscape and interacting with the environment or rather on the economic needs and social prerequisites movement implies and the technology and skill it involves. There has been little in archaeology on the importance of studying residence and locality as expressive of identity rather than economic strategies or environmental pressure. Residence has rather been investigated for in its connotation as the 'lived-in space', i.e. the home, particularly in terms of place where social relations are kept and individual identity is expressed (Sorensen, 2000).

Anthropological studies, on the other hand, have often used the concept of locality as representative of ontological aspects. Works by Andrew Strathern (1973) and Marilyn Strathern (1987), for example, have focused particularly on how for Highland and Lowland groups of New Guinea the idea of locality is strictly related to that of identity of the individual and of the group. The land is in fact the material expression of kinship and provenience: moving from one territory to another for Highland women signifies choosing to acquire a 'new' identity, which in their case assures agnatic descent. This implies nurturing their children through food coming from their husbands' land. Investigating mobility in terms of locality and residence could thus reveal kinship system and social dynamics in past communities as it does in modern ones.

Movement is linked to diet and food consumption through the relationship between resources and the environment. For subsistence economy, the relationship is expressed through the type of movement performed to gather and exploit foodstuffs within the ecosystem chosen or experienced. Within kinship organisation and residence patterns, food can be conceived as part of the *habitus* (*sensu* Bourdieu, 1977) in as much as it is connected with cultural and ideological phenomena as well as environmental ones. Food - gathered, produced and consumed - is the vehicle through which economic activity and social relations as ways of engaging with the lived-in space are expressed. The relevance of the concept of habitus is connected to its definition as a "system of durable, *transposable* disposition (…) which generate and organise practices and representations that can be objectively adapted to their outcomes" (Bourdieu, 1990: 53, emphasis added). For Bourdieu, knowledge is constructed and not passively experienced; in this perspective food consumption can contribute in the definition of knowledge and be used within practical relations. Particular relevance is given in this work to how such practical relations might have be transferred and adapted to other settings.

The disposition that regulated food consumption in the Bronze Age of Italy could have easily been moved across groups or households and may have been one of the means of expression of the *habitus* objectively transported.

Through this work, economic and social dynamics will be examined via mobility through the identification of locality – as the place of residence – rather than of the movement *per se* in a way that has seldom been discussed before in archaeology. Pastoral economy, post-marital residence and social exchanges will be approached through the identification of movement within groups. Particularly, the concept of gender will be explored (see below), and the way this has been dealt with in Italian prehistory. In order to better examine Puglisi's ideas on Bronze Age social structure and gender ideology, patterns of movement within the community – revealed through the link between food resources and the environment – will be commented upon.

Diet is perceived as invariably connected with the environment and hence linked with the notion of locality. Furthermore, the role of food in its expression of cultural identity (i.e. the use of food production strategy in the categorisation of the ethos) as well as that of a vehicle of the affirmation of the Self will be argued.

Before describing how mobility can be traced archaeologically it is however important to introduce how and with what effects this has been treated in Italian later prehistory.

MOBILITY AND ITALIAN PREHISTORY

The strong correlation between pastoralism and recent prehistory is often expressed in the reconstruction that Italian scholars have offered of the Bronze Age. Bronze Age economy is seen as founded on the herding of cattle and caprovids performed by semi-sedentary groups partially engaged in specialised or opportunistic forms of hunting, foraging and farming (Barker, 1986; Pellegrini, 1992; Albore Livadie, 1994; Malone *et al.*, 1994; Cazzella, 1994a; Bietti Sestieri, 1996). Such a perspective implies a number of economical, social and cultural presuppositions. These follow Salvatore Puglisi's (1959) work on the Bronze Age groups of Central and Southern Italy. In particular, for Puglisi, Central and Southern Italian Bronze Age societies descended from a '… nomadismo patriarcale e guerriero' (*ibid.*: 23) with nomadic male-dominated patrilineal and virilocal communities, based on transhumant pastoralism, where men were responsible for the larger part of the economy while women took care of all alternative means of subsistence such as gathering and food processing.

Puglisi's interpretation of material culture and mortuary practices carried two core concepts that will be explored in this work: i) the reconstruction of a herding economy model, and ii) the supposition of patrilineal kinship.

Both entail a specific kind of social dynamics that would have implied mobility performed differently by different members of the group. In Puglisi's idea, in an economy-specific mobility pattern men were likely to transfer to highland pastures seasonally while women remained in the village throughout the year, perhaps only moving on a daily basis. Conversely, in a descent-related mobility pattern, in this case a patrilineal one, females were likely to move during adulthood out of their group of origin and into the marital one while men were permanently resident within the natal community. A potentially valuable archaeological tool in the exploration of these models is bone chemistry used as a means to reconstruct past lifeways.

THE CLASSICAL PROBLEM I. MOBILITY IN PASTORAL SOCIETIES OF THE ITALIAN BRONZE AGE

In the late 1950s Salvatore Puglisi's book '*La Civiltà Appenninica. Origine e sviluppo delle comunità pastorali in Italia*' (1959) changed archaeology's perspective on the Bronze Age of Italy. In his work, Puglisi expanded on Rellini's (1932) concept of 'Apennine Culture' as a unifying process that included regions of Central and Southern Italy (those in contact with the Apennine Mountains). He argued that for a period that extended from the later phase of the Copper Age (2000 BC) to the end of the Bronze Age (900 BC), so-called Apennine groups showed a significant homogeneity in material evidence, economic strategies and social complexity, in a way that gave new meaning to the concept of 'culture', no longer defined by historicist tradition or typological sequences.

Despite its age, Puglisi's book is still an innovative piece of work in the Italian archaeological tradition, especially when considering how some Italian scholars tend to have excessive reliance upon pottery studies. Puglisi's Marxist approach set the agenda on the importance of environmental conditions in the definition of Apennine groups' economic strategies, while still managing not to fall into the environmental determinist trap. For Puglisi, Apennine groups originated from earlier Gaudo and Rinaldone cultures, considered nomadic by virtue of the lack of large settlements and the use of isolated collective tombs. His reconstruction of Bronze Age pastoral communities implied a precise type of economic dynamics with herders likely to move on a seasonal basis, transferring the animals to highland areas during the summer season only to return later during the year. Within Puglisi's reconstruction, and in accordance with later theories (Barker, 1981), not all the members of the group were involved in this transhumance. Only a selection of people, supposedly men, left a relatively sedentary group to spend several months in a different environment. This movement implied specific differential effects in terms of food consumption for those who were leaving as well for those who were staying. For traditional material culture-based archaeology these may be difficult to detect as a different perception or significance attached to an individual or an activity may not leave traces in the archaeological record. However, the one aspect Bronze Age people were differently experiencing as a consequence of their mobility that might be identified archaeologically is diet. For transhumant herders living somewhere different from the rest of the community meant eating different foodstuffs, and despite a number of resources they might have carried with them from the village, they must have relied on the local environment for survival. Such an environment might have been (ecologically and geochemically) very different from the one they departed from, and left – through diet – a series of traces in their bodies.

THE CLASSICAL PROBLEM II. SOCIAL DYNAMICS AND GENDER ROLES IN THE BRONZE AGE OF ITALY

In recent Italian works, the idea of patriarchal Bronze Age societies has been accepted *a priori* rather than discussed, and used as a means of interpreting archaeological data rather than being the object of investigation itself. The discussion of social organisation and gender roles in Italian recent prehistory has suffered the hegemony of 'wider' issues such as that of the emergence of social complexity. Gender and ideology have been conceived as a 'solved' problem, so that male power and female 'subjection' to a male-dominated system needed not be further investigated. This very crude reconstruction does not imply that no contribution has been made to the identification of social identity nor that gender has been ignored *tout court*. Scholars like Cazzella and Moscoloni (1995) and Bietti Sestieri (1992) have focussed on the study of kinship systems and gender roles. Archaeological evidence from recent prehistory of Italian contexts does not allow the subversion of traditional assumptions although it provides sufficient data to attempt innovative approaches. Others like Robb (1994) and Barfield (1986), for example, have tackled the issue of gender roles in a constructive way coming to conclusions that integrate well with the existing evidence and offer a pioneering perspective within Italian studies. More generally, the need to come to alternative theories has been successfully discussed by Whitehouse (1998).

Puglisi (1959) and other Italian archaeologists (Cazzella and Moscoloni, 1995) identify the social structure of Italian communities of the Bronze Age as patrilineal, characterised by progressive complexity originally based upon gender ideology with kin organisation through descent along the male line (see for example Cazzella, 1984). Puglisi's idea of Italian Bronze Age society is based on kinship organisation and social dynamics of patriarchal groups organised in virilocal systems, with female mobility related to post-marital residence. Agnatic descent in fact implied the movement of women out of the group of origin and into the marital one. This fell within traditional interpretations applied in kinship studies (cf. Lévi-Strauss, 1969) but may also be the result of the strong correlation, proposed even by more recent Italian scholars, between systems of lineage and residence models (cf. Bietti Sestieri, 1992). Bronze Age females were thus mobile by virtue of the matrimonial system adopted by the community they lived in. Workers adopting this model have implied that if they were to marry out of the group or household of origin, they could have carried with them their (original) cultural and ideological beliefs and later adopted new ones. If women were moving within set kinship systems, the traces of this movement would have been reflected in a change in dietary habits, if not in terms of the type of resources used then surely in terms of their chemical properties as a result of geochemical interaction with the environment. If women and men were moving in different ways and at different stages of their lives this must have had an effect on their dietary system.

GENDER AND MOBILITY

As a substantial part of this work there is the identification of gender-related behaviour through the analysis of mobility and residence patterns, with a particular emphasis on how gender relations are able to define social phenomena not only through the recognition of women, as no more invisible to the archaeological eye, but rather through the identification of systems of connection based on gender ideology and identity.

More recent archaeological works (Whitehouse, 1998; Sorensen, 2000; Whitehouse, 2001) seem to emphasise the definition of social relations through an engendered perspective rather than trying to participate in the feminist battle against masculine domination.

This position is of relevance to the present study as in Italian archaeology the issue of gender is rarely approached and could represent a valuable tool in the re-consideration of social relations and identity in the past. In Italian archaeology, the question of gender has rarely been addressed if not through a 'naive' approach (Whitehouse, 2001: 50), where sex and gender had a one to one relationship. Italian prehistorians have restricted their attention to very limited fields of the theoretical debate, focussing on more general concepts, mostly associated with 'society'. The latter has been studied in terms of its formation and development or in the structuring of its complexity mainly in light of the consequences it has for the generation of material culture. An understanding of internal dynamics, the need to – borrowing Whitehouse's idea – 'challenge the stereotypes' (Whitehouse, 1998) has seldom been on the agenda, leaving open questions that were more likely to be interrogated by Anglo-American scholars.

Within Italian archaeology, Bronze Age prehistoric groups have been traditionally conceived as patrilineal and patrilocal (Puglisi, 1959), and female mobility has been read in this context as a sign of women's subjection to male power and control over social or cultural phenomena. Conversely, when mobility was performed by men this was believed to be the sign of an exclusive male system of networking either in economic or social milieu. This is clearly a case of what has been defined as the maleness of the agent (Gero, 2000), in a vision of the world that limited women's participation within the community (Wylie, 1997). This evident dualism, this active-male/passive-female *cliché*, raises a fundamental question: how can the same phenomenon (mobility) lead to such different interpretations in a supposedly uniform socio-cultural context. In many traditional ethnographic studies women's mobility within different kinship systems has been implicitly conceived as her 'natural' inferiority to man. In Lévi-Strauss's words, either within patrilineal or matrilineal kinships, it is 'men who exchange women and not *vice versa*' (Lévi-Strauss, 1969: 115). Marylyn Strathern (1987) identifies this western cultural misconstruction with our tendency to interpret women's mobility within patrilineal systems as their natural negative asymmetry with men. In her view, the inferiority of women who move from one community to the other as if they were 'objects' is taken for granted rather than questioned and this distracts from the real object of attention: the study of socio-historical processes. Strathern's work undeniably centres the question. In Italy, several attempts (*e.g.* Bietti Sestieri, 1992; Robb, 1994; Robb, 1997; Barfield, 1998) have been made to identify mobility in connection to gender roles within recent prehistory. The main focus has been on material culture or skeletal studies, both likely to carry ideological meaning. Food consumption has seldom been approached in this perspective although it could potentially represent a methodological alternative to traditional approaches.

FOOD AND IDENTITY

The main contribution to the study of food and consumption in archaeological discourse comes from social anthropology and cultural studies (*e.g.* Lévi-Strauss, 1966; 1970; Douglas, 1983; Harris, 1986; Fischler, 1988; Lupton, 1996). Scholars have dealt with food and diet in modern and past societies, demonstrating how the apparently automatic action of eating can carry deeper significance.

The importance of food is understood here as a means to reveal cosmological concepts as well as personal ones, in particular identity. Fischler (1988: 275) well explains how food is essential to express 'people's oneness and the otherness of who eats differently'. In archaeology, this pattern of dietary/identity association is traditionally used as a means to distinguish different *ethos* both in cultural and chronological terms (hunter-gatherers, foragers, farmers, herders). However, if we agree that food identifies people, any archaeological investigation should concentrate on two main aspects of this process of identification: 1) how can we recognise food production and consumption, and, mainly 2) how do we interpret it.

Whereas investigations into food production have a long tradition in archaeology that encompasses technology to archaeozoology and paleobotanics through art and representation, interest in food consumption is relatively recent. Harris's (1986) materialist view on how food has a main nutritional purpose that goes beyond any structuralist symbolic investment forms part of a point of departure, although his subversion of Lévi-Strauss's dictum and his idea of 'good or bad food to eat' as 'good or bad food to think' oversimplifies the question. Food is normally culturally (and socially) constructed, just as its 'norms for consumption' are frequently culturally and socially transmitted. Consumption, moreover, obviously carries a metaphysical role and importance that surpasses its biological function, beyond any environmental influence or economic system. In archaeology, a good example is Hamilakis's work (1999) on Cretan contexts, where environmental factors may have influenced a group's productive economy but the significance and the scope of this production are endowed with deeper values.

The process of interpreting food and consumption is however a far more complex one than that of identifying its origin and mode of production. The core issues are:
- how can food affirm oneself, and
- how can food be an instrument of interaction.

Food, the body and the self have been the object of many significant works in cultural studies (Fischler, 1988; Lupton, 1996; Counihan, 1999). The debate on food and personal identity is still an ongoing process, although detailed discussion of this topic is beyond the scope of this work. In this work emphasis will be placed on how food expresses natural or cultural 'categories' of people in the expression of their *social* identity.

To eat is to live, but not only this; when we are born one of our first experiences is expressed through nourishment, and if we consider it more closely the act of receiving milk from our mother is also our first 'social interaction'. This mechanism of *consuming/connecting* is perpetuated throughout our lives. Although feeding ourselves is innate and follows an instinctual mechanism – even after weaning – the process of experiencing what to eat and who to eat it with is far from being a straightforward matter. If we would choose not to eat or drink we would abdicate our life not only in its biological form but also in its social and cultural expression. By performing an essential activity we thus cement social, cultural, and environmental experiences.

For Hastorf (1991: 132), the distribution of food 'can express political, social, and economic relationships as well as nutrition'. This range of relations leaves us with a virtually unlimited field of investigation. What is important to identify here is the level upon which this information can be deciphered. In Fischler's (1988) work, the archaeological discourse seems to suffer the vulnerability of one interpretative level, which stands between the ability of food to identify the collective and its capability to identify the self. The power of food to assert collective identity into the external world is unequivocal. Lupton (1996) points out how the experience of eating and drinking is essential to the way we live *in* and *through* our body. This mechanism is explicit in modern societies (anyone who is vegetarian or had a vegetarian guest for dinner knows how much food habits influence a social experience), where the notion of edibility is in certain circumstances culturally constructed. For past populations the equation subsistence/culture is even more rooted, and has sometimes been overexploited. What is questioned here is how within an inside/outside opposition (one culture as opposed to other cultures), deeper levels of insight can be reached. Fischler's oneness/otherness concept seems to be based mainly on an inter-societal level, but how does food distinguish within the same context or community? In modern societies, food emphasises the boundaries between natural categories such as age and gender (*e.g.* some foodstuffs are considered not suitable for children; others are strongly associated with one gender as opposed to the other). In the past, did food differentiate within natural or cultural classifications? Were age, sex, and gender differently perceived? And if so, was this different perception expressed through consumption?

Without falling into the biological deterministic trap and considering the importance of the social and cultural investment in natural concepts, if we were to start from a general level, we could agree that past societies have demonstrated the recognition of at least two cosmological values embracing individuality: age and gender (see Robb, 1994). In European archaeology these cosmological values are expressed in spheres such as material culture or burial practice and have been used for a long time as an immediate way of perceiving past human beliefs. The advent of gender archaeology has demonstrated that not only have these categories been overlooked for a long time but also that the focus on a simplistic reading of them has failed to reveal how socially complex they can be. In her book Sørensen (2000) reviews how the cultural nexus of gender is often disregarded and attached to its biological significance. Sofaer Derevenski (1997; 2000a, in prep.) further demonstrates how the issue of age in archaeology undergoes harder treatment, often being ignored *tout court*.

Age, sex and gender are all vehicles of one's identity. We define ourselves and others through the recognition of our biography (*sensu* Robb, 2002), both through our biological sex and our cultural gender. According to the Cartesian model our identity is somehow twofold; it is expressed both through our body and our mind. Phenomenology rejects this idea of a distinction between the mind and the Being, or as Heidegger puts it, between the Being and the Man (Heidegger, 1969: 31). Nevertheless this concept of duality is often repeated – at different levels of expression – in the debate of self-consciousness. Thomas's (1996: 11) description of Lacan's idea of the Self places the accent on how identity is cognitively 'built-up' from childhood, and only completed through verbalisation (language), primarily, through the discovery of the 'non-self', *i.e.* the Other. This dichotomy of oneness/otherness is the core concept to be developed here. What is argued is the coexistence of different levels of identity for a single individual or group. A good example for this comes from Robb's (1994) idea of stigmatisation (of other individuals – such as witches or criminals – or other groups) as a source of coalition within Italian prehistoric societies. The opposition between the Self and the Other is thus an undoubted means of expressing one's identity, but how many contrapositions can one convey at the same time? If we think of ourselves, we can recognise several cognitive levels through which we can express our identity: our age, our sex, our gender, our language, our ethos or our political beliefs. All of these factors bond us to different categories of people and describe us in different ways. So alongside a Self/Other dichotomy, should also coexist multiple levels of oppositions that relate the Self to the external world. One of these relations is expressed through food consumption. Differences in food consumption among groups of individuals will thus be examined at Sant'Abbondio as a way of identifying social categories sharing communal identities.

DIET IN ECONOMY, SOCIETY AND IDENTITY

The use of food production and consumption in archaeology in general and in prehistoric archaeology in particular has been mainly directed towards the reconstruction of a past people's identity in a rather categorical fashion. Either chronologically or culturally, subsistence economy has had the ability to identify past *ethos* through the reconstruction of prehistoric communities of hunter-gatherers, foragers, herders or farmers, and very rarely has their culture been divorced from their economy. This tradition mirrors the tendency to identify pots with people and originates in what could be renamed the tradition of 'food as people'. It should be borne in mind that, just as material culture is not the direct equivalent of past identities, food consumption could lead to interesting outcomes that diverge from an economy-driven identification of past histories.

It is indisputable that food has a social and ideological dimension (Sorensen, 2000). Today, as in the past, the act of eating and drinking is one of the principal practices of connecting; it is a basic process through which we express our complexity as a 'social hearth' around which we can assess our relationship with the 'external world'. In this work, the relationship between people and food is used through the material trace it leaves in the human body and explored in the ideological significance it may carry within a society as well as across cultures. Specifically, it is used as a means to understand social relations and beliefs within a community. For this purpose, it is conceived in its twofold nature, as described by Fischler (1988: 275): i) food as 'from biological to cultural' (from its nutritional function to its 'symbolic' one); ii) food as 'from individual to collective' (linking the psychological to the social).

Diet is not seen as a system of symbols through which pre-existing categories are expressed. Overall diet is not perceived as a symbol at all; if body and mind are two ways of expressing the same thing (Ingold, 2000), food is perceived here as an aspect interacting with both.

Through skeletal studies, trace element analysis can be conceived as the most direct way to elucidate past lives, through the study of the producer of culture rather than the product itself. The strong limitation osteological investigations have often entailed, as a result of the state of preservation of the skeletal remains, have however often generated a partial reconstruction. Such limitations can be overcome through the employment of bone chemistry. In bioarchaeology, sometimes nature and culture coincide, leaving little space for constructive conclusions (cf. Sofaer Derevenski, 2000a). Recent works stand as good examples of how osteological data allow deeper inferences on past lives and offer the chance to reconstruct 'archaeological biographies' (sensu Robb, 2002) that move away from biological ones. The only limitation of this approach is the quality of the material available. In this case the poor state of preservation of Sant'Abbondio's skeletal material encourages us to pursue alternative routes to traditional osteological analysis. Bone chemistry does not require wholesale preservation of skeletal series, and may provide a methodological link to identify ontological concepts within prehistoric societies. Through trace element analysis, diet is the bridge used to connect (or better, re-connect) past individual histories to collective ones, moving from one to the other.

TRACING MOBILITY ARCHAEOLOGICALLY. FOOD TO GO

Tracing movement of people in relation to the reconstruction of social dynamics poses the question of how this can be identified archaeologically. The most common approaches would bring us to trace the circulation of objects in order to define that of people. This however limits our ability to capture the complexity of cultural phenomena, as objects, as opposed to people, do not have age, sex, gender or bodies. Furthermore, the analysis of material culture is also restricted by the level of preservation of such objects.

The use of trace element analysis of human bones could be conceived as a methodological alternative for the study of mobility in ancient communities, tracing movement through *people* rather than *things*. The human skeleton is considered as a biological archive of past lifeways that offers a precious opportunity to detect 'adaptive and behavioural shifts in the past' (Larsen, 1997: 5). In this perspective, the nexus between mobility and people is expressed via food, as where we eat is where we live, and what we eat is how we live. Food and diet can help us to define past dynamics and can be traced osteoarchaeologically. As Sanford (1992: 80) stated, 'bone has the ability to exist in a dynamic relationship with the environment'. In this case for 'bone' we mean the entire human skeleton, including teeth, and for 'environment' we should consider the geological background of the area in which the sample studied is situated. Bone has a 'life span' that ranges between 7 to 10 years, during which it undergoes a process of complete chemical remodelling through elemental absorption and excretion (Mays, 1998). The intake of minerals in the form of either major or trace elements through the gastrointestinal tract is achieved via food and ground water. The analysis of the elemental composition of bone can therefore illustrate the elemental intake from a specific environment during the last 7-10 years of an individual's life. Hence trace element variation relates to, and can record, both diet and the geological environment in which a person lived. Teeth, on the other hand, do not remodel and are considered in Groupe's (1998: 337) words, 'archives of childhood'. Their chemical matrix is formed during a growth process that starts *in utero* and continues until early adulthood. Specifically, dental enamel is formed during childhood (as the tooth grows from the point to the root) over a period between first 10 to 15 years of life. They thus record developmental processes and diet during early life within a specific geological environment. Dealing with samples reflecting two different stages of life characterised by two different chemical histories allows us to trace two different moments of the 'dynamic relationship' between people and environment, described by Sanford (1992). Social dynamics, in this case mobility, can be traced through the observation of patterns of variation or consistency between the tissues, of a single subject or between individuals. This can be achieved – life span-wise – either synchronically or diachronically and will be examined in this work through food.

Trace element analysis, diet, and mobility: are we what we eat or are we where we eat?

Bone chemistry has been applied to trace past economy and environment (see Schoeninger, 1981), to identify social differences (see Larsen, 1997; chapters 2 and 7), and in numerous cases to inform us of life and health conditions (see for example, Martin *et al.*, 1985; Stuart-Macadam, 1989). The association between trace element studies and mobility is only relatively recent. Work on North American populations has been undertaken by several scholars (Schneider and Blakeslee, 1990; Price *et al.*, 1994; Ezzo, 1997). Within European prehistory a similar investigation, on Bell Beaker groups, has been carried out by Price *et al.* (1998). All of these works have used human bone *and* enamel in a comparative perspective based on the histological differences of these two tissues. Despite the innovative nature of these studies, two major issues need to be discussed. First of all, each of these works has concentrated on one or a small spectrum of elements (among which strontium generally had the leading role). Secondly, but most importantly, the use of the results in terms of population dynamics has been rather circumscribed.

Strontium has a long tradition of studies in archaeology that has been codified in the so-called 'strontium model' (Sandford, 1993) allowing bone chemistry investigations to be informative and reliable, especially when it comes to diagenesis. Nevertheless, Strontium is not the only element that can describe past diet, and is not as informative on its own as it would be if associated with other elements. The advantages of multi-elemental investigations have been intensively described by Sandford (1992) and are further discussed below. It is however important to point out a number of issues relevant to this research. Not all elements have a similar biochemical function in the human organism, and not all elements follow a similar pattern of behaviour. There are considerable differences in the order of magnitude of the elemental concentration, the level of synergy or antagonism with other elements, the potential nutritional or toxic effect, and the variance in accordance with sex and age or health status. Each of these elements can contribute to archaeological discourse especially in relation to the biochemical significance they carry within human metabolism.

A further limitation to mobility-oriented trace element studies consists of the restricted application these have entailed nearly systematically. Price *et al.*'s works, although extremely constructive, have focussed on the explication of mobility through one phenomenon: kinship relations in terms of post-marital residence within prehistoric groups. In other words they assume mobility is a unidimensional social phenomenon. This leaves us with a rather discouraging picture leading us to the belief that trace element analysis of human tissues can *either* represent past diet (and therefore economy) *or* past mobility (and therefore society). No attempts have been made to reconstruct the two at the same time, or simply to explore further issues. Trace elements – just like stable isotopes – are seen as paleonutrition detectors that seldom offer the chance to infer on alternative levels.

The use of multi-elemental trace element analysis is perceived in this research not only as a way of reconstructing the social *and* economic scenario of Italian recent prehistory through the identification of patterns of mobility, but also as the vehicle of deeper levels of significance that relate to ontological concepts such as gender ideology and social identity. The use of a mobility-related bone chemistry study is pioneering in Italian archaeology and, on a wider scale, could represent an alternative to the tradition of single-elemental approaches. ICP-MS results will be understood not only as the direct consequence of changes within the economy or the society but also in relation to issues that, especially for Italian recent prehistory, are in strong need of further debate.

THE CASE STUDY: SANT'ABBONDIO

In this research, trace element analysis is carried out on human skeletal remains from the Middle Bronze Age cemetery of Sant'Abbondio (Pompeii, Naples – Southern Italy) (see Figure 4.1). The site represents one of the few Middle Bronze Age necropolises from Campania and offers a good context to test the theoretical premises outlined earlier. Archaeological (Mastroroberto, 1998) and anthropological (Chapter Two, this volume; Tafuri *et al.*, 2003) analyses have identified a large, homogeneous, community settled in an area geographically ideal for the practice of transhumance where contact with nearby groups was assured by the presence of natural pathways. Excavations were undertaken by the *Soprintendenza Archeologica di Pompei* between 1992 and 1996, and although the cemetery has not been fully published yet, preliminary data are already available (Mastroroberto, 1998). A total of 70 burials were excavated (*ibid*.: 135) and the remains of 62 individuals were recovered.

Bone and dental enamel samples were collected from each individual and treated for chemical analysis according to methods available in the relevant literature (Lambert *et al.*, 1990) (see Chapter Three this volume). Trace element analysis was performed through Inductively Coupled Plasma-Mass Spectrometry (ICP-MS) with a procedure tailored according to the sample tested (bone as opposed to enamel). The decision to use the ICP-MS procedure has originated from the intention to pursue a multi-elemental approach. As stressed by a number of authors (see for example Hatcher *et al.*, 1995; Jarvis, 1997) plasma analyses can be carried out at relatively high temperatures, facilitating the detection of a wide spectrum of elements at a very low resolution. Moreover, as will be discussed more extensively further on, plasma methods are considerably faster and more inexpensive compared to others. A spectrum of 32 elements from the categories of essentials, non-essentials, and Rare Earth Elements, was selected to gather a range of different information in relation to the biochemical role of each element within the human organism and their function in terms of the relationship (via food and water) between humans and the environment. In this perspective, the volcanic nature of the area under study is not only a good historical source but also a geological specific that provides us with a wide range of information. It is evident that under strong geological and pedological variation, the detection of short-term as well as long-term mobility can have less problematic results. ICP-MS data were tested for diagenesis and post-depositional effects in accordance with the standard procedure available, and analysed through a range of statistical approaches.

The theoretical framework described earlier in this chapter produces a set of expectations in terms of trace element data. Transhumance economy models according to Puglisi's perspective (but also according to Barker 1981) should imply short term or seasonal movements of smaller groups of people within a fundamentally residential system. In this case, trace element data should yield clusters of small numbers of individuals bearing the traces of such movement, in relation to their adulthood. We might especially expect males to be moving between groups. A supposedly virilocal model would result in male homogeneous chemical compositions for bone and enamel as a consequence of men's residential system. Females, on the contrary, would present heterogeneous patterns across bone and enamel with homogeneity with the group for adult life (bone) and differentiation in the chemical reflection of childhood (enamel).

Having described a plausible socio-economic scenario we should not assume that patriarchal pastoral communities necessarily implied exclusive female mobility versus male stability or exclusive male pastoral transhumance. Such an assumption would inevitably lead to the idea of mobility as a monolithic feature, expressed in schematic units of pre-determined conditions. It would suggest that only one type of movement could relate to one type of society and occur at one time. An essential part of this analysis argues for the concept of mobility as multidimensional, represented within a single context at many different levels of expression. Bronze Age society used mobility in different spheres of daily life. Movement was used in the formation of social relations, and for economic purposes, it was also part of trade and contacts between different communities.

SUMMARY

When outlining the cultural scenario of Bronze Age Central and Southern Italy, it becomes evident how important it is to further investigate its social dynamics. The Bronze Age is a period of profound transformation in Italy as elsewhere in the Mediterranean. New economic models are adopted; material culture increases in diversity and sophistication, while the social system seems to move towards more complex schemes. Within such a scenario it is essential not only to critique known interpretations but to address new questions and diversify theoretical as well as methodological approaches. A means through which a new approach can be reached lies in the analysis of mobility in its significance and complexity within a context.

The previous pages have highlighted the different types of mobility, which appeared to have taken place in the Bronze Age contexts of Central and Southern Italy. Economic, social, and political needs might have been involved, all of which could have brought different categories of individuals the need to be mobile across various levels of distance and time. It becomes evident how a multidimensional approach to mobility becomes important. Mobility is differently motivated and approached. Single phenomena as accountable for movement (*cf.* Kelly 1992) are no longer appropriate to consider. From this perspective, mobility in the Bronze Age of Italy cannot be treated as a monolithic issue. Movement of people and therefore ideas, ideologies, and identities originates from different causes (*i.e.* trade, migration, intermarriage) and can lead to different effects. In Puglisi's (1959) interpretation these causes are either pastoralism or patrilocality and apply respectively to men and women in a way that imposes a scheme of reasoning that applies only one type of mobility to one specific gender, leaving little space for alternative patterns. In this work it is proposed that, within single communities, different types of mobility could apply to different groups of individuals, across social or natural categories. Through mobility, further levels of social complexity can be reached, as in accordance with social relations that are defined by systems of "individual and collective practices" (Bourdieu, 1990: 54).

LINKING THE THEORETICAL BACKGROUND TO DATA EXPECTATIONS

A series of expectations, deriving from the theoretical premises described in this chapter, can be created in terms of trace element results. The consumption of food gathered or produced in a specific environment is able to reveal locality in past Bronze Age society, as dietary regime can be identified through trace element analysis on human bone and enamel. This can, in turn, be connected with the various patterns of mobility through the identification of the different environments with which people interact through food. Table 1 is offered as a general guideline for the use and interpretation of trace element data for a range of archaeological scenarios. It is intended as a methodological bridge between the theoretical framework offered here and the data analysis and interpretation presented in Chapter Five. In this scheme, the two main issues involved in the analysis of mobility are the time implied (short-term or long-term mobility) and the space covered by the movement.

Given the different types of mobility that characterise the Bronze Age, we should expect to be confronted with multiple patterns of movement connected to different dietary regimes, resulting from linked sets of trace element data. In Campania in particular, we could predict movement due to subsistence strategies, and specifically pastoralism in the surrounding Apennines Mountains according to a seasonal vertical system (cf. Khazanov, 1983). Transhumant pastoralism would have involved episodic movements, producing differences in the chemical composition of the bone for the people involved in such a nomadic lifestyle. However, mobility due to trade and exchange is also likely to produce a similar pattern of bone elemental composition. It is therefore essential to use archaeological data to back up trace element results in order to distinguish between one mobility scenario as opposed to the other.

In terms of social relations, multifaceted patterns of variation in the elemental composition of bone and enamel are likely to be encountered on the level of categories of individuals. Heterogeneity between enamel and bone values could be related to a movement reflected in the difference in chemical life during childhood as opposed to adulthood. Groups of females with contrasting composition of bone and enamel could reflect marriage exchanges between communities, while sub-groups of a wider community, represented by classes of age and sex presenting different elemental concentration, could reflect a dissimilar access to resources, as in connection with social differentiation within the group.

The nature and complexity of the patterns of variation emerging from the observation of the chemical composition of human hard tissues can lead to a series of interpretations regarding differences in the diet, which can be associated with the various types of mobility considered. The contribution of archaeological data is of utmost importance in the reconstruction of patterns of movement, providing the key to interpret trace element results.

1. Mobility and Social Dynamics

CAUSE OF MOBILITY	EXPECTED DIETARY and GEOCHEMICAL REGIME	EXPECTED TRACE ELEMENTS DATA
Mobility and mass migration	Rapid shift in the dietary regime as a consequence of change in the residential environment	Trace elements for bone: general homogeneous pattern among individuals and between individuals and environment (geochemical coherence for ongoing diet). Trace elements for teeth: general homogenous pattern among individuals but divergence between individuals and environment (geochemical incoherence between early and late diet).
Economic Mobility (Foragers)	Heterogeneous diet with different subsistence sources. Frequent mobility possibly causing intervals in the interaction with the environment.	Trace elements for bone: general homogeneous pattern among most individuals but possible divergence between individuals and environment. Trace elements for teeth: general homogeneous pattern among individuals but possible divergence between individuals and environment.
Economic mobility (Pastoralism)	Seasonal mobility with shifts in the residential environment. Sources of food may be varied but plausibly recurrent.	Trace elements for bone: few individuals showing different patterns from the rest of the group (as a sign of seasonal movements and/or leave from the group during adult life). Trace elements for enamel: general homogeneity (as a result of general stability within the group during childhood)
Mobility and trade and exchange	Periodical mobility outside or inside a specific environment. Episodic dietary shifts.	Picture 1 Trace elements for bone: few individuals (adult males?) showing different pattern as a result of recent movement/return within the group Trace elements for enamel: individuals (adult females?) showing different bone patterns display homogenous enamel values as a sign of original residence within the group. Picture 2 Trace elements for bone and enamel: few individuals showing different pattern as a result of recent movement into the group.
Mobility and social relationships (exchange of individuals–elites)	Differentiated diet for sub-groups of the community, either in relation to enhanced mobility or in connection with different access to resources.	Picture 1 Trace elements for bone: inter-group discrepancies and patterns showing different groups associated by similar values as a result of different life conditions and/or diet within the community. Trace elements for enamel: patterns similar to the one showed by bone with possible correlation or divergence with the environment. Picture 2 Trace elements for bone and enamel: few individuals showing different pattern as a result of recent movement into the group.
Mobility and social relationships (Marriage exchanges)	Permanent shift in the residential environment. Possible coherence between early and late diet although under different geochemical influence.	Picture 1 Trace elements for bone: homogenous patterns for most of individuals as a result of co-residence Trace elements for enamel: few individuals (adult females?) showing different pattern as a result of movement after childhood. Picture 2 Trace elements for bone and enamel: few individuals showing different pattern as a result of recent movement into the group (adult males/females).
Mobility and social differences	Differentiated diet for sub-groups of the community, either in relation to different mobility or in connection with different access to resources.	Trace elements for bone: inter-group discrepancies and patterns showing different groups (*i.e.* of women) associated by similar values as a result of different life conditions and/or diet within the community.

Table 1.1 Methodological framework and ICP-MS data expectation.

Chapter Two
Sant'Abbondio. Archaeological data and anthropological analysis

Introduction

The case study of this research is the Middle Bronze Age cemetery of Sant'Abbondio (Pompeii, Naples). The use of Sant'Abbondio offers a significant advantage, on the one hand, the cultural background of the site can be fully inserted in the framework of Middle Bronze Age of Southern Italy, as its geographical location makes it ideal for investigations related to either farming or herding, as well as fishing economy, and it offers numerous areas for the practice of transhumance and routes to nearby territories. However, the cemetery presents funerary ritual and cultural evidence that offer multiple insights. The use of single inhumations – at first considered a unique feature for Bronze Age Southern Italy, but now supported by the new data from Gricignano and San Paolo Belsito (Albore Livadie and Marzocchella, 1999) – makes Sant'Abbondio an ideal context, the mortuary data of which offers a large scale as well as detailed set of information. The use of single burials contrasts with the prevailing evidence of collective rite attested in the rest of the southern part of the peninsula. This represents the best condition to infer issues of individual identity within a context that integrates well with the cultural framework of Bronze Age Italy.

Both archaeological and anthropological data will partially be discussed. The former have already been preliminarily published by Mastroroberto (1998) in a brief excavation report, however some of the archaeological information used in this work was gathered by the author via personal communication and limited documentation from the excavators. A report of the paleobiological investigation has been recently published (Tafuri *et al.* 2003), therefore a synthesis of the anthropological data is presented here.

the hill of Sant'Abbondio at the time of use of the cemetery (Mastroroberto 1998) (Fig. 2.2).

The *Soprintendenza Archeologica di Pompei*, under the supervision of Dr. Marisa Mastroroberto, undertook excavations on the site between 1993 and 1997 through two campaigns (1992/93 and 1996/97) carried out by different teams. The stratigraphy of the area has revealed the presence of Roman cultivation, associated with the southern suburbs of the ancient city and covered by the 79 AD eruption. Below the Roman evidence the Middle Bronze Age burials emerged. The latter were covered by a dark layer of volcanic material dated to the Middle Bronze Age (defined as BM2 by the excavators) and associated with the abandonment of the site (Mastroroberto 1998). The presence of this volcanic evidence represents a *terminus ante quem* for the necropolis and has provided further demonstration of Mount Vesuvius' activity after the so-called *Pomici di Avellino* eruption (for a detailed review see Albore Livadie *et al.*, 1986). The latter is not attested in the Sant'Abbondio stratigraphy, as the site does not fall under the area of dispersion of the pyroclastic flow. The volcanic event attested in the area of Sant'Abbondio might be recognised as a transitional episode, which occurred during an undefined moment between the Middle Bronze Age and Late Bronze Age (Mastroroberto 1998).

Fig. 2.1 Location of Sant'Abbondio.

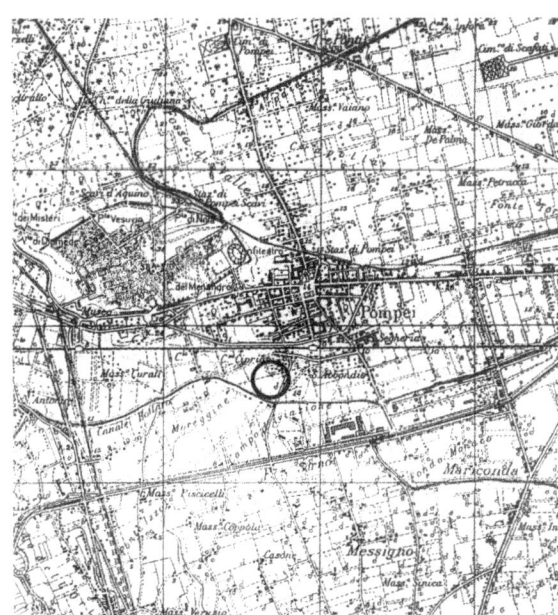

Fig. 2.2 Location of the cemetery within Pompeii's area. The River Sarno is visible south of the site (IGM 1:25.000) (after Mastroroberto 1998).

Some data from the excavations

The necropolis of Sant'Abbondio is situated in the modern city of Pompeii in the province of Naples, Southern Italy (Fig. 2.1). The area where the prehistoric cemetery lies is slightly elevated above the surrounding plain of Pompeii, close to the sea (approximately 1 km) and along the River Sarno that, although at some distance now, ran just few meters away from

Radiocarbon determination from Sant'Abbondio yielded a date between the 17th and the 15th centuries BC (Marisa Mastroroberto pers. com.). In terms of relative chronology, it is rather difficult to ascertain the period of use of this funerary site, although a series of features such as material culture –

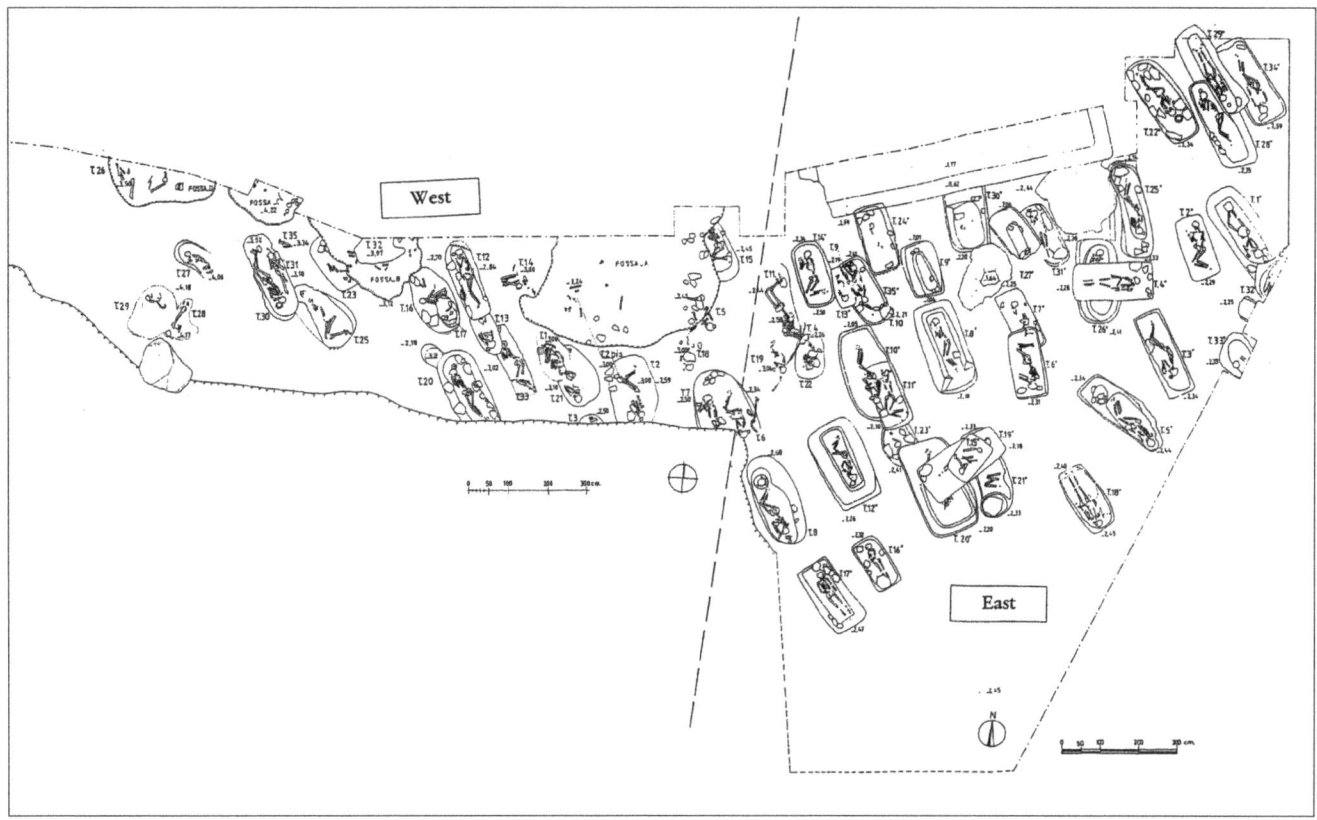

Fig. 2.3 Sant'Abbondio. Plan of the Middle Bronze Age cemetery. East and West areas (respectively the long stretch and the wider section) relate to the two different seasons of excavation. The two sections also correspond to the hilltop (East) and its E-W slope (West) towards the river (after Mastroroberto 1998 modified and integrated).

referred to a period between the later phase of Palma Campania and earlier Protoapennine B – topographical organisation, burial construction and orientation, presence of primary and secondary deposition, seem to suggest a continuous occupation of the site by a single community sharing and preserving a uniform ritual.

Beneath the Middle Bronze Age necropolis an earlier layer characterised by the presence of numerous postholes has been interpreted as the remaining portion of an Early Bronze age site. A double line of postholes orientated East-West along the southern edge of the slope could have formed part of some kind of fortification of the settlement or, according to the excavators, as a elevated structure built on what was considered to be a wetland area (Marisa Mastroroberto, pers. com.). Pottery from the Early Bronze Age settlement is referable to the Palma Campania phase (Marisa Mastroroberto pers. com.) and provides one of the very few indications of continuity between Early Bronze Age (site/structure) and Middle Bronze Age (necropolis) evidence in the area. Further investigation in the Sant'Abbondio area could represent a precious testimony of such an important phase, especially for what concerns the Campanian area.

The area of the excavated Middle Bronze Age cemetery (Fig. 2.3) covers approximately 315 m². It is limited on northern, southern and western sides by modern buildings, while the modern road cuts the eastern border. Within the cemetery, some areas were disturbed by Roman interventions that destroyed some of the inhumations. A total number of 72 burials were identified, thirty-seven of which were excavated in 1992/93, over an area of 171 m², while the remaining 35 were excavated during the 1996/97 campaigns, over an area of 144 m². The excavated area may have represented the southern portion of a wider cemetery (of approximately twice its size; cf. Mastroroberto 1998) that is today partially obliterated by the modern road, and for which further investigations in the area north of the *Cavalcavia* are being planned. The necropolis is placed on a wide terrace on top of the small hill named 'Sant'Abbondio' that would have been unoccupied along its southern and western limits where the River Sarno flowed. The low hill has an East-West slope that is hardly noticeable today but must have been more so during ancient times. The morphology of the portion of land occupied by the cemetery creates a natural division between two areas: an eastern portion (roughly corresponding to the 1996-1997 excavations) that occupies the Sant'Abbondio hill, and a western part (related to the 1992-1993 excavations) sloping in East-West direction towards the ancient riverbank of the Sarno.

In terms of topography, the cemetery seems to follow a general pattern: burials are placed in what seems to be a series of rows roughly oriented north-west/south-east. Groups of tombs are sometimes associated, either through connecting pits (*i.e.* 28-29-34/93) or through a single large pit containing double inhumations (*i.e.* 30-31/93), and sometimes with mixed ritual (*i.e.* 5/96 consisted of an adult inhumation next to the deposition of an infant within a large vessel). A number of burials cut through previous depositions (*i.e.* 4/96 and 19-15/96) or rest on top or earlier tombs (*i.e.* 5-18/93). This illuminates us on the consistency of Sant'Abbondio population, which, in cases of secondary depositions seem to have made the effort to preserve the earlier burial maybe as a result of the remembrance of the deceased. All burials were of the *fossa* type, with elongated pits dug directly into the reddish bedrock. The grave structures included simple pits, double pits, pits with an internal subsidiary pit located at the feet of the deceased, pits with a lateral area for the deposition of grave goods, and pits with a side step. The graves were marked externally with mounds of grey tuff and white fluvial stones, often containing fragments of an intentionally broken vessel.

Some of the burials were dug into the bedrock, as is evident from the marks of digging tools preserved on the walls of some of the graves. Each grave was surrounded by a series of small- and medium-sized tuff and lava stones that resembled those placed as external markers. This has led the excavator to hypothesise a double ritual that involved a primary deposition of the corpse and the grave goods, performed by a smaller section of the community (perhaps the restricted family of the deceased) and marked by the placement of the inner stones, and a second phase, performed by a larger section of the group, marked by the positioning of external signs and ritual breakage and deposition of pottery vessels (Mastroroberto, 1998: 143-144). Most burials were single although a number of multiple inhumations were identified (6-7/93; 30-31/93; 10-11/96). The group of tombs numbered 15-19-20-21/96 has also been considered as a multiple burial. Double or multiple burials consist of a primary event and one or more secondary depositions showing the skeletal remains partially moved to give space to the later burial. Most of the inhumations are oriented north-south with a regular distance between each other, according to an apparently pre-defined spatial organisation. In all the burials the body was slightly contracted, on one side, oriented north-south with the head at the south or at the north, normally facing west. Grave goods consisted of one or more vessels associated with one or more lithic object or a bronze weapon. These were generally placed near the head and by the hands of the deceased. Occasionally they were found near the pelvis and only rarely were they recovered in a different position from the ones just described.

It is worth noting that a small number of individuals seemed to display particularly 'rich' burials either in terms of quantity and quality of grave goods or architectural features of the tomb. As an example, the number and nature of objects from burial 8/93 has led the excavator to describe it as a possible "warrior" tomb (Mastroroberto, 1998: 147), related to a supposed key figure within the community (rightly interpreted as a male on an archaeological basis, now confirmed by the anthropological study). The 'coherence' of the cemetery is however evident from the funerary ritual that tends to recur with a consistent model of grave goods composition, architectural features and spatial distribution. The presence of double or multiple depositions could reflect the importance given to social criteria such as kinship relations. All of these aspects, as well as a detailed study of material culture deserve better attention in a thorough archaeological investigation that is currently being completed.

The ritual of single inhumations can be considered a distinct feature, which has now become characteristic of the known Middle Bronze Age Campanian contexts (see Albore Livadie and Marzocchella, 1999), given the collective burial practices that characterise the Middle Bronze Age of other Central and Southern Italian regions. The theoretical and methodological approach of this study makes the use of single inhumation an ideal condition: each individual is inserted in a definite 'cultural' setting that allows general as well as specific considerations. Such a detailed insight would not be possible in collective contexts where the data on single individuals is obliterated by the use of such practice. Early Bronze Age funerary evidence in Italy tends to concentrate in the southeastern regions of the peninsula and burials are almost always of the collective type. Despite the lack of extensive archaeological data from Campania, it is immediately clear that the Sant'Abbondio cemetery represents one of the very few Middle Bronze Age funerary contexts excavated. Investigations in progress are demonstrating the recurrence of single inhumations at other sites in the area, although much work is needed before any general pattern can be drawn. Very recent excavations carried out at San Paolo Belsito near the site of Palma Campania in the province of Avellino and in the Gricignano area, north of Pompeii (*ibid.*, 1999), have yielded funerary evidence considerably similar to that of Sant'Abbondio.

GEOGRAPHICAL, GEOLOGICAL AND PALEOENVIRONMENTAL DATA

The geomorphology of the portion of Campania under study is rather varied despite its limited size. The Pompeii plateau is surrounded by the coastline of the Gulf of Naples with Mount Vesuvius to the west-northwest, the Sorrento promontory with its high cliffs overlooking the sea to the south, and the final stretch of the Campanian Apennines to the east-northeast, with the mountain ridges of Mount Partenio, Mount Sarno, and the Avella Mountains. The landscape changes from highland plateaus surrounded by sloping mountainsides and cliffs interrupted by river courses (the Sarno, Clanio, Lauro and Sabato river valleys) to lowland costal areas, surrounded by hills and river estuaries.

The geology and geomorphology of the area under study is invariably influenced by the presence of Mount Vesuvius. A volcano dominates any changing environment and has a strong impact not only on its inhabitants but also on its 'inanimate' features. Mount Vesuvius is still - technically speaking - an 'active' volcano, since its last eruption falls within historical and contemporaneous times. In the period that precedes the 20th century, for which data are available through historical sources and geological studies, several eruptions are described in the literature. Ancient sources such as Vitruvius (*De Architectura*, II, 6), Diodorus Siculus (*Bibliotheca Historica*, IV, 21), and Strabo (*Geographica*, V, 246-247) describe the activity of Vesuvius, although the most famous event is the 'Plinian' eruption that destroyed the city of Pompeii in 79 AD. Recent works by Rosi and Santacroce (1986) and Albore Livadie *et al.* (1986) have attempted a summary of Mount Vesuvius' activity through time. Numerous events are known today, although their description and interpretation is beyond the scope of this research. What can be considered relevant to this analysis is the influence that prehistoric eruptive phenomena have had on the environment and the geology of the Pompeii plateau before the historical occupation of the area.

The Neapolitan volcano consists of two distinct cinder cones: an earlier one - Mount Somma – whose activity ceased with a collapse of the top, and a later one – Mount Vesuvius – that originated from a new formation of the earlier cone (Fig. 2.4).

Several studies have attempted to ascertain the date of beginning of its activity and, although research is still in progress, Delibrias *et al.* (1979) set it around 17.000 BP, with the eruption of the *Pomici di Base* and the formation of the main mouth of Mount Somma. In terms of archaeological evidence for recent prehistory, the most important eruption is the ca. 3.800 BP event (Rosi and Santacroce, 1986) of the *Pomici di Avellino*. This events sets a *terminus ante quem* for the dating of the Early Bronze Age Palma Campania phase, a new cultural phenomenon (Albore Livadie, 1994) that differs from earlier Copper Age evidence and terminates with the disruptive event of the *Pomici*. As the Pompeii plain, south of Mount Vesuvius, is unaffected by this event, it comes as no surprise that the site of Sant'Abbondio does not show any trace of the *Pomici*, providing unique evidence of continuity between the Early and Middle Bronze Age. For the period preceding the *Pomici*, and after the Agnano-Monte Spina eruption (ca. 4100 BP), Marzocchella (1998: 113) has identified a series of eruptive phenomena, defined as 'Flegrea 1, 2 and 3' and referred to the chronological interval 2800-1800 BC. Following the *Pomici di Avellino* two main prehistoric and protohistoric eruptive events have been identified before 79 AD. They are defined by Albore Livadie *et al.* (1986) as 'horizon A' and 'horizon B' and consist of two layers of pumices and ashes.

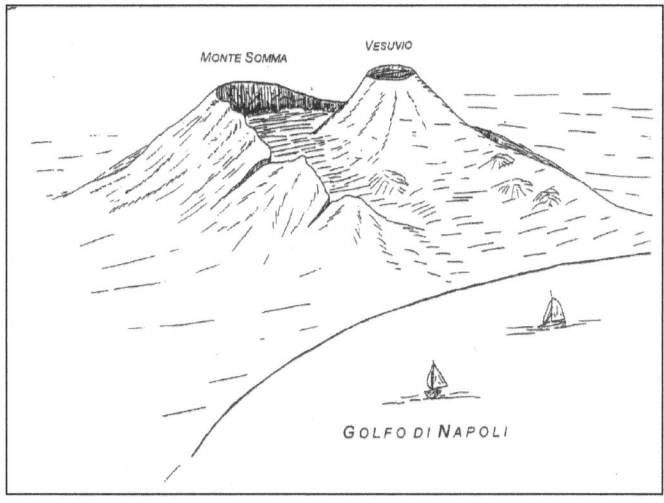

Fig. 2.4 The Somma-Vesuvio volcanic complex (after Civetta *et al.* 1998).

The 'horizon A' event is particularly relevant to the case study as it refers to a period that shortly follows the *Pomici* with a flow that corresponds to the area south-southeast of Mount Vesuvius, in the vicinity of Pompeii. The date of this event is set approximately between a later phase of the 16th century BC (corresponding to part of the Protoapennine B) and an imprecise moment of Late Bronze Age. The 'horizon B' refers to the area northeast of the volcano and does not involve the Pompeii plain. The dating of the event is set to a moment preceding the 7th century BC, a period for which sure stratigraphic data are available. The 'horizon A' described by Albore Livadie *et al.* almost certainly corresponds with the eruptive phenomenon indicated by Mastroroberto (1998: 146-147) as covering the Sant'Abbondio cemetery.

Geological data of the area under study were provided by IGM (*Istituto Geografico Militare*) maps of the *Servizio Geologico d'Italia*, and data obtained via the World Wide Web (*Centro di Geotecnica* at the University of Siena – www. e-geo.unisi.it). The Pompeii plain is covered by a large area (approximately surrounding the volcano) of eruptive material and eroded soils from Mount Somma-Vesuvio. The plain is also occupied by a stretch of sand, mud, and peat soils corresponding to River Sarno's present and ancient bed; these sediments fill the Holocene formation of the 'Lagni Nolani'. Northeast of the Pompeii plain is the series of Holocene volcanic formations of the Paleosomma and Neosomma mainly consisting of pyroclastic deposits of lavas, lapilli, and pumices. South and west of Pompeii is a series of different geological settings corresponding to the lowland-highland intervals characterising the geomorphology of the area. To the north they mainly consist of Cretaceous limestone of marine formation and Pleistocene tufa of volcanic origin, partially separated by stretches of sandstone related to the Lauro and the Sabato riverbeds. To the south a series of Trias and Giura-Lias marine formations of limestone are again interrupted by sandstone beds of smaller river courses.

The reconstruction of paleoenvironmetal conditions during the Bronze Age of Campania is beyond the scope of this work. Nevertheless, in order to understand how the Sant'Abbondio people interacted with the environment through their diet it is important to tackle the nature of such environment. The aim here is to briefly examine data describing the nature of the vegetation – and partially the type of animal occupation – in the Early and Middle Bronze Age of the Pompeii area. Data available in the literature will be used to discuss environmental capacity, land use and economy. Most of the paleoenvironmental data available for the region are provided by Albore Livadie's (1994b) survey of a series of Early Bronze Age sites buried under the *Pomici di Avellino* eruption. Despite belonging to a period slightly earlier than the one under study, Albore Livadie's work is virtually the only evidence available to reconstruct the ancient environment of Campania. Data from extensive surveys and palynological analyses of a series of sites date prior and subsequent to the *Pomici* eruption are therefore combined in a composite scenario.

The investigation of a number of settlements has led Albore Livadie (1994) to suggest an economy strongly directed towards transhumant pastoralism; sites are located in strategic areas, mainly at the crossroads between highlands used for the seasonal movement of herds, and nearby hills and valleys with fertile soils and water resources. Lowland areas and riverine zones are less known although new investigations at Gricignano should help to fill gaps in the research. Traces of ploughing together with animal tracks at Palma Campania and Ottaviano (Albore Livadie 1994b: 229; Albore Livadie *et al.*, 1998: 60-61) and evidence of a series of hoe/plough furrows at Gricignano (Marzocchella, 1998: 122) are clear signs of an intense use of lowland areas for cultivation that was carried out in zones sometimes contemporaneously occupied by animals (Albore Livadie, 1994b: 229). Faunal remains from the sites investigated mainly referred to caprovids and cattle (*ibid.*: 236) and the alternation of highland and lowland occupation in relation to herd movement seems to be confirmed by the presence of seasonal Early and Middle Bronze Age highland sites (*i.e.* Camposauro at ca. 1000 m., Taurano at 510 m., and Visciano at 496 m. above sea level). In addition to this, pottery analysis from Palma Campania assemblages has revealed the presence of a number of vessels almost certainly used for dairy production. Land use for gardening or intensive agriculture is attested by the presence of ploughing activity and by the use of highly productive area in terms of soil conditions and water resources. Palynological data from a number of sites (Palma Campania, San Paolo Belsito, Visciano, Schiava, Tufino, and Avella) analysed for periods immediately before and after the *Pomici* eruption reveal a situation that seems to undergo a significant change in the period of re-occupation of the area following the eruptive phenomenon.

SANT'ABBONDIO SKELETAL SAMPLE

The human skeletal remains from Sant'Abbondio add up to a total of 62 individuals (32 related to the 1992/1993 campaign and 30 related to the 1996/1997 one) preserved from the 72 burials excavated. The state of preservation of the sample is, overall, highly fragmentary. Fragile or small bones such as ribs or hands and feet are systematically absent, while those remaining only exceptionally are intact. None of individuals preserved the epiphyses of upper or lower limbs (for a detailed descriprion of the burials see Tafuri *et al.* 2003). The bad state of preservation could be related to the volcanic nature of the soil in the area of the cemetery, which is known to badly maintain human remains. Nevertheless, a pH test performed to measure the level of acidity of the soil has revealed neutral to alkaline values (mean pH 7.3), which generally provides the conditions for better conservation of osteological material. Hence, the causes of the poor state of preservation must be searched elsewhere – maybe in the burial practice. The only exception to the overall bad state of the sample is represented by teeth, which, being very well preserved, form a key source of anthropological data.

For the anthropological analysis, sex determination was carried out following Acsàdi and Nemeskéri (1970), with the observation of 14 morphological traits for the skull and 11 for the pelvis. The method was further integrated with Phenice's (1969) work on the subpubic region. Metric analysis could not complement morphological data, as the state of preservation of the sample did not permit the measurement of sexually dimorphic bones. The level of accuracy of morphological methods has been tested by several authors (Meindle *et al.*, 1985; Lovell, 1989; Sutherland and Suchey, 1991). Phenice's method, for example, has an accuracy that ranges between 83% and 96%. The use of cranial data has similar levels of accuracy, varying between 80% and 90% (Meindle *et al.*, 1985; St Hoyme and Iscan, 1989). When the two methods are combined, accuracy rises considerably, reaching 97-98% (Meindle *et al.*, 1985; Molleson and Cox, 1993). As a general note, it should be borne in mind that a number of studies have proven how the diagnostic potential of some traits remains highly population-specific (for a review see Mays and Cox, 2000).

For Sant'Abbondio most of the bones used for estimating sex were highly fragmentary; not a single individual preserved a complete skull or reasonably complete hip bones. Sexing was thus performed using single characters of diagnostic bones. The grade of completeness of the skull and the pelvis is very important when recording the general observation of dimorphic traits that is separated from the analysis of single features. For this reason the estimation of sex presented here should be considered more subject to error than is normally the case with well preserved material.

The choice of the procedure for the calculation of age at death was restricted by the state of preservation of the sample. For adult individuals, the main approach consisted of the observation of dental wear, following Lovejoy (1985), combined with Scott (1979) and Smith (1984). The latter two techniques have the great disadvantage of not offering an appropriate system to correlate wear patterns to age ranges. Therefore in this study wear patterns were converted in accordance with Lovejoy's age categories. However, since dental wear rates vary between cultures these age estimates should be considered relative to the sample, and indicative rather than definitive. As Lovejoy's method tends to be excessively specific, in this study large age classes (Young Adult, Adult, Mature) of adult individuals were selected instead. The examination of cranial suture closure in adults (Lovejoy, 1985) could only be performed for a very restricted number of individuals that preserved a complete skull. Interestingly, the results agree with those coming from the analysis of dental wear. Other methods such as the pubic symphysis scoring system (Todd, 1921a; 1921b) or auricular surface changes (Lovejoy, 1985) could not be applied.

For infant and juvenile individuals, age at death was determined through the observation of dental eruption and development, following Ubelaker (1989). Analysis of the fusion of epiphyses and diaphyses and primary ossification centres together with osteometric procedures (*ibid.*) could not be used due to the state of preservation of the skeletal remains.

In order to better understand how representative the skeletal sample could be of the Sant'Abbondio living population, the *sex ratio* (M/F; defining the ratio between male and female individuals) and the *index of juvenility* or Bocquet & Masset (1982) index (D5-14/D20-x; expressing the balance between individuals dying between 5 and 14 and older ones, that for ancient human groups this is expected to vary between 0.1 and 0.3) were calculated.

Given the nature of the sample no cranial measurements could be recorded while post-cranial metrics were obtained for a limited number of individuals and restricted to a few measurements. Consequently, no cranial or postcranial indices are available. For the same reason estimated stature could not be calculated and Krogman and Işcan's (1986: 327-332) standard to estimate stature from fragmentary long bones could not be applied as in most cases the segment of bone required for calculation was not preserved.

Methods for the observation of cranial and post-cranial non-metric traits to reconstruct genetic relationships were not applicable. Dental analysis however involved the recording of the bucco-lingual (B-L) and the mesio-distal (M-D) diameters and of non-metric traits (Arizona State University – ASU method; Turner *et al.*, 1991). Dental pathologies such as caries, calculus, abscesses and enamel defects were observed according to Buikstra and Ubelaker's (1994) standards. The observation of skeletal pathological conditions was, again, greatly influenced by the state of the sample preventing the observation of skeletal loci focal to pathological conditions (*i.e.* the thoracic girdle) or of modifications of the bone such as activity-related markers of stress. Signs of metabolic pathologies such as porotic hyperostosis and cribra orbitalia were observed where possible.

THE BIOARCHAEOLOGICAL ANALYSIS

Once sex and age at death were estimated, the sample was divided in the following age groups:

1. Infant I   0-6 years
2. Infant II   7-12 years
3. Juvenile   13-20 years
4. Young adult   21-30 years
5. Adult   31-40 years
6. Mature   + 40 years
7. GA   generic adult

Overall, the Sant'Abbondio skeletal sample appears to be fairly homogeneous in its paleobiological characters. The population seems relatively 'gracile' with no evidence of strong muscular insertions or marked robusticity.

The sex ratio (1.11) and Bocquet and Masset's index (0.3) indicate a population well represented by sexes and different age classes. It is, however, interesting to observe a trend of high frequencies of females between the juvenile and young adult classes as opposed to low numbers of males in the same classes, and a generally greater male longevity (Fig. 2.5). A possible explanation could lie in a high incidence of female mortality in relation to phenomena such as pregnancy and childbirth.

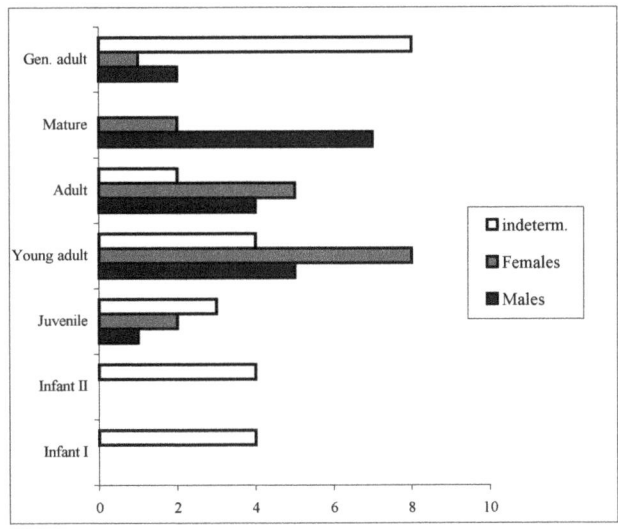

Fig. 2.5 Paleodemographic summary of the Sant'Abbondio sample.

OSTEOMETRIC ANALYSIS

Despite the state of preservation of the sample allowing a very restricted set of osteometric data, it has been possible to test, for differences in the cross-sectional geometry of the lower limbs of Sant'Abbondio adults in relation to the sex of the deceased. This type of analysis has been used by Ruff (1987) to measure sexual dimorphism in bone structure and infer behavioural differences, subsistence strategies, and the sexual division of labour. For Sant'Abbondio, this test could be particularly useful to examine possible sex-specific differences in the use of lower limbs especially in light of Puglisi's idea of predominance of male engagement in the practice of transhumance. If males, as opposed to females, were engaged in long, seasonal movements this should be reflected in the geometry of their bone and could be revealed through the calculation of postcranial indices. For the femur the ratio I_x (Antero-Posterior diameter) (A-P) /I_y (Medio-Lateral diameter) (M-D) was calculated, while for the tibia the antero-posterior and medio-lateral mid-shaft diameter (I_{max}/I_{min}) was considered. Table 2.1 depicts sex differences in femoral and tibial cross-sections at Sant'Abbondio.

Cross-section of lower limbs – male vs. females			
	Males	Females	
Section	mean	mean	(M-F)/F × 100
Tibia – right	1.4	1.2	16.6
Tibia – left	1.4	1.4	0
Femur – right	1.4	1.0	40
Femur – left	1.4	1.1	33

Table 2.1 Sex differences in femoral and tibial cross-section. For femur the ratio I_x (A-P diameter)/I_y (M-L diameter) was calculated, while for the tibia I_{max}/I_{min} was considered.

For the femur, males have a higher ratio indicating a relatively greater A-P bending strength. In Ruff's interpretation, a relatively higher A-P bending strength is associated with higher levels of mobility. It is interesting to note that the Sant'Abbondio group displays a very high sexual dimorphism in lower limb cross-sectional indices, and hence, if we follow this line of interpretation, a dimorphism in activity more typically found in hunter-gatherers than in sedentary agriculturalists (Ruff 1987). This could be related to accentuated mobility of male as opposed to female, possibly in relation to the pastoral activity and the tending of the herd to distant pastures.

PALEOPATHOLOGIES

The state of preservation of the sample prevented the systematic recording of pathologies. The few cases presented should be considered 'surviving' evidence. Among metabolic defects, cribra orbitalia and porotic hyperostosis are strongly related to iron deficiency anaemia and associated with multiple phenomena such as malnutrition, reduced iron absorption, enhanced iron utilisation, blood loss or infections (Stuart-Macadam, 1998). The correlation between anaemia and infectious diseases is confirmed by a number of studies (e.g. Weinberg, 1992) that have demonstrated how pathogens are able to bind serum iron causing reduced absorption of this mineral through food (hypoferremia). In paleoanthropological studies, iron deficiency anaemia is not attested in the Paleolithic and rare in the Mesolithic, only starting to appear after the Neolithic period (ibid: 53). Strong correlations with the emergence of sedentary lifestyle has been suggested, as modern studies on hunter-gatherer societies have demonstrated that mobile people are free from such a condition (Metz et al., 1971). Porotic hyperostosis could not be observed for all Sant'Abbondio individuals although the orbital roofs were generally better preserved than the frontal area. Of the 27 individuals observed for porotic hyperostosis, four (14.8 %) registered the pathology through cribra orbitalia (specifically, burials: 12/93, 2/96, 10/06, 25/96 – Fig. 2.6), while none gave evidence of the same on the frontal bone.

Post-cranial pathological conditions are registered for two individuals (18/93, 22/96), they consist of periosteal reactions localised on the diaphyses of upper or lower limbs and probably associated with traumatic episodes or infections of moderate severity.

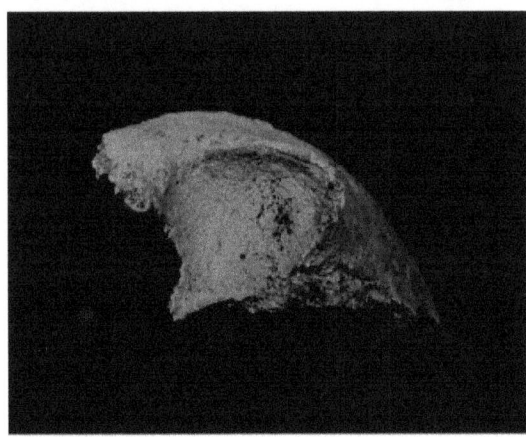

Fig. 2.6 Individual 2/96, roof of the left orbit- cribra orbitalia.

DENTAL ANALYSIS

Forty-nine of the 62 individuals observed preserved either upper or lower dentitions, either permanent or deciduous. A dental inventory was made for each individual according to the synthetic form proposed by Buiskstra and Ubelaker (1994). A total of 1012 teeth were recorded. For subadults both deciduous and permanent dentitions were documented, although deciduous teeth were not included for some of the analyses, and subadults, as an age class, were excluded from some of the investigations.

Dental dimensions were measured through maximum mesiodistal (M-D) and bucco-lingual (B-L) diameters. The lack of preservation of alveolar bone may have produced measurements that are slightly larger than expected.

Dental wear was observed and compared between the two sexes in order to verify gender-specific variation in relation to a possible differentiated diet. Pathologies such as caries and calculus were observed and their distribution plotted in relation to sex and age classes. Periodontal diseases, abscesses, or ante-mortem loss could not be fully investigated because of the loss of alveolar bone in most of the individuals considered. Enamel defects were observed and recorded despite the rather bad state of preservation of buccal and lingual surfaces. Given the nature of the sample, for most analyses the ratio individual affected/individual observed rather than tooth affected/alveolus observed was used to calculate prevalence.

Occlusal surface wear

Occlusal wear was recorded to estimate age at death according to Lovejoy's (1985) age groups. Wear follows the helicoidal plane described by Hillson (1996: 237-238), which consist in the normal pattern of wear on dentition. Among a limited number of individuals there is an unusually high incidence of occlusal wear on the upper and lower anterior dentition (from canine to canine). In some cases this wear pattern could led to a misinterpretation of age at death; as an example, individual 18/93 was initially aged as mature (over 40 yrs) due to the strong wear on the anterior dentition, but a double check on the molars instead revealed an age range of 20-30 years. The extreme contrast between anterior and posterior wear can best be explained through the extra-masticatory use of incisors and canines and, in very few cases, prevented the observation of enamel hypoplasia.

OCCLUSAL WEAR – KOLGOMOROV-SMIRNOV TEST MALES VS. FEMALES						
	M1			M2		
AGE CLASS	n	Z	p	n	Z	p
20-40	19	0.725	0.669	18	0.843	0.476
>40	8	0.554	0.498	8	0.919	0.965

Table 2.2 Results of the Kolgomorov-Smirnov test for occlusal wear on M1 and M2 using the scoring system of Scott (1979).

To examine the possible relationship with sex of the individuals for distribution of occlusal wear a Kolgomorov-Smirnov test was performed. Scores were calculated for the maxillary and mandibular left M1 and M2 using Scott's (1979) standard and divided according to two large age classes: adult (20-40 years) and mature (>40 years). The division into very large groups was made to overcome the bias that derives from having used occlusal wear as an aging system, which would have created a pattern of wear that followed age classes. Significant variation in the distribution between the sexes is not appreciable for either age categories (Table 2.2).

Dental caries

Dental caries has been defined by Hillson (1996: 269) as 'a destruction of enamel, dentine, and cement resulting from acid production by bacteria in dental plaque'. This pathology is probably the most commonly used indicator of past diet in archaeological investigations not least because it is easily observable. The aetiology of this oral disease is directly connected to the quality of food ingested, as the bacterial breakdown of carbohydrates (sugars and starches) is the principal reason for the occurrence of caries. For this case study, caries was observed according to Moore and Corbett's (1971) method, modified by Buikstra and Ubelaker (1994). The latter considers 7 different surface locations but does not provide a grading system. Therefore, in order to grade severity of the pathology, the method was modified further and caries was recorded as '0' (absent); '1' (slight); '2' (moderate); '3' (severe/disruptive). For the purpose of data collection, individuals and teeth affected were considered separately although, as caries is an infectious disease, several lesions are likely to be registered for the same individual. Among the 25 individuals affected, 68% of them had multiple lesions. Both adults and subadults were recorded although no caries was registered on deciduous teeth except for the case of individual 13/96 - who had both deciduous upper M1s affected.

Results for the distribution of caries are reported in Figure 2.7. Upper and lower teeth are grouped together for the analysis. Not surprisingly the posterior dentition is the most affected, with M2 being most affected since most involved in mastication. Anterior dentition is less affected despite being better preserved than posterior one. Maxillary teeth are slightly more affected than mandibular ones (58% vs. 42%). Occlusal and interproximal lesions are the most frequent, in relation to the areas of the teeth that are more likely to experience food and plaque accumulation.

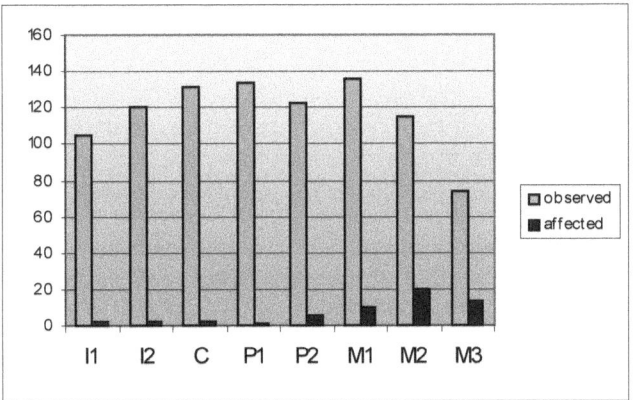

Fig. 2.7 Distribution of dental caries according to teeth affected. The total of teeth affected is compared to the total of teeth observed.

In the examination of the prevalence of caries, *ante-mortem* loss should be considered as one of the consequences of this type of phenomenon however, for the Sant'Abbondio sample the observation of *ante-mortem* loss has been dramatically reduced by the lack of preservation of alveolar bone which made it impossible to determine whether the loss of tooth was biological as opposed to taphonomic. For this reason *ante-mortem* loss is not discussed in relation to carious lesions.

The distribution of caries according to sex and age at death is depicted in Figure 2.8.

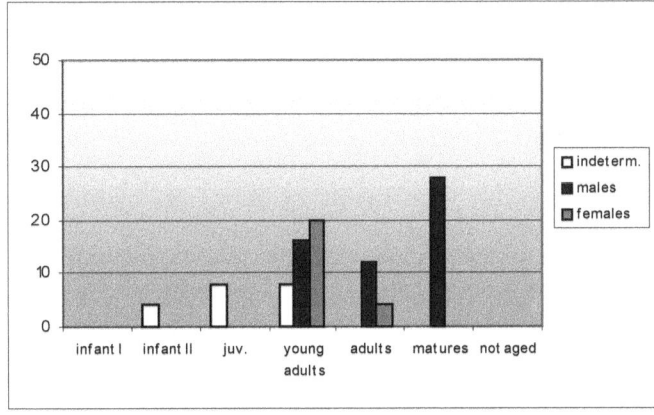

Fig. 2.8 Frequency (in % of individual affected/individual observed) of caries distributed by sex and age at death. N=25.

Among females, a high prevalence in young-adult individuals drastically decreases in the adult class and disappears in the mature one. Males show an increasing trend that follows age. Both patterns seem to follow the paleodemographic framework of the sample and they are very likely influenced by it. Females are, in fact, largely distributed in young classes, while male are generally older. Furthermore, the high incidence among mature males may be also associated with a normal progression and increase of caries with age.

Dental calculus and periodontal disease

The role of dental calculus and periodontal diseases in archaeological investigation is similar. Both pathologies reflect general oral hygiene, although calculus is more closely connected to carbohydrate consumption and diet in general. Supra-gengival calculus was observed here according to Brothwell's (1981) three-point scoring system. Out of the 49 individuals examined, 28 (57.2%) showed calculus, which normally affected more than one tooth (85.7% of individuals affected had multiple lesions).

The distribution of calculus according to sex and age at death is not dissimilar to that shown by caries. A slightly higher number of females are affected, skewed towards younger age classes while males are distributed in all age classes (Fig. 2.9). The total absence of abscesses or other periodontal diseases (see Figure 2.11) is explained by the post-mortem loss of alveolar bone in all individuals.

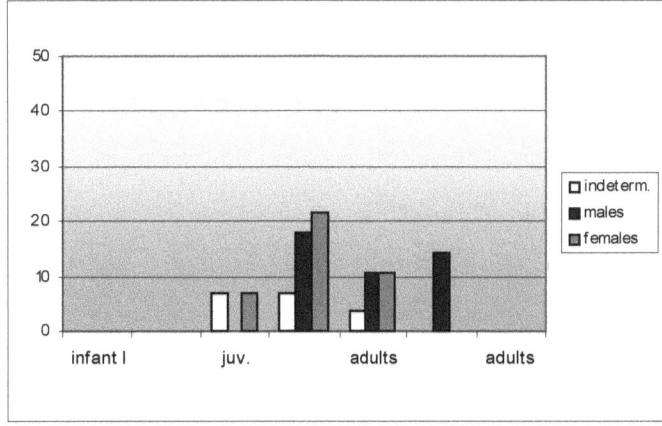

Fig. 2.9 Frequency (in % of individuals affected/individual observed) of calculus distributed by sex and age at death. N=20.

Enamel defects

Enamel defects can occur in different forms: hypoplasia, opacities, and discolourations (Hillson, 1996: 165). All of these are used in bioarchaeological analysis to detect disease or metabolic stress during childhood, both of which leave a visible trace on enamel while this is forming.

Enamel defects observed at Sant'Abbondio were predominantly expressed through linear horizontal grooves localised on the buccal surface of the tooth (linear enamel hypoplasia). Only defects visible to the naked eye were recorded. Hypoplasia was examined and measured according to Buikstra and Ubelaker (1994) on permanent dentition. Of the 49 individuals observed, 25 (51%) had traces of hypoplasia, 40.8% of which showed multiple defects. Generally, dental assemblages show a lower presence of frontal teeth as opposed to premolars and molars. At Sant'Abbondio however, this phenomenon is not observed and the distribution of preserved teeth (as seen in figure 2.7) is homogeneous. This works in favour of the exclusion of an intra-population under-representation of the pathology.

The age of occurrence of the lesion was calculated on upper I1 and I2 and where possible on the canines. Measurement of the hypoplastic lines was not always possible as the buccal surface of the teeth was often damaged in a way that enabled recognition of the trait but not accurate measurement.

Measurements were recorded as the distance between the midpoint of the buccal cemento-enamel junction and the most occlusal portion of the line. Values were compared with age ranges provided by Goodman and Rose (1990) and were calculated for a total of 13 individuals (52% of the total individuals affected). Individuals affected had lesions referring to the 3rd or 4th year of life. Hypoplasia is equally distributed between the sexes in adult individuals (Fig. 2.10).

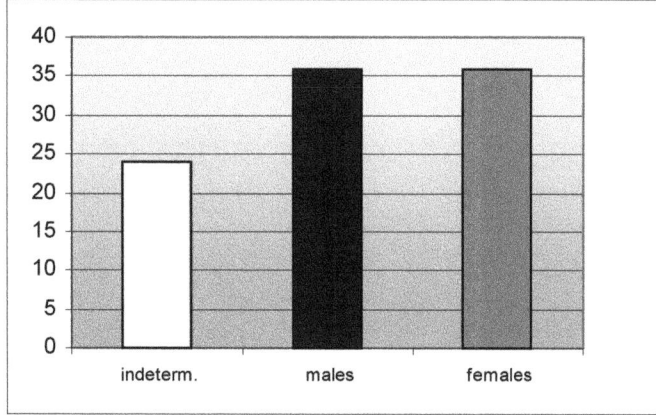

Fig. 2.10 Frequency (in % individual affected/individual observed) of enamel hypoplasia distributed by sex. N=25.

Dental non-metric traits

The observation of dental non-metrics is used to test genetic relationships within a population on the basis of the heritability of these characters (for a review see Larsen, 1997, chapter 9). For the Sant'Abbondio population comparison between adult males and females and east and west section of the cemetery was made to explore the genetic variability of the sample.

Fisher's Exact Test
ASU traits in the maxilla, East vs. West section

Trait	Males		Females	
	N	p	N	p
I1 WING	14	0.280	14	0.156
I1 SHOVELING	14	0.714	14	0.308
I1 TUB. DIST.	14	0.689	14	-
I2 SHOVELING	14	0.280	14	0.154
DOUBT	14	-	14	0.692
CTD	14	0.670	14	0.406
CMR	14	0.714	14	0.429
CDAR	14	0.495	14	0.615
M1 MET	14	0.594	14	0.385
M1 HYP	14	0.594	14	0.385
M1 CUSP 5	14	-	14	0.429
M2 MET	14	0.280	14	0.175
M2 HYP	14	0.280	14	0.704
M2 CUSP 5	14	0.714	14	-
M2 CARABELLI	14	-	14	0.571
M3 MET	14	0.670	14	0.692
M3 HYP	14	0.670	14	-

Table 2.3 Fisher's Exact Test measuring the difference in occurrence of non-metric traits on the maxilla according to area of deposition in the cemetery (East vs. West).

Morphological traits were observed for all adult individuals following the Arizona State University (ASU) method (Turner et al., 1991). Superior and inferior dentitions were recorded separately, and both antimeres were observed. To produce a final score for each trait, Turner and Scott's (1977) criterion was followed therefore the antimere exhibiting the highest score was the one considered for analysis (Fig. 2.11).

The application of Fisher's exact test for males and females in accordance with the area of deposition (Table 2.3 and 2.4) shows no significant differences for both antimeres. This suggests that the sample is genetically homogenous. However, the extremely low frequencies of the traits and the relatively small sample for which observations could be made, makes it difficult to treat these conclusively.

Fisher's Exact Test
ASU traits in the mandible, East vs. West section

Trait	Males		Females	
	N	p	N	p
P1 LING.CUSP.VAR.	12	0.342	11	0.978
P2 LING.CUSP.VAR	12	0.613	11	0.308
M1 ANT. FOVEA	12	0.385	11	-
M1 DEF. WRINKLE	12	-	11	0.634
M1 CUSP 5	12	0.623	11	0.954
M2 CUSP NO.	12	0.412	11	0.129
M3 CUSP NO.	12	0.623	11	0.643
M3 CUSP 5	12	0.594	11	-
M3 CUST 6	12	-	11	0.156
M3 CONG. ABS.	12	0.156	11	0.332

Table 2.4 Fisher's Exact Test measuring the difference in occurrence of non-metric traits on the mandible according to area of deposition in the cemetery (East vs. West)

Discussion and comparisons

Comparison of the Sant'Abbondio anthropological data with those from other coeval contexts from Central and Southern Italy, allows an examination of how representative the paleobiological characteristics of the population are. However, the state of preservation of the sample prevented the performance of a number of anthropological analyses. Data from other contexts used for the comparative analysis, derive partly from the anthropological literature, as for the case of Grotta Vecchi (Rubini et al., 1990), and partially from Borgognini Tarli et al.'s (1996) and Minozzi (1994; 1999) works on Middle Bronze Age sites of Central and Southern Italy (Madonna di Loreto, Toppo Daguzzo, Lavello, Grotta dello Scoglietto, and Marcita). In addiction, data from Coppa Nevigata and Luogovivo are used with kind permission of Dr L. Salvadei and Prof. G. Manzi (Museo Preistorico Etnografico "L. Pigorini" – Rome; University of Rome "La Sapienza").

Post-cranial pathologies, in the form of periosteal reactions due to infection or trauma, show comparative frequencies with other sites (Fig. 2.12). According to Borgognini Tarli (1992) a low occurrence of conflicts among Italian prehistoric populations could be the cause of low incidence of skeletal pathologies and traumas. Moreover, as Robb (1997) stresses, it is possible that weapon display as a symbolic idiom of prestige and competition with the potential of conflict acting as a

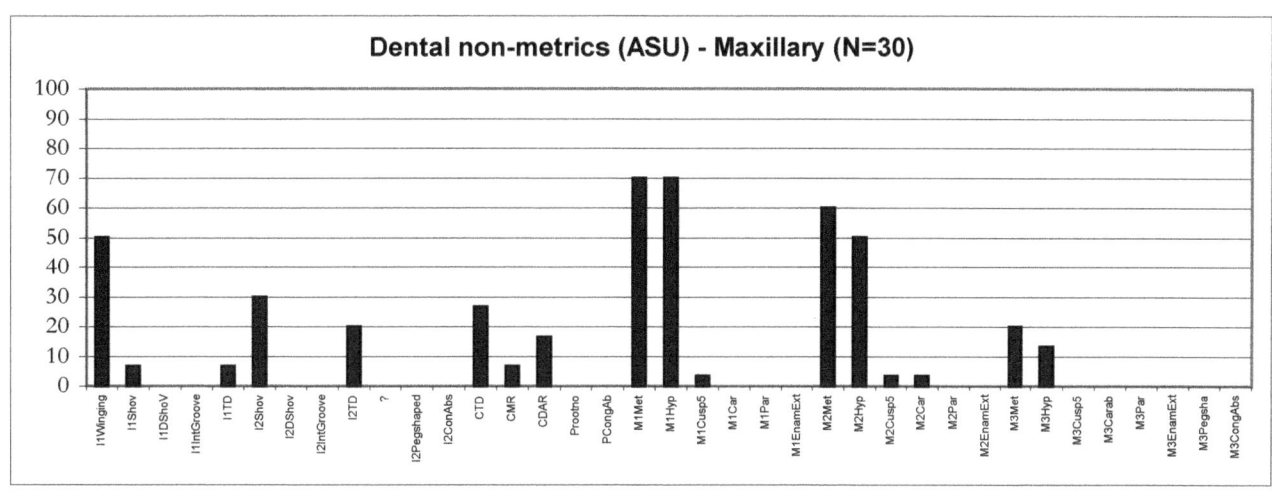

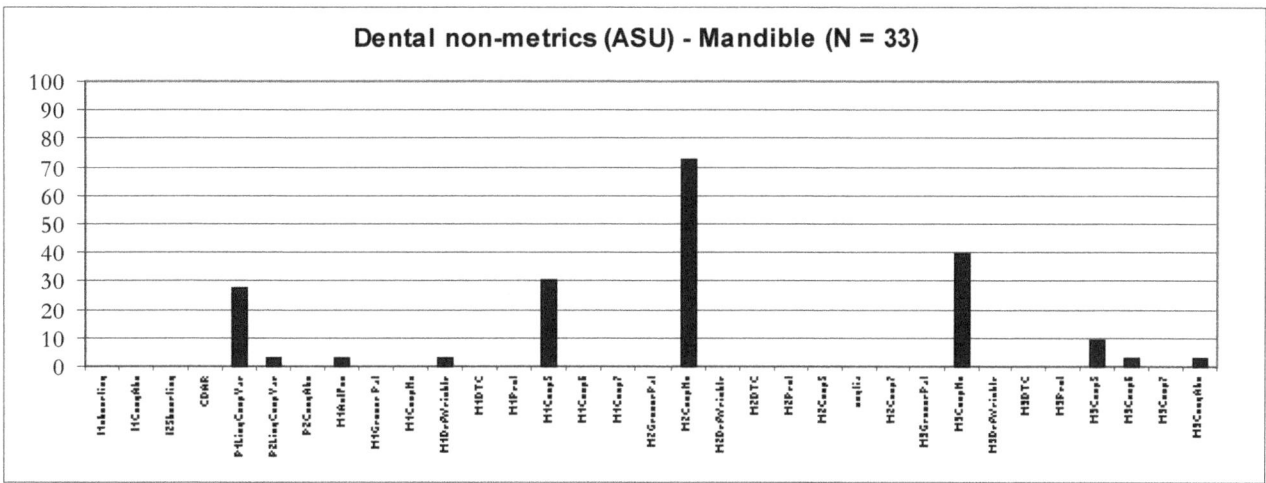

Fig. 2.11 Frequencies (%) of non-metric traits (ASU methods) for upper and lower teeth. Values express individuals showing the trait/individuals observed.

deterrent of actual violence, resulted in lower rates of trauma in Copper and Bronze Age societies.

In terms of dental pathologies it is worth observing that at Sant'Abbondio there is a higher prevalence of caries in relation to the other series observed (Fig. 2.13).

The lower incidence of abscesses at Sant'Abbondio is related to the lack of preservation of alveolar bone and should not be considered. Similarly the ante-mortem was unobservable in the Sant'Abbondio assemblage. The higher prevalence of caries at Sant'Abbondio may indicate a higher amount of carbohydrates consumed by the Sant'Abbondio population and could be related to a greater contribution of herding, gardening or farming of cereals and other grains to the economy of the group. It could also be explained by a relatively higher longevity of the Sant'Abbondio population resulting in a higher frequency of pathological conditions. Data on the age at death of the comparative populations are unfortunately not available; this limits the quality of the results obtained and should be considered only generically indicative of the differences in the incidence of carious lesions.

A comparison between enamel hypoplasia and porotic hyperostosis (Fig. 2.14) reveals that Sant'Abbondio is the only site showing a greater frequency of enamel defects as opposed

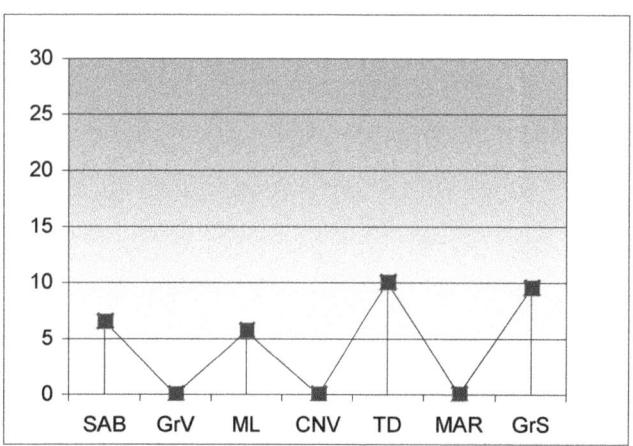

Fig. 2.12 Frequencies (in % of individuals affected/individuals observed) of post-cranial pathological conditions (periostitis) at Sant'Abbondio and other comparative samples. SAB=Sant'Abbondio; GrV= Grotta Vecchi; ML= Madonna di Loreto; CNV= Coppa Nevigata; TD= Toppo Daguzzo; MAR= Marcita; GrS= Grotta dello Scoglietto.

to hyperostotic stress. All other sites present the inverse trend, except for Grotta Vecchi, which shows a ratio near to 1. Borgognini Tarli (1992) explains the high prevalence of porotic hyperostosis in Bronze Age Italian contexts as the result of cohabitation with animals. The high frequency of these pathologies among groups that could have assured themselves a sufficient intake of animal proteins, and supposedly did not suffer from nutritional deficiencies, is explained by Borgognini Tarli (*ibid.*) as the result of the occurrence of infectious disease caused by enteric bacteria present in secondary products and meat. A further cause could have been poor levels of hygiene conditions and increasing sedentism and aggregation of people, responsible for the transmission of various infections (Stuart-Macadam, 1998).

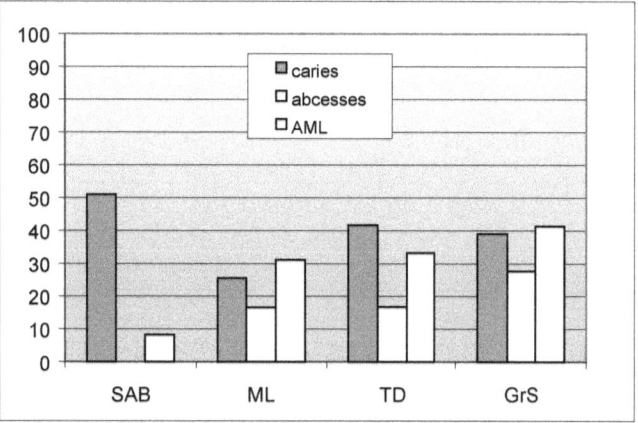

Fig. 2.13 Frequencies (in % of individuals affected/individuals observed) of dental pathologies at Sant'Abbondio and other comparative sites. SAB=Sant'Abbondio; ML= Madonna di Loreto; TD= Toppo Daguzzo; GrS= Grotta dello Scoglietto.

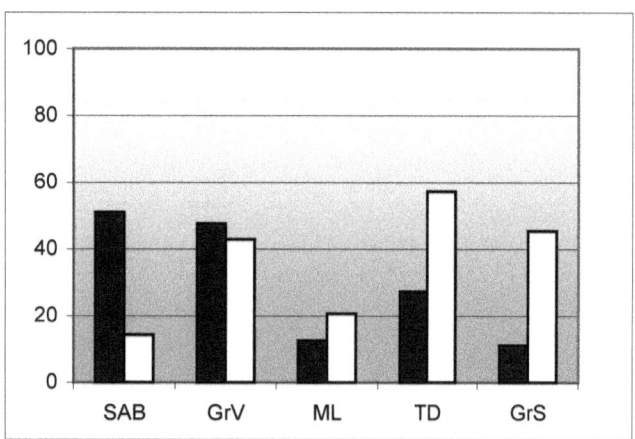

Fig. 2.14 Frequencies (in % of individuals affected/individuals observed) of enamel hypoplasia and porotic hyperostosis at Sant'Abbondio and other comparative sites. SAB=Sant'Abbondio; GrV= Grotta Vecchi; ML= Madonna di Loreto; TD= Toppo Daguzzo; Grotta dello Scoglietto.

In contrast with other contemporary contexts, the Sant'Abbondio sample shows a relatively low incidence of cribra orbitalia (14% of total individuals observed). It is important to stress that this result could be due to the lack of preservation of the regions affected by this pathology (preserved only for 56% of the total sample), nevertheless it could represent alternative scenario from that depicted by Borgognini Tarli (1992). The low incidence of this pathology could reflect overall good dietary and health conditions that generated a low level of metabolic stress in adults. The occurrence of iron-deficiency anaemia in the Sant'Abbondio population could be due mainly to physiological, rather than pathological, conditions especially considering that 75% of the individuals are females in their reproductive years, probably experiencing physiological iron deprivation as a result of pregnancy and lactation.

In a comparative perspective, the two striking results from Sant'Abbondio are the high frequency of caries as indicative of a higher consumption of carbohydrates, and the high level of physiological stress during childhood identified through enamel hypoplasia that could hint at a lesser contribution of proteins (meat, milk and derivates) to childhood diet or general metabolic stress suffered during growth. Although defects in the enamel are considered the result of multiple causes including hereditary anomalies, localised trauma and general social or environmental stress (Larsen, 1997: 45-46), a strong relationship between enamel hypoplasia and systemic physiological stress has been argued (see Hillson, 1996), particularly in the case of malnutrition (see for example Goodman and Rose, 1991; Zhou, 1995). For the Sant'Abbondio people, the occurrence of enamel hypoplasia could be explained either in relation to a greater contribution of grains to the diet – normally associated with an increase in enamel defects in North-American populations (Goodman *et al.*, 1980; Goodman, 1989) – an interpretation that might be supported by the high prevalence of caries. In this perspective, the low incidence of iron-deficiency anaemia, seen trough cribra orbitalia, does not necessarily contrast with these results. The possible high consumption of carbohydrates is in agreement with Barker's (1984) model of a mixed economy, recently supported by Albore Livadie (1994: 205-207). This does not exclude the possibility of an economic regime that was exclusively pastoral with the dietary contribution of plants (therefore carbohydrates) through the practice of gathering and/or opportunistic gardening. A more definite suggestion cannot be made for the Sant'Abbondio group's economy without the contribution of faunal data and further results from palynological and paleobotanic investigations. The Sant'Abbondio people broaden the 'traditional' paleobiological model proposed for Bronze Age groups (see Borgognini Tarli, 1992: 259-268), as they are not entirely typical of the conditions believed to be indicative of pastoral communities (*i.e.* low prevalence of caries and high frequency of metabolic stress). Explanations for such a scenario could lie in a general improvement in the living condition of the Sant'Abbondio group expressed through a low prevalence of metabolic stress and a low frequency of post-cranial pathological conditions. However, nor they contradict such a patter but rather force us to expand the range of possibilities in the reconstruction of past lifeways for Bronze Age groups.

Archaeological and anthropological data

Anthropological data from this research can be examined in association with limited archaeological information obtained from the excavators. In particular, it is worth examining whether there are differences in the composition of grave goods in accordance with the sex of the deceased.

Contingency tables were created according to the following categories of objects: a) ceramics; b) metal weapons (bronze daggers); c) lithic weapons (flint arrowheads and daggers); d) metal objects (undetermined metal objects or objects not considered as weapons); e) tools (lithic artefacts such as scrapers or blades) and f) ornaments (generally metal pins). Normally, male burials seem to contain more objects than female ones for a number of categories of objects (ceramics, metal weapons, tools), while females have more objects in the categories of lithic weapons and ornaments (Table 2.5). Adult graves are not necessarily richer than infant or juvenile ones and all categories of objects are equally represented in child burials, although in smaller quantity.

CATEGORY - Ceramics					
	f	j	m	u	Total
0	(10	9	6	10	35
1	8	2	12	3	25
Total	18	11	18	13	60
CATEGORY – Metal Weapon					
	f	j	m	u	Total
0	15	11	14	12	52
1	3	0	4	1	8
Total	18	11	18	13	60
CATEGORY – Lithic Weapon					
	f	j	m	u	Total
0	16	11	18	12	57
1	2	0	0	1	3
Total	18	11	18	13	60
CATEGORY – Metal Object					
	f	j	m	u	Total
0	14	10	18	12	54
1	4	1	0	1	6
Total	18	11	18	13	60
CATEGORY – Tool					
	f	j	m	u	Total
0	18	11	16	13	58
1	0	0	2	0	2
Total	18	11	18	13	60
CATEGORY – Ornament					
	f	j	m	u	Total
0	17	11	18	13	59
1	1	0	0	0	1
Total	18	11	18	13	60

Table 2.5 Crosstabulation for categories of individuals and grave goods. 0=absent; 1=present. f=females; j=juveniles; m=males; u=unknown sex.

It is particularly striking to observe how weapons (either metal or lithic), despite being limited in number, are not necessarily more frequent in male graves. Given the archaeological *cliché* that identifies Bronze Age male burials as richer in symbolic objects of power and masculinity (*i.e.* weapons), the evidence from Sant'Abbondio suggests a different scenario. It is not impossible that the state of preservation of the sample led to a misassignment of the skeletal morphological traits and generated incorrect sexing of some of the individuals. However, chemical data are coherent with the anthropological ones and results from trace elements for adult males and females (as skeletally sexed) follow the expected chemical behaviour (see Chapter Four). Although the two sets of data have been independently ascertained, such coherence represents an additional motive of reliance on the anthropological results. This therefore finds us in need of an alternative cultural explanation for the presence of weapons in female tombs.

In light of the small sample size, the significance of differences in the composition of grave goods between sexes was statistically tested using Fisher's exact test. Results are summarised in table 2.6. No significant differences are appreciable, however despite the lack of statistical significance, the variation observed is undoubtedly indicative of different trends.

Fisher's Exact Test – males vs. females				
Category	n	X^2	df	p
Ceramics	36	1.800	1	0.315
Metal Weapons	36	0.177	1	1.000
Lithic Weapons	36	2.118	1	0.486
Metal objects	36	4.500	1	0.104
Tools	36	1.895	1	0.487
Ornaments	36	1.150	1	0.472

Table 2.6 Results of the Fisher's exact test for categories of grave goods in accordance with sex of the individuals.

As described earlier, the cemetery is naturally divided in two topographically distinct halves (East and West). A contingency table (Table 2.7) was carried to test whether there are differences in the composition of grave goods for the two areas in accordance with sex and age of the deceased. Although the sample is rather small and therefore not ideal for statistical analysis a Fisher's Exact Test was performed (Table 2.8). Women are systematically associated with lithic daggers while men are not. Such evidence adds to that of the presence of metal weapons in female burials and seems to suggest a symbolic significance attributed to weapons that circulates across gender, possibly entailing multiple meanings that are not clearly definable with the traditional equation weapon=male power.

Although there is no difference between the two areas of the cemetery according to biological categories (sex) or cultural ones (deposition of grave goods) there is a difference in the incidence of a number of pathologies. When comparing oral health between individuals buried in the two halves of the cemetery it is interesting to observe a considerably higher frequency of enamel defects in individuals buried in its eastern section (Figure 2.15). Equally, it is worth noting how three of the four individuals observed for porotic hyperostosis came from the eastern area.

This type of evidence suggests that the eastern section of Sant'Abbondio population experienced a higher degree of systemic physiological stress (*i.e.* enamel hypoplasia and porotic hyperostosis) ascribable to a multitude of factors that vary from insufficient nutrition to infections and/or pathological conditions. Such a phenomenon speaks in favour of a differentiation within the population that is related to the topographical characterisation of the burial space. Such a pattern will be explained in the analysis of the chemical composition of bone and dental enamel of the Sant'Abbondio sample (see Chapter Five) and will be more thoroughly discussed further in the text.

2. Archaeological Data and Anthropological Analysis

Crosstabulation (Counts)

CATEGORY - Ceramic									
CERAMICS	e-f	e-j	e-m	e-u	w-f	w-j	w-m	w-u	Total
0	6	5	3	4	4	4	3	6	35
1	2	2	6	2	4	2	6	1	25
Total	8	7	9	6	8	6	9	7	60

Crosstabulation (Counts)

CATEGORY – Metal Weapon									
METAL WEAPON	e-f	e-j	e-m	e-u	w-f	w-j	w-m	w-u	Total
0	7	6	7	6	7	6	7	6	52
1	1	1	2	0	1	0	2	1	8
Total	8	7	9	6	8	6	9	7	60

Crosstabulation (Counts)

CATEGORY – Lithic Weapon									
LITHIC WEAPON	e-f	e-j	e-m	e-u	w-f	w-j	w-m	w-u	Total
0	8	6	9	5	7	6	9	7	57
1	0	1	0	1	1	0	0	0	3
Total	8	7	9	6	8	6	9	7	60

Crosstabulation (Counts)

CATEGORY – Metal Object									
METAL OBJECT	e-f	e-j	e-m	e-u	w-f	w-j	w-m	w-u	Total
0	5	7	9	6	7	5	9	6	54
1	3	0	0	0	1	1	0	1	6
Total	8	7	9	6	8	6	9	7	60

Table 2.7 Crosstabulation for categories of individuals and grave goods according to area of deposition (east vs. west). 0=absent; >1=present. (e-f=eastern female; e-j=eastern juvenile; e-m=eastern male; e-u=eastern unknown; w-f=western female; w-j=western juvenile; w-m=western male; w-u= western unknown).

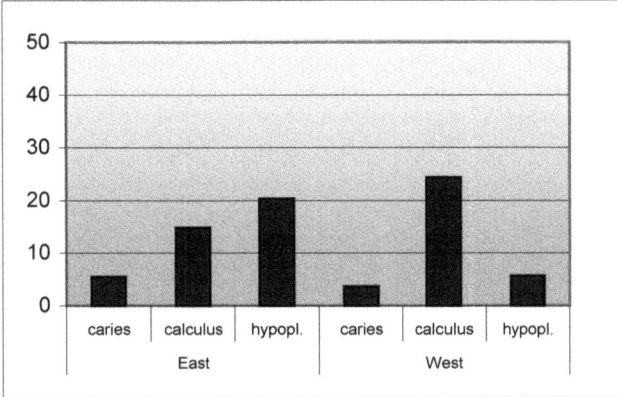

Fig. 2.15 Frequency (% of teeth affected/observed) of dental pathologies for individuals buried in the two halves of the cemetery.

SUMMARY

Archaeological and anthropological data from the Sant'Abbondio cemetery have revealed evidence of a multifaceted nature. Firstly, the cemetery itself represents, together with the recent discoveries at Gricignano and at San Paolo Belsito, near Naples (Albore Livadie and Marzocchella, 1999), an alternative scenario, in terms of funerary rituals, from that traditionally perceived for Bronze Age Southern Italy. However, despite the original significance of mortuary practices, the cultural coordinates for southern Italian Bronze Age remain unchanged. Material culture, plausibly economic strategies, and possibly social aspects may have been shared by prehistoric groups of the southern peninsula. The addition of Sant'Abbondio data, however, allows us to revise Puglisi's work in a more comprehensive perspective, and contributes to the reaffirmation of some of his propositions, while it offers the chance to expand some of his ideas and propose more complex archaeological as well as anthropological scenarios.

Fisher's Exact Test – East vs. West				
males	n	X^2	df	p
Ceramics	19	0.277	1	1.000
Metal Weapons	19	0.130	1	1.000
Lithic Weapons	19	----	----	----
Metal objects	19	----	----	----
Tools	19	1.626	1	0.485
Ornaments	19	----	----	----
females				
Ceramics	17	1.633	1	0.335
Metal Weapons	17	0.562	1	0.576
Lithic Weapons	17	0.008	1	1.000
Metal objects	17	1.639	1	0.294
Tools	17	----	----	----
Ornaments	17	1.105	1	0.471
juveniles				
Ceramics	24	0.253	1	1.000
Metal Weapons	24	1.043	1	1.000
Lithic Weapons	24	1.043	1	1.000
Metal objects	24	2.182	1	0.086
Tools	24	----	----	----
Ornaments	24	----	----	----

Table 2.8 Fisher's Exact Test for males and females and juveniles to measure differences in the composition of grave goods in accordance with the area of deposition in the cemetery.

The combination of known archaeological information with the anthropological data emerged from this work have made it possible to infer the cultural scenario of Sant'Abbondio context. It seems arguable a homogeneous cultural background for the group, as no evident chronological differentiations are appreciable. This coherent context refers to a population skeletally homogeneous, for which patterns of variation (as the ones described earlier on) are more likely to be ascribed to socio-cultural phenomena than to biological ones.

Sant'Abbondio represents a suitable sample for this study, as it appears to be representative in key archaeological and anthropological aspects such as material culture and skeletal biology, of the Bronze Age of the southern part of the peninsula. However, by expanding our knowledge of this moment of Italian prehistory with new and complementary data, it offers the chance to propose more complex interpretations.

CHAPTER THREE
ARCHAEOLOGICAL BONE CHEMISTRY. METHODOLOGICAL FRAMEWORK

THE CHEMISTRY OF ANCIENT HUMAN BONE

The application of chemistry in archaeology is best expressed in the analysis of human bones. The use of the human body as a "biological archive" (Borgognini Tarli and Pacciani, 1993: 23) relates to the identification of past biographies. If the determination of past demography or health conditions is among the primary questions, the understanding of past diet and hence subsistence still remains a frequently approached line of investigation. Bone chemistry is the most direct and reliable method to determine paleonutrition according to the principle that "the reading of chemical signatures passed from the foods being eaten to the consumer allows the documentation of diet" (Larsen, 1997: 270).

The chemical composition of human bone

The chemical structure of human bone is composed of an organic and an inorganic fraction (Table 3.1). The organic matrix forms up to 30% of the dry weight of bone and is primarily constituted by Type I collagen. Bone ash on the other hand, is a mineral combination of calcium phosphate that forms the hydroxyapatite and phosphorus (Price, 1989). Collagen represents 90% of the organic matrix of bone and is the main protein in the human organism. Its function is related to the maintenance of the structural integrity of various tissues and organs of which it is part. It can be present in different quantities, in combination with other components, and can have different molecular sequences, sizes and tissues that classify it into different types.

COMPOSITION OF MINERALISED TISSUES

	Bone		Developing enamel		Mature enamel	
	Weight	Volume	Weight	Volume	Weight	Volume
Inorganic (%)	88 (80-100)	70	37		16	≥96
Organic (%)	30	19		20		<0.2->0.6
Density (g/cm³)	2-2.05		1.45			2.9-3
Calcium (%)	24					34-40
Phosphorus (%)	11.2		16-18			
Ca/P ratio (weight)	2.15		1.92-2.17			
CO_2 present as carbonate (%)	3.9		1.95-3.66			
carbonate (%)	0.5		0.25-0.9			
Sodium (%)	0.3		0.25-0.56			
Magnesium %	5000		<25->5000			

Table 3.1 Chemical composition of human enamel and bone (after Hillson 1996 modified).

The inorganic matrix of bone, on the other hand, is formed by a microcrystalline structure of carbonate apatite, tricalcium phosphate hydrate and hydroxyapatite (Carlstrom and Engstrom, 1956). Bone tissue is formed by a series of layers of mineralised bone called lamellae. These are of three different types: the first form what is called the circumferential lamellar bone, that shapes the outer surface of the bone; the second type constitutes the interstitial lamellar bone, found between multicellular units of the bone, while the third type is placed concentrically around a central vascular canal (the Haversian canal) and forms osteons (Fig. 3.1).

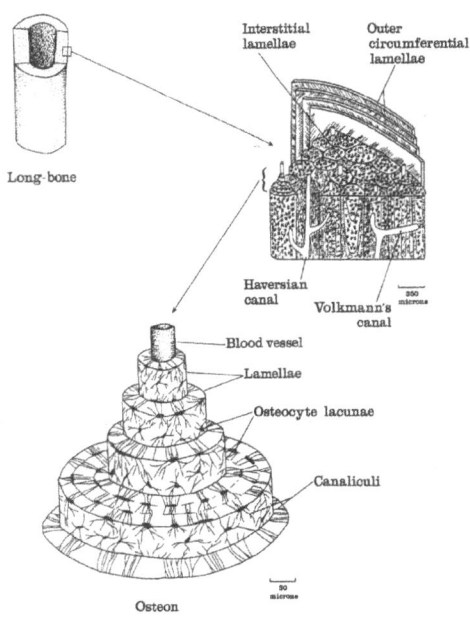

Fig. 3.1 Microscopic structure of cortical bone (after Mays 1998).

Osteons are tissue cylinders that respond to changing physiology and act as homeostatic regulators of calcium metabolism, bone repair and maintenance. Their function is carried out by two cells (osteoblasts and osteoclasts) responsible for the formation and resorption of new tissue, which is performed to maintain the structural consistency of bone and to control the concentration of calcium in body fluids. Through the activity of osteoblasts and of osteoclasts, the human skeleton undergoes active remodelling throughout the entire life span of an individual. Bone turnover generally involves only 3-5% of total osteons. For the femur an approximate estimate of 3% has been calculated (Radosevich, 1993). Formation of new bone takes several months while resorption is completed in a few weeks. Turnover tends to be fairly rapid in the trabecular fraction of the bone and slower in the cortical. The duration of the overall cycle varies between three months and a year and appears to be related to the age and health conditions of the individual. Complete remodelling of the skeleton requires from seven to ten years. (Mays, 1998: 3).

The chemical composition of teeth

The histology of teeth is very different from that of bone. Teeth have a growth process that starts from the cuspal terminus and proceeds to the extremity of the cementoenamel junction. They are constituted of three different tissues, enamel, dentine, and cement, that have different histological settings (Fig. 3.2). Dentine and cement form respectively through odontoblasts and cementoblasts, cells responsible for the creation and mineralisation of their matrix. The organic portion of these tissues, as for bone, is mainly constituted of collagen together with a non-collagenous component called ground substance. The collagen fibres are able to turn over rapidly – although not as fast as those of bone – allowing dentine and cement to remodel its matrix throughout life (Hillson, 1996). Enamel is a non-cellular tissue despite being formed by a series of cells called ameloblasts. Its organic portion constitutes around 5% of the total weight (Table 3.1).

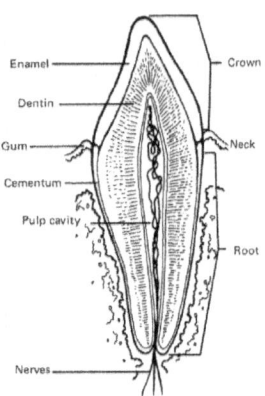

Fig. 3.2 Section of a human tooth (from Mays 1998 with modifications after Hillson 1996).

The main matrix of enamel is inorganic, consisting of calcium phosphate and hydroxyapatite, and its composition varies in accordance with substitution of the inorganic matrix that is normally carried out by elements such as carbonate and fluorine (Hillson 1996). A protein called amelogenin, together with other non-amelogenin proteins, is responsible for the process of formation of the matrix. Enamel development is based on phases of matrix secretion and maturation. At the initial stage, ameloblasts produce a matrix filled with apatite crystals, subsequently breaking down its organic component and allowing the crystals to grow and organise themselves into prisms that make the enamel tissue almost entirely mineral (*ibid.*: 149). Prisms of developing enamel form an angle of approximately 120° with the crown surface so that when observed with a Scanning Electron Microscope they give a so-called *cross striation* pattern. It has been observed (see for example Boyde, 1989) how cross striations are related to the variation of enamel matrix secretion interval. The latter, in humans, has a rate of 4.5 µm per day (Schour and Hoffman, 1939) so that cross striations represent a 24 hours interval or circadian rhythm (Hillson 1996).

HUMAN METABOLISM AND TRACE ELEMENTS

During the formation of bone and enamel tissue the uptake of minerals influences its biochemical composition. The absorption of elements is carried out by the gastrointestinal tract through food (along the food chain from plant to animal) and is a reflection of the lived-in environment through soil and groundwater. Excretion, contrarily, is provided directly by the faeces or indirectly by biliary and pancreatic secretion, urine and sweat.

Elemental uptake in the human tissues occurs at two different levels in accordance with concentration in the organism. These two levels categorise elements under the definition of major and trace elements, with the latter further divided into dietary essentials, non-essential, and potentially toxic (Underwood, 1977) (see Table 3.2). Major elements are present in large quantities and are indispensable for the functioning of the organism. They include carbon (C), hydrogen (H), nitrogen (N), calcium (Ca) phosphorus (P), oxygen (O), potassium (K), sulphur (S), chlorine (Cl), sodium (Na), and magnesium (Mg), constituting 96% of the total body weight (Sandford, 1993). Trace elements are only present at very low levels (less than 0.01% of the total body mass (Schroeder, 1973)), and are associated with three main functions within the animal and human organisms. Firstly, they functionate as enzyme activators. Secondly, they release or attract electrons in oxidation-reduction reactions, and finally they the act as metalloproteins, binding, transporting, and releasing other minerals. Ultimately, they are necessary in the maintenance of cell growth and reproduction, the support of the immune system and the regulation of brain activity (Sandford, 1992).

The process of absorption and excretion of minerals – or element homeostasis – can vary in accordance with the sex, age, nutritional status, and health conditions of an individual. Studies have demonstrated, for example, the influence of phenomena such as pregnancy and lactation on elemental uptake (see Blakely, 1989). Strontium/calcium (Sr/Ca) ratios in pregnant and breastfeeding women have shown lower values of strontium as a result of discrimination against the latter in favour of calcium in the placenta and the mammary glands (Sillen and Kavanagh, 1982). Higher bone turnover in women has also been related to these factors and can produce sex-specific differences in element concentrations (Kent *et al.*, 1990). In relation to age, infants can show high elemental concentrations as the result of gestational body storage and altered absorption and excretion due to the incompleteness of the gastrointestinal tract (Underwood, 1977). Mineral uptake is also influenced by physiological stress deriving from pathological conditions (Hambridge, 1974) and nutritional deficiencies (Underwood, 1977).

A further aspect that can influence homeostasis is the interaction between single elements as synergic or antagonistic with one another. Elemental synergy has been adequately discussed only for minerals such as iron, zinc and copper, although available data are not always as informative as one would like. By contrast, antagonism between elements has been widely investigated (see for example Underwood, 1977; O'Dell, 1985). As an example, an excess of zinc can cause a deficiency in copper, calcium, iron, cadmium, and chromium (Sandford, 1992). The intake of calcium, moreover, can promote the formation of chelating agents with dietary phytates from grains, forming insoluble complexes that inhibit the uptake of essential trace elements. High levels of iron increase aluminium excretion while phytate can inhibit the uptake of zinc, iron and magnesium (Sandford, 1992). All trace elements play specific roles in the biochemical composition of bone. It is therefore difficult to make a general synthesis of the functioning of each in the human organism as they can affect and are affected by a wide range of factors. As a general example, although essential trace elements (chromium, cobalt, copper, zinc, arsenic, lithium, nickel, silicon and vanadium) are not considered as nutrients, their presence in the organism regulates the absorption of vitamins and the functioning of enzymes (O'Dell, 1985).

Essential	Symbol	Proportional uptake in bone	Non essential	Symbol	Proportional uptake in bone	REE	Symbol	Proportional uptake in bone
Vanadium	V51	n.a.	Nickel	Ni60	n.a.	Lanthanum	La139	n.a.
Chromium	Cr52	n.a.	Strontium*	Sr88	90% (Ezzo 1994b)	Cerium	Ce140	n.a.
Manganese	Mn55	25% (Ezzo 1994b)	Zirconium	Zr90	n.a.	Praseodymium	Pr141	n.a.
Cobalt	Co59	14% Underwood (1977)	Niobium	Nb93	n.a.	Neodymium	Nd146	n.a.
Copper	Cu63		Tin	Sn118	n.a.	Samarium	Sm147	n.a.
Zinc	Zn66	28% (Ezzo 1994b)	Gold	Au197		Europium	Eu151/153	n.a.
Arsenic	As75	n.a.	Lead	Pb208	90% (Underwood 1977)	Gadolinium	Gd157	n.a.
Selenium	Se77/82	n.a.	Uranium	U238	n.a.	Terbium	Tb159	n.a.
Rubidium	Rb85	n.a.				Dysprosium	Dy163	n.a.
						Holmium	Ho165	n.a.
						Erbium	Er166	n.a.
						Thulium	Tm169	n.a.
						Ytterbium	Yb172	n.a.
						Lutetium	Lu175	n.a.
						Hafnium	Hf178	n.a.
						Tantalum	Ta181	n.a.
						Thorium	Th232	n.a.

Table 3.2 List of the elements considered for ICP-MS analysis. * Although strontium is technically a non-essential element, it has proved to have potential as a paleodietary indicator (Ezzo 1994b). n.a. = data not available.

According to Ezzo (1994), for an element to be used in paleodietary studies, it must fulfil a series of conditions that would automatically reduce biogenic and diagenetic biases. Features such as measurability and molecular stability can be seen as prerequisite. Furthermore, the ability of some elements to act as bone-seekers – that is to be highly absorbed by bone as opposed to other tissues – make them a preferred choice over others. The advantage of studying non-essential elements – normally preferred over essentials – is thus not always understandable. The specific homeostatic behaviour of essential elements can represent an *advantage* rather than a disadvantage for paleonutritional investigations, precisely because of their well-known functions within the human organism.

Elemental homeostasis, biochemical function and bioavailability

The term homeostasis is used in biology to describe the capacity of complex organisms to maintain a "stable internal environment" (Sandford, 1993: 23). In the human organism, homeostasis regulates elemental concentration through the creation of elemental body stores and the regulation of their mechanism of absorption and excretion. At a general level, elemental deficiencies or abundance are regulated through enhanced absorption or limited excretion and *vice versa*. At a greater level of complexity, homeostasis can also be achieved through physiological control that ensures that important sites are the first to receive mineral contributions.

For this study, a total of 35 elements are considered, divided among: essential, non-essential (together with possible toxic) and lanthanides or Rare Earth Elements (REE) (Table 3.2). The latter were initially selected as believed to better give a measure of the interaction between living species and the environment and are applied as an indicator of diagenesis. Unfortunately very little is published on the biochemical role of REE in the human organism. A description of elemental homeostasis, biochemical role, and bioavailability of the essential and non-essential elements considered for ICP-MS analysis is provided below. Because of the lack of published information, no description for Rare Earths is provided. The function of lanthanides and actinides within the human organism is virtually unstudied. At present, no extensive material has been found on the matter, despite the extensive literature searched. Data presented are gathered from the relevant literature and though the Internet (Goodman, 2001). They are however mainly understood for modern diet and cannot be directly equated to past situations.

Vanadium (V)

The great majority of vanadium in the human body is absorbed with diet and excreted through faeces. Human food varies greatly in vanadium concentration. Meat, fish and liver contain about 2-10 ppb while wheat and cereal contain between 6.5 and 20 ppb. Very high amounts of vanadium are present in dill (140 ppb) and radishes (790 ppb). Daily requirements are difficult to determine although a quantity of

15 μg/day is suggested (WHO, 1996) and the daily dietary intake is calculated around 0.04 mg (Goodman, 2001). In terms of toxicity, a study by Diamond and co-workers (1963) has demonstrated that a daily intake of 10 mg can cause serious toxic effects. A study on pigs and rats (Kruger, 1958) demonstrated that the addition of vanadium (as for strontium) in the diet can promote mineralisation of bone and teeth and reduce caries. Work by Strasia (1971) has shown how low-vanadium diets result in higher amounts of iron in blood and bone. Levels of vanadium in bone normally ranges around 0.006 ppm (Goodman, 2001).

Chromium (Cr)
Chromium is essential to the human metabolism, being responsible for the absorption of carbohydrates, lipids and proteins. Its function is also associated with the receptivity of insulin (Mertz, 1969). Trivalent chromium is normally not toxic and chromium poisoning is rarely attested. Cases of toxicity can be encountered as a result of oral ingestion or a high quantity of chromium in the air. By contrast, chromium deficiency has proven to be extremely recurrent in highly purified diets and seems to have a role in metabolic disorders such as diabetes-like syndromes and insulin resistance and ischemic heart disease (Shroeder, 1966).

The daily dietary intake of chromium ranges between 0.01 and 1.2 mg (WHO, 1996). The major contribution of this mineral to diet is given by meat, wholemeal grains, legumes and spices. Milk, cheese, fruits and vegetables only contain small amounts of chromium (Anderson, 1988).

Infants and juvenile individuals might show chromium deficiency as a result of deficiency in protein. Multiparous women have proved to have lower chromium levels than nulliparous (Hambridge, 1974) although the direct correlation between chromium deficiency and pregnancy has not been fully proven (Mertz, 1982). According to Mertz (*ibid.*), aging can be associated with gradual chromium depletion. Levels of chromium in the bone normally vary between 0.1 and 0.3 ppm (Goodman, 2001).

Manganese (Mn)
Manganese is an enzyme activator, hence related deficiency could cause defects in growth processes, skeletal abnormalities, and malfunction of the reproductive system. The quantity of manganese in the human organism varies between 12 and 20 mg (WHO, 1996) showing high concentrations in bone tissue (2-3 μg/g fresh weight (Asling and Hurley, 1963)). Daily dietary intake varies between 0.4 and 10 mg. Daily requirements and toxicity level are still unknown although according to Friedman (1987), the minimum amount required is approximately 0.70 mg/day. Bioavailability of manganese in human diet is provided in descending order (from 20 to 0.2 ppm) by nuts, dried fruit, whole cereals, roots, tubers, fruits and leafy vegetables (Underwood, 1977). Its concentration in animal tissues has proved to be very low (Wenlock *et al.*, 1979), in bone they can range between 0.2 and 100 ppm (Goodman, 2001). Highly processed diets based on refined cereals, meat and dairy products tend to have lower amounts of this mineral.

Studies have demonstrated how manganese absorption is directly correlated with iron level in the organism and how these two elements seem to have similar mechanisms of absorption resulting in chemical antagonism (WHO, 1996). Greater absorption of manganese occurs in iron deficient metabolism, while high levels of iron tend to inhibit manganese assimilation (WHO 1996). A correlation between age and manganese requirement has been demonstrated by Spencer *et al.* (1979). Middle-aged men seem to require more than 2 mg/day as opposed to younger individuals for whom this value seems to be sufficient.

Cobalt (Co)
Of total body content, approximately 14% of cobalt is stored by the bones (Underwood, 1977). Cobalt function in the human organism is mainly related to its form as vitamin B_{12}. Deficiency and toxicity in humans have not been extensively investigated although a few studies on animals have demonstrated how a lack of this mineral in the organism results in vitamin B_{12} synthesis inhibition and subsequent metabolic inefficiency (Andrews, 1960). It can be argued that the contribution of cobalt to diet is relatively unimportant when it is not associated with its vitamin B_{12} status. Cobalt uptake from diet is mainly provided by green leafy vegetables. Dairy products and cereals are extremely poor in this mineral. Daily dietary intake is around 0.005 to 1.8 mg (WHO, 1996). According to Underwood (1977), cobalt does not accumulate in human tissue with age and, unlike iron and copper, it is not stored in the liver. Moreover, studies on newborn lambs and calves have demonstrated that the cobalt content of the liver is reduced significantly when the mother is cobalt deficient. Levels in human bone vary between 0.01 and 0.04 ppm (Goodman, 2001).

Cobalt absorption increases with iron deficiency as cobalt and iron's transport pathway in the intestine is governed by the same mechanism and results in an antagonism between the two elements in terms of absorption.

Copper (Cu)
The biochemical function of copper is mainly related to the role of blood in the human body. In the plasma, copper is connected with the mobilisation of iron through the maintenance of iron stores (Hart *et al.*, 1928).

The effects of copper deficiency are still under study, but normally insufficient quantities of this mineral can cause anaemia, skeletal fragility and osteoporosis. A study by Klevay (1974) has demonstrated that the daily requirement of copper is 1.3-1.5 mg/day, mainly absorbed through food. Other sources raise the daily requirement to 6 mg/day (Goodman, 2001). Copper toxicity is generally caused by ingestion of contaminated food (as a result of the use of copper-rich vessels and utensils). This can cause severe liver failure and eventually death. The highest amounts of copper in human food (from 30 to 400 ppm) derive from crustaceans and shellfish (oysters in particular) as well as animal organs such as liver. Dried fruits in general, and nuts in particular, have high concentrations of this mineral as well as legumes and cocoa. Smaller amounts (between 2 to 0,5 ppm) are contained in dairy products, fresh fruits and cereals.

Copper deficiency in humans has never been attested (Underwood, 1977) and Scheinberg (1961) has demonstrated that most diets are even excessive in this element. Soft water has been demonstrated to provide higher copper concentration if compared to hard water (Schroeder and Balassa, 1966). Zinc/copper (Zn/Cu) ratio has been associated with breastfeeding, as it has been demonstrated to be lower in human milk than in cow milk (Klevay, 1974). Copper concentration is highly differentiated in adult and infant/juvenile individuals. In infants the amount of copper in the liver can be 6-10 times higher than in adults (WHO, 1996) as a result of retention from neonatal life. The liver acts as a copper store to overcome the low quantity of this mineral found in human milk. Over a period of approximately four years, hepatic copper levels gradually fall to normal values (Bloomer and Lee, 1978). Among adults, women normally show values 10% higher than men. During pregnancy this discrepancy tends to rise up to levels that are 3 times greater. Biological levels in bone are attested at 1-26 ppm (Goodman, 2001).

Several minerals are antagonists to copper; among them, cadmium, iron, lead and zinc can interact with copper absorption, although the circumstances of this antagonism are still under study (WHO, 1996).

Zinc (Zn)
The importance of zinc is related to its function as a stabiliser of molecular structure. The effects of zinc deficiency vary from dermatological problems to defects of skeletal growth and sexual maturity. Zinc insufficiency causes immune suppression as a result of zinc dependency of the hormone timuline. Known toxic effects are few, although it has been demonstrated that a high quantity of zinc can affect copper absorption (Fischer *et al.*, 1984). Daily dietary intake is estimated at 5-40 mg. The richest source of this mineral is seafood (in particular oysters), together with meat and nuts.

Bone and teeth have high values of zinc (150-250 ppm) (Underwood, 1977). Its absorption is mainly controlled and regulated by the duodenum, which is responsible for the preservation of homeostasis (*ibid.*). Infants can show high values of zinc as a result of retention *in utero*, although breast milk is relatively rich in this element and can supply 80% of daily requirements. During pregnancy and breast-feeding, women overcome high zinc requirements by an enhanced absorption and reduced excretion (WHO, 1996).

Arsenic (As)
Arsenic is largely present in the environment (soil and ground water) as part of many different minerals. Although its toxic potential has been intensively investigated, studies of the role of arsenic in the human diet are still very limited.

The human organism normally metabolises arsenic transforming it into different minerals such as strontium and rubidium, which are then excreted by the body through urine. Normal levels in the bone are around 0.08-1.6 ppm (Underwood, 1977). Fish and marine products, that contain considerably higher amounts of this mineral compared to other types of food, make the major contribution of arsenic to human diet. Daily dietary intake ranges between 0.04 and 1.4 mg. It is however important to stress that ground water intake is one of the major components of arsenic variation in the human organism.

Rubidium (Rb)
Rubidium has been shown to act as a substitute for potassium in human nutrition and its chemical relationship with this element is the object of several studies (*e.g.* Underwood, 1977). Concentrations of this element are relatively low in bone (0.5-5 ppm), although an overall extremely high concentration of this mineral in comparison to others is registered in other human tissues (*i.e.* brain and stomach).

Meat is relatively rich in rubidium, while the contribution of cereals through diet is rather limited. Daily intake normally ranges between 1.5 and 6 mg (WHO, 1996). Rubidium has no biological role but, being chemically similar to potassium, it is normally stored in the human tissues once absorbed from food. No extensive studies on possible sex and age differences in rubidium concentration have been undertaken. Further investigations on the biochemical role of this mineral are needed.

Strontium (Sr)
Despite the dominance of strontium in archaeological chemistry studies, the biochemical role of this element in the human organism has still not been fully investigated. Its behaviour is mainly observed in relation to calcium, as mammals discriminate against strontium in favour of calcium and the two elements have similar biochemical mechanisms. The use of strontium in elemental studies is based on the principle that its concentration within living organisms varies inversely to their position in the trophic pyramid (Sandford, 1992). It is therefore evident that strontium concentration in the human organism allows us to identify the position of the population under study within the food chain, leading to precise inferences in paleonutritional studies.

Levels of strontium in bone are believed to vary between 36-140 ppm (Goodman, 2001), although much higher levels have been attested (*e.g.* Underwood, 1977; Iyengar *et al.*, 1978), and trace element studies in archaeology normally present rather high values (Price *et al.*, 1998). The major implication of strontium in physiological processes is related to its behaviour in accordance with biological factors such as age and sex. Absorption is higher (ca. 60%) in children in their first year of life. Dietary intake is 0.8-5 mg/day. The reduction of levels of strontium in the tissues in relation to physiological stress such as weaning, and pregnancy and lactation, has proven to be essential to the archaeological investigation to reconstruct past dynamics (Blakely, 1989).

Nickel (Ni)
It has been observed that nickel absorption from the human gastrointestinal tract is relatively low, although several studies have concentrated on the differences in nickel absorption according to meat diets (low-nickel contributors) as opposed to vegetarian diets (high-nickel contributors). Approximately 50% of the daily requirement (0.3-0.5 mg) is provided by cereals (WHO, 1996).

During pregnancy and breast-feeding and in cases of iron deficiency it has been demonstrated that nickel absorption tends to be higher (Underwood, 1977). Nickel/iron (Ni/Fe) antagonism is demonstrated by high nickel absorption in iron-deficient diets. A sex-based difference is revealed during breast-feeding with an enhanced mechanism for absorption and retention of this element. Levels of nickel in the bone are not clearly determinable; values range between 0.7 (Goodman, 2001) to 110 ppm (Iyengar *et al.*, 1978).

Zirconium (Zr)
The function of zirconium in the human organism is still unknown, although this element is extremely abundant in the lithosphere (Underwood, 1977). Several studies (see for example Schroeder and Balassa, 1966) have demonstrated that relatively high quantities of zirconium are found in human tissues (0.1 ppm in bone).

The dietary contribution of zirconium is provided mainly by vegetable oil and tea (between 3 and 11 µg/g). Meat, diary products and cereals have lower amounts (1-3 µg/g) (Underwood, 1977). Daily dietary intake ranges around 0.05 mg (WHO, 1996).

Tin (Sn)
The biochemical function of tin is still unknown (WHO 1996), although it is believed to be an essential element. Daily requirements have been established through studies of animal diets and vary around 0.5 mg (*ibid.*). No exhaustive data on tin deficiency and toxicity are provided although the toxic potential of tin has been generally recognised. Johnson & Greger (1982) have demonstrated that low intake of tin results in high absorption and retention in the human body and *vice versa*. In diets providing approximately 50 mg/day of tin, absorption was of about 3%, while with 0.11 mg of daily intake absorption increased up to 50% (WHO, 1996). A good degree of tin absorption could be due to contamination derived from metal cooking vessels, although tin's toxicity mechanisms are rather complex. The ingestion of tin has low toxic potential as it is normally not retained in the tissues, while even a considerable amount of this mineral in the diet of rats has demonstrated no inhibition of growth and health in general (Underwood, 1977). Biological levels in bone range between 0.1 and 5 ppm (Goodman, 2001).

Lead (Pb)
The biological role of lead is still relatively unknown despite having been intensively studied for its toxic potentials. According to Underwood (1977) the highest concentrations of lead are found in bones (3.6-50 ppm) while Schroeder and Tipton (1968) have demonstrated that 90% of total human lead is found in the skeleton.

Lead toxicity is not easily observable though dietary intake because of lead enhanced excretion in cases of higher absorption, although a substantially higher contribution from the diet is registered in the tissues as a result of poisoning.

Within the human organism age-related differences are clearly visible. Infants and juveniles have systematically higher lead concentrations as a result of incomplete development of the intestine and kidneys that results in higher absorption and lower excretion. A study by Zigler (1978) has demonstrated how infants are capable of storing up to 50% of lead absorbed while on average adults only retain about 10%. During pregnancy and breast-feeding, lead (and other heavy metals) can be transferred from the mother to the child via placenta and milk. A study by the World Health Organisation (1996) has demonstrated a correlation between liquid diets and lead intake.

Cereals are the main contributors of lead to the diet (35% of total dietary contribution). Daily dietary intake ranges between 0.06 and 0.5 mg although values in the human organism are also related to the geochemistry of the living environment. The retention of lead is affected by the amount of calcium, phosphorus, iron, copper and zinc present in the organism. In particular, a study by Quarterman *et al.* (1974) has demonstrated that as dietary calcium increases, lead intake tends to decrease. The level of absorption by the human organism is highly dependant on calcium, potassium, iron, copper and zinc concentrations. The antagonism of calcium and potassium with lead results in a higher concentration of lead with calcium and potassium deficiency. The same mechanism is repeated in low iron diets and in greater proportions if compared to iron/manganese or iron/cobalt antagonism. The antagonism between lead and copper is still under study although work from Klauder *et al.* (1972) has demonstrated that high lead concentration in the body can result in lower copper storage.

The identification of dietary intake for each of these elements can be summarised through the classification of different contributors. Water is the main contributor of elements such as lead and arsenic. Meat contains high levels of chromium and rubidium, while fish is rich in copper, zinc, vanadium and strontium. Cereals and grains contain vanadium and chromium, while dried nuts are rich in manganese and copper. Finally, leafy vegetables are high contributors of copper, strontium, nickel and zirconium.

THE USE OF TRACE ELEMENT DATA. PROBLEMS OF DIAGENESIS AND 'ELEMENTAL MODELS'

Post-mortem changes in bone tissue are caused by elements that, if absorbed, migrate into the matrix of the bone to fill the void left by the decay of organic material and replace structural ions in the apatite crystal (Lambert *et al.*, 1989). After deposition bone can change its elemental composition. Some minerals such as calcite or barite, as well as iron and manganese may fill in the void and pores of the bone at a very initial stage of diagenesis. As the process proceeds, ionic substitution can take place and elements such as strontium, barium and lead can substitute calcium as cations (Sandford, 1992). This chemical reconstitution, or diagenetic process, can alter the original composition of bone following its burial by leaching, decomposition, and exposure to soil and ground water, and can result in enrichment, depletion or substitution of the original element composition in the bone (Price *et al.*, 1985a).

Other post-depositional processes are related to features such as soil pH (Gordon and Buikstra, 1981), texture and mineral and organic content as well as groundwater, temperature and microorganism attack (a study by Grupe and Piepenbrink 1988, for example, demonstrated the capacity of fungi to transport barium).

The influence of diagenesis on trace element analysis has been widely discussed (see for example Price *et al.*, 1985a; Sillen, 1986; Lambert *et al.*, 1989; 1990) although early studies underestimated its importance. Some authors have argued that post-depositional effects may be sex-specific; Lambert (1989), observed that males and females have different lead, iron, and manganese concentrations that disappears after bone surface removal. In terms of the histology of bone, no particular differences between the two sexes are recognisable and it is therefore necessary to better investigate this issue before being able to make further inferences. Differences in mineral concentrations are, however, appreciable in accordance with the type of bone used for analysis. The use of different skeletal regions has already been shown to produce different results (see for example Lambert *et al.*, 1982; Grupe, 1988).

Bone element composition in prehistoric populations can vary by 40% for some minerals (Price, 1989). In addition to diagenesis, such differences can be related either to environment and diet or to variation in human metabolism (in most cases related to sex and age). Several works in the last decades have focused on different ways of detecting – through interbone variations – and removing – through sample preparation procedures – non-biogenic compounds (Lambert *et al.*, 1990). Strontium concentration and Sr/Ca ratio were used initially as ways of identifying strontium uptake from the soil (Sillen and Kavanagh, 1982), as it is known that living mammals discriminate against strontium in favour of calcium. Work by Sillen (1981) on Natufian and Aurignacian samples demonstrated that there were no significant differences in strontium content among herbivores, carnivores and humans and that it could not be used as an indicator of ancient diet. The same method was applied by Williams (1988) who argues that strontium must not be considered as a the only reliable dietary indicator.

Neutron activation analysis has demonstrated vanadium, manganese and aluminium contamination in bone (Hancock *et al.*, 1987). Utilizing this, combined with electron probe microanalysis, Williams (1988) demonstrated that elements such as scandium, lanthanum, cerium, hafnium, thorium and uranium had higher concentrations in archaeological remains when compared with modern bone cortex and thus resulted from post-depositional uptake. X-ray diffraction was used by Nelson and co-workers (1986) to compare trace element composition in modern and prehistoric terrestrial and marine feeders. Strontium levels showed different trends in the samples suggesting groundwater contamination. X-ray fluorescence and diffraction was also used by Kyle (1986) on bone and teeth samples from Papua New Guinea, who showed that only bone was contaminated by aluminium, iron, strontium, silicon, barium and zinc taken up from the soil of deposition. Methods such as crystallographic examination of the bone has been used in the estimation of diagenetic effects indicating that post-depositional element uptake has to be considered as a main issue in spectroscopic analysis. It must, however, be borne in mind that inter-bone differences cannot be directly informative of diagenetic processes. As Price (1989) and Sillen (1981) have demonstrated, the lack of such differences could be the result of chemical equilibration of bone matrix that can disperse formerly existing variation. In this regard, ratio studies have been proposed as a good way to overcome this problem (see for example Price *et al.*, 2000).

The only tangible way to overcome the problem of diagenesis is through sample preparation (either chemically or physically) and correct interpretation of trace element data, especially in terms of the biochemical function of minerals, sex and age-specific variance, and elemental models. In this study, sample preparation procedures have been specifically directed towards the control of diagenetic effects on bone and teeth and focus on ways of removing their non-biogenic portion. Their accuracy and effectiveness will be discussed further.

SINGLE-ELEMENT INVESTIGATIONS AND STRONTIUM STUDIES

In archaeology, the single-elemental approach follows two main directions: paleopathological studies and reconstruction of health conditions, and toxicological analysis. The most commonly used element in paleopathological investigation is iron. Work by Fornaciari *et al.* (1983) on the relation between iron deficiency in human bone and hypoplasia stands as a good example of this. Although all elements can be toxic if ingested in high quantities, toxic effects resulting from working activities or daily exposure normally involve minerals such as lead, manganese or uranium. The use of lead in the manufacture of lead-glazed pottery or as a result of drinking and eating from contaminated vessels (Aufderheide *et al.*, 1981) has been used to reconstruct past economic and social frameworks.

Within such an approach some elements have played a key role, strontium being the principal one. The application of strontium concentrations and Sr/Ca ratio studies to paleonutritional investigation represents the first appearance of trace element analysis in archaeology (Toots and Voorhies, 1965). The basis for strontium studies is that "… at each level of the trophic pyramid there is a metabolic discrimination against strontium as opposed to calcium" (Radosevich, 1993: 271), so that, along the food chain, higher concentrations of this element are found in plants (that absorb it from soil and groundwater) and decreasingly in herbivores, humans and carnivores.

Sr/Ca ratios have been used to trace past diet, building on the principle of discrimination of strontium in favour of calcium in mammals. This kind of study has proved to be effective in comparing the concentrations in humans, herbivores and carnivores (Sillen, 1981). It has also been linked to dietary differences related to social differentiation and ranking (Schoeninger, 1979) or to features involving human metabolic processes such as weaning, pregnancy, and lactation (Blakely, 1989). It has provided a good means of detecting dietary changes over time in relation to pre-agricultural vs. agricultural populations (Schoeninger, 1981).

The drawback of strontium investigations as for all trace element studies is diagenesis. The influence of diagenesis on the elemental composition of human skeletal remains has been already discussed, although it is important to stress that post-mortem alterations related to strontium have been especially investigated as a result of the importance given to this element in archaeological studies.

Recently, strontium (together with other elements) has been used for non-dietary studies in a pioneering way. Price and co-workers (1994; 1998; 2000) and Ezzo and his colleagues (1997) have begun to identify patterns of residence and mobility within past populations. Strontium concentrations and strontium isotope analysis are examined in both bone and enamel tissue and correlated with the geological background of the area under study to trace patterns of mobility related to social features (marriage, migration, conquest, colonisation). This type of analysis has opened a whole series of new avenues for research. This research has similar interest although a multi-elemental approach has been preferred and could lead to even more interesting results, as it offers a multidimensional perspective.

MULTI-ELEMENTAL STUDIES

The monopoly of strontium in bone chemistry studies has resulted in a limited knowledge of the potential of other minerals for archaeological investigation. The multi-elemental approach has mainly been used to trace ancient diet (cf. Lambert *et al.*, 1979) and to detect diagenetic effects (Katzenberg, 1984; Lambert *et al.*, 1984). Levels of concentration of zinc, copper and magnesium have been studied by Blakely and Beck (1981) to determine social status. Beck (1985) associated the different concentrations of zinc and strontium in males and females with gender-based diet.

This research represents an attempt to use the multi-elemental approach to overcome the strontium monopoly in bone chemistry investigations. While being aware of the importance of providing elemental models that are sufficiently informative of human metabolic processes, it is essential to stress that inter-elemental relationships and variance deserve particular focus when dealing with this type of investigation. The potentials of the multi-elemental approach are primarily related to the multi-dimensional nature of the results obtained. Through the observation of more elements it is possible to infer biological as well as cultural phenomena with a greater level of precision. Biochemical information on elemental synergy or antagonism, for example, can be used to investigate past health conditions. The paleonutritional perspective some elements provide helps define past dynamics, not only in relation to subsistence but also in accordance with socio-economic phenomena.

PREVIOUS MULTI-ELEMENTAL INVESTIGATIONS AND METHODS FOR DATA ANALYSIS

Multi-elemental studies tend to be rather 'neglected' within trace element analysis, possibly as a result of the trend to focus on the use of single minerals, particularly strontium and lead, to examine specific questions. They have been criticised mainly for the difficulty of isolating the different properties of each element within the human organism and for the diverse effects they carry in terms of diagenetic forces.

Within traditional bone chemistry studies, the main goal of multi-elemental investigations has been to determine subsistence shifts, especially in terms of the introduction of maize horticulture (Lambert *et al.*, 1979). This kind of approach to paleodietary reconstruction has been applied on the basis of the ability for some minerals to discriminate between diets centred on plant rather than meat sources. Elements such as magnesium, manganese, and vanadium, together with strontium and calcium, have been considered as informative of plant contribution to diet, while zinc, selenium, copper, and molybdenum have been employed as indicators of meat consumption (Sandford, 1993). As an example, Lambert *et al.* (1979) studied the Middle and Late Woodland sites of Gibson and Ledders, Illinois (USA), using Atomic Absorption (AA) on rib samples. Strontium, zinc, magnesium, calcium, sodium, copper, iron, aluminium, manganese, potassium, cadmium and lead were used. Statistical analysis consisted mainly of intra- and inter-site elemental variation, through parametric tests, in accordance with groups of individuals categorised by age and sex. Results from bone specimens were examined in comparison with soil values in order to detect possible ion exchange. Elements such as iron, aluminium, manganese and potassium were considered to be highly subject to diagenesis; all other elements were used for dietary interpretation. Values from intra- and inter-site analysis reflected differences related to shift in diet throughout time, while sex- and age-based data reflected metabolic and biological influences on mineral concentration.

Baraybar & de la Rua (1997) applied a multi-elemental approach, using zinc, iron, magnesium, vanadium, copper, strontium, barium, phosphorus and calcium through Atomic Emission Spectrometry (ICP-AES) to a Chalcolithic site in Northern Spain. The sample preparation technique followed that of Szpunar *et al.* (1978). Data were processed through bivariate plots and calculation of correlation coefficients, while multivariate analysis was carried out through Principal Components Analysis. Elemental concentrations were presented as a ratio to calcium determining relative elemental abundance. Bivariate plots were used to trace differences between terrestrial vs. marine, and herbivore vs. carnivore diet. Strontium, barium, vanadium and zinc were considered to be the most reliable in discriminating along the trophic chain.

Francalacci and Borgognini Tarli's (1987) approach was also directed to the reconstruction of dietary habits and to the identification of the nutritional contribution of various species within traditionally conceived subsistence systems. The authors used Atomic Emission Spectrometry (ICP-AES) trace element analysis and stable isotopes data on a range of elements (barium, copper, magnesium, manganese, strontium, vanadium and zinc) on human and animal bones from Epigravettian, Mesolithic, and Neolithic Italian sites to compare the reliability of the various methods (especially in terms of intra-individual variation and diagenetic alteration) and reconstruct paleonutrition. The authors used multi-elemental investigation to reconsider generalisations on Neolithic economy, demonstrating the significant contribution of meat and fish proteins to the diet of Late Neolithic groups, as opposed to plant (cereal and nut) consumption. Bivariate statistics, through parametric and non-parametric tests, indicated high intra-individual and inter-site variation. A few elements such as barium, copper and zinc were considered good paleodietary indicators, yielding results that met expectations in terms of biochemical behaviour and confirming the reliability of elements other than strontium in the detection of past nutrition.

The common approach of all of the studies described is the investigation of dietary shifts and variation within ancient human populations, focussing on subsistence strategies. What is believed to be a limit to such approaches is that the question is mainly paleonutritional, with little or no concern for social dynamics.

METHODOLOGICAL FRAMEWORK

INDUCTIVELY COUPLED PLASMA-MASS SPECTROMETRY

In the initial part of this chapter a review of past approaches complemented the presentation of the biological and chemical basis for the analysis applied for this research. In the following part of the chapter, the specimens studied and the method used (Inductively Coupled Plasma-Mass Spectrometry) will be discussed. The analytical method will be described and a review of sample preparation procedure will be provided in order to better understand the choice for the procedure applied in this work. Methods for the assessment of the reliability of results obtained are also presented.

Inductively Coupled Plasma-Mass Spectrometry (ICP-MS) is one of many laboratory techniques that can be used to provide trace element data. The principle upon which this method works has been partially described earlier in this chapter and is founded on the separation of electrically charged atoms on the basis of their atomic mass. A mass spectrometer (Fig. 3.3) is generally formed of five components: an inlet system, responsible for receiving the sample and transforming it into a gas; an ionic source, that converts the gaseous molecules into a ion beam; a mass analyser, that separates the ions according to their mass-to-charge ratio; a detector, responsible for measuring the concentrations of the separated ions; and a computer, that can read the signals from the detector and translate them into a numerical value presented in a database (Braun, 1987).

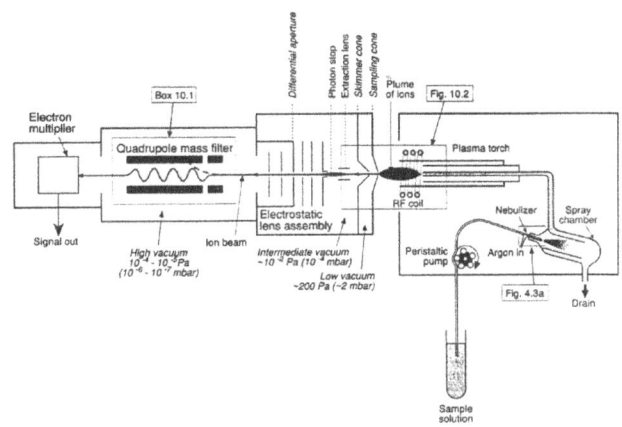

Fig. 3.3 Inductively Coupled Plasma-Mass Spectrometer (after Jarvis 1997 modified).

In order for spectroscopic analysis to take place, the sample must be in the form of a solution so that it can be converted into a gas. This aspect initially restricted the types of samples that could be analysed, although new instrumentations and techniques are now able to investigate almost any biochemical compound.

The distinctiveness of ICP-MS from other forms of spectroscopic analyses is evident in the name of the technique itself, which is based on the use of a plasma. In order for all elements in a compound to become dissociated, it is sometimes necessary to raise the temperature at which analysis is carried out. Other forms of spectroscopic analyses are performed at relatively low temperatures (*e.g.* for atomic absorption the limit is about 4,000°C) that allow efficient identification for most elements. However, if a large multi-element detection is desired it is necessary to achieve intense heating. In this case, it is possible to operate with a plasma torch. When ICP-MS is performed, the sample to be analysed is introduced in the form of a solution – the plasma – that is converted by a nebuliser into an aerosol dispersed in a stream of argon gas and introduced into a plasma torch (Jarvis, 1997). Ion detection is generally obtained by Thermal Ionisation Mass Spectrometry (TIMS), which can use different methods (for example, the Faraday Cup, the electron multiplier of petrographic plates), based on the principle that ions with different mass to charge ratios (m/z) will react differently.

The plasma torch is generally formed by three concentric silica tubes: the outermost one containing the plasma gas, the intermediate one containing the auxiliary gas supply and the inner one that carries the sample. Once the argon gas supporting the plasma enters the torch, it is activated with a high-power radio frequency alternating current that produces the motion of free electrons of the argon gas. Ionisation is thus created by collision between free electron and argon gas atoms, at a temperature that reaches about 10,000°C, avoiding unnecessary chemical interferences. As the sample is volatilised, dissociated and ionised, it comes out the plasma torch as a mixture of atoms and ions. As a result of a decrease in pressure, the ion beam is vacuumed into the mass spectrometer through two conical openings: the sampling cone and the skimmer that deflects away all uncharged molecules and atoms. Through a series of electrostatic lenses the ion beam is then introduced into the mass analyser. This generally consists of a quadrupole mass filter (Fig. 3.3) that accepts ions of only one mass/charge ratio through the detector.

The slow introduction of ICP-MS analysis was initially caused by the high cost of instrumentation involved in it. As an alternative, Atomic Absorption Spectrometry (AAS) was used and has been held in high regard as fast, effective but also easily accessible and low-cost (Sandford, 1992). Further studies (Jarvis, 1997) have, however, demonstrated that the ICP-MS method is able to provide advantages such as high sensitivity for most elements, exceptionally low detection limits, simultaneous multi-element determination (AAS, for example, implies a different run for each element), high precision and accuracy, rapid analysis (1 minute per sample) and a low amount of sample required for analysis (less than 10 µl).

SAMPLE PREPARATION METHODS IN THIS STUDY

Two main types of procedure for sample preparation are known in archaeological bone chemistry: 'physical methods' and 'chemical methods'. Both focus on removing the non-biogenic portion in the hard tissues. Chemical methods have proven to be excessively aggressive on the biogenic portion of the bone (Lambert *et al.*, 1990) because of the use of reagents, while various studies have demonstrated (cf. Lambert, 1989, 1990; Groupe, 1988) how physical removal of the outer surface of the sample can drastically reduce the impact of diagenetic factors without having to chemically attack the tissue and contaminate it further. The first study to apply the physical method was that of Szpunar *et al.* (1978), later developed by Lambert and co-workers (1989). It is carried out through the abrasion of a 1-3 mm layer of the outer surface of the cortex, where ions are more likely to substitute from the soil into the matrix and *vice versa*. A review of sample preparation procedure (Lambert *et al.*, 1990) has proven the effectiveness of this method, hence it was the one selected for this study.

SAMPLE COLLECTION

In bone chemistry studies, many different regions of the skeleton have been used, although there is a general consensus on which are the most reliable bones (see Grupe, 1988). Trabecular bone has been demonstrated to poorly reflect the chemical composition of the whole skeleton and has been considered unreliable in terms of diagenetic effects (Pate and Brown, 1985). Grupe (1988) also stressed the difference in concentration between trabecular and compact bone. In this perspective, femur or tibia shafts supply a sufficient thickness to enable the physical sample preparation procedure through the removal of the outer surface of the bone, where most post-depositional chemical substitution takes place (Lambert *et al.*, 1990).

For this study, collection of bone tissue took place from the cortical fraction of the femur mid-shaft. In most individuals in the Sant'Abbondio assemblage the femur was present; only ten individuals were lacking this bone in which case a fragment of the tibia or of another long bone was selected instead (Table 3.3).

The collection of enamel samples was carried out from the lower or the upper canine of each individual. The choice of the canine was motivated by the grade and interval of maturation and eruption of this tooth, representative of a precise and relatively limite d interval of juvenile age (see Moores *et al.*, 1963; Goodman and Armelagos, 1985; Ubelaker, 1989).

3. Methodological Framework

Burial	Year	Sex	Age	Enamel	Bone	Soil	Notes
1993	**n= 32**						
1	1993	m	adult	C_{right}	left femur		In Pompeii
2	1993	m	adult	C_{right}	right femur		
2 bis	1993	j	inf II	C_{right}	limbs		
3	1993	-----	--------	------------	------------------	----------	No skeletal remains
4	1992	f	adult	C_{left}	right femur	sampled	
5	1993	f	adult	C_{left}	right femur		
6 Q.I	1993	m	adult	C_{right}	femur?		
7	1993	j	inf II	C_{left}	limbs		
8	1993	m	adult	C_{right}	right femur		In Pompeii
9	1993	u	adult	no teeth	right femur		
10	1993	-----	--------	------------	------------------	----------	No skeletal remains
11(B)	1993	f	adult	no teeth	left femur		
12	1993	f	adult	C_{right}	left femur		
13	1993	m	adult	C_{right}	femur		In Pompeii
14(B)	1993	j	juv.	C_{left}	right femur		
15(B)	1992	u	adult	no teeth	right femur		strong muscol. insertions
16	1993	-----	--------	------------	------------------	----------	No skeletal remains
17	1992	j	inf I	$C_{right} + C_{right}$	limbs		*Enchytrismos* + green tr.
18Q.I	1993	m	adult	C_{right}	femur		
19	1993	-----	--------	------------	------------------	----------	No skeletal remains
20	1993	f	adult	C_{right}	right femur	sampled	
21QIII	1993	u	adult	no teeth	right femur		
22	1993	j	inf I	no teeth	left femur		In Pompeii, in sarcophagous
23	1993	-----	--------	------------	------------------	----------	No skeletal remains
24	1993	m	adult	no teeth	no postcranial		
25(B)	1993	u	adult	no teeth	right femur		
26(B)	1992	u	adult	C_{right}	tibia		teeth with green traces
27	1993	f	adult	C_{left}	femur		
28	1993	u	adult	no teeth	femur		
29(B)	1993	f	adult	C_{left}	humerus		
30	1993	m	adult	C_{right}	right tibia		
31	1993	f	adult	C_{right}	right femur		
32	1993	-----	--------	------------	------------------	----------	No skeletal remains
	1993	m	adult	C_{right}	left femur		
34	1993	u	adult	no teeth	right femur?	sampled	
35	1993	-----	--------	------------	------------------	----------	No skeletal remains
36	1993	u	adult	no teeth	limbs		
37	1993	f	adult	C_{left}	right tibia		
Skull	1993	f	adult	no teeth	no postcranial		
1996	**n = 30**						
1	1996	f	adult	C_{right}	right femur		
2	1996	f	adult	C_{right}	right femur		
3	1996	m	adult	C_{right}	right femur		
4(B)	1996	f	adult	C_{left}	right femur	sampled	
5 bis	1996	m	adult	no teeth	right femur		
5 n. 2	1996	j	inf I	C_{right}	limbs		*enchytrismos*
6	1996	m	adult	C_{right}	femur		
7	1996	u	adult	C_{right}	limbs		(bone from soil)
8	1996	f	adult	C_{right}	right femur	sampled	
9	1996	-----	--------	------------	------------------	----------	No skeletal remains
10	1996	f	juv	C_{left}	right femur		
11	1996	m	adult	C_{left}	right femur		
12QVIII	1996	m	adult	C_{right}	right femur		
13	1996	j	juv	C_{right}	limbs		
14	1996	f	adult	C_{right}	right femur		
15	1996	u	adult	no teeth	left femur		Comm. Remains?
16	1996	j	inf II	C_{right}	right femur		
17	1996	u	juv	C_{right}	right femur		
18	1996	m	adult	C_{right}	right femur		
19	1996	m	adult	C_{right}	right femur		
20	1996	u	adult	no teeth	femur?		
21	1996	u	adult	C_{left}	right femur		
22	1996	m	adult	C_{left}	left femur		
23	1996	-----	--------	------------	------------------	-------	No skeletal remains
24	1996	j	inf I	C_{left}	limbs		
25	1996	m	adult	C_{right}	left femur		
26	1996	f	adult	C_{right}	left humerus	sampled	
27	1996	-----	--------	------------	------------------	----------	No skeletal remains
28	1997	f	adult	C_{right}	left femur		
29	1997	f	adult	C_{right}	left femur		
30	1996	-----	--------	------------	------------------	----------	No skeletal remains
31	1997	u	adult	C_{right}	right femur		
32	1996	-----	--------	------------	------------------	----------	No skeletal remains
33	1996	-----	--------	------------	------------------	----------	No skeletal remains
34	1997	m	adult	C_{left}	right femur		
35	1997	j	juv	C_{right}	left femur		

Table 3.3 Record of Sant'Abbondio bone, enamel and soil collection.

The left canine was systematically chosen in order to exclude potential laterality biases. The choice of a lower tooth was a result of the state of preservation of the assemblages that have yielded a higher number of mandibles as opposed to maxillae. When the left lower canine was missing, the right one was selected as an alternative, and when this was missing the left and right upper canines were used (Table 3.3). For juvenile individuals both deciduous and permanent canines were selected in order to determine possible differences in elemental composition. In order to provide a duplicate following the destruction during preparation, a cast of each tooth was made. Double samples of enamel were collected from 5 individuals to test method accuracy. Enamel extraction was carried out systematically from the same area on each tooth (Fig. 3.4) and a record of the area of collection was kept.

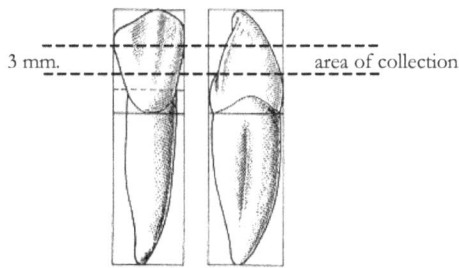

Fig. 3.4 Area of collection of enamel from the canine (after Mallegni and Rubini 1992 modified).

During collection any event causing possible contamination (*e.g.* breakage of the tooth while grinding resulting in the possible presence of dentine) was recorded. The area of extraction measured 2-3 mm along the central section of the labial surface of the crown. The middle labial region – corresponding, in an adult tooth, to approximately 3 years of age - was preferred although the buccal surface was used in cases where the enamel on the labial surface was not fully preserved.

Samples – either human or animal – from other contexts were collected to provide material for comparative analysis. The presence of comparative samples is essential to test both preparation procedures and instrumental accuracy, founded on the principle that any contamination would produce similar data in supposedly heterogeneous samples. Furthermore the analysis of faunal samples from Sant'Abbondio as well as other sites provides evidence of the elemental concentration in animals as opposed to humans and could provide additional information. The comparative samples consisted of a total of eight specimens (2 human adults from the Romano-British cemetery of Huntsman's Quarry; one human adult from an unspecified Medieval Anglo-Saxon cemetery; one human juvenile from the Bronze Age site of Huntsman's Quarry[1]; one human adult from Roman Pompeii and two animal samples – pig and sheep – from unspecified Anglo-Saxon sites).

Soil samples were also collected from different parts of the Sant'Abbondio cemetery and in general from the Sarno Valley and the Sorrento Peninsula to better assess the level of interaction between individuals and local environment.

SAMPLE PREPARATION FOR ICP-MS ANALYSIS

The method used to prepare the samples for spectroscopic analysis was that proposed by Lambert and co-workers (1989; 1990). Bone and dental enamel were treated differently as they have a different chemical composition, mainly related to the fact that bone has a higher organic matrix (20-30%) than teeth, which are almost entirely inorganic. Preparation took place in the Geochemistry Laboratory of the Southampton Oceanography Centre and throughout the entire procedure sterile gloves and mask were worn to avoid contact with the sample. Tools (spatulas, tweezers, abraders) were washed with deionised water each time they were used and double washed from one sample to the other. Samples prepared were always placed on sterile paper or in sterilised containers (crucibles or vial).

During the bone preparation procedure the sample was:

- weighed (W1) to a 0.1 g level of precision;
- repeatedly washed with deionised water to remove outer impurity;
- abraded to remove of the outer surface (1-3 mm) using a DREMEL tool mounting a 3.2 mm aluminium oxide abrasive wheel;
- weighed (W2) to a 0.01 g level of precision;
- soaked in deionised water for 1-3 hours to remove further impurity;
- placed in glass vials and dried overnight at ca. 100°C in a GRIFFIN incubator to return to dry weight;
- ashed at 900°C in sterile 15 ml porcelain crucibles to destroy the organic component;
- powdered into a fine grain in a porcelain mortar;
- weighed (W3) to a 0.01 g level of precision;
- placed in sterile glass vials for solution.

Although a number of more volatile elements such as zirconium (Lambert *et al.*, 1990), are normally affected at high temperatures, the choice of 900°C as ashing temperature was made to ensure that all of the organic fraction of the bone was dissolved; this was mainly due to the consideration that the use of a physical procedure as opposed to a chemical one, could guarantee the purest biogenic composition to be extracted with the removal of any residual diagenetic portion of tissue.

The preparation procedure for teeth was considerably different, as no ashing was required to remove the organic fraction (being enamel mostly inorganic), and the enamel was already extracted in form of a powder. Each tooth was:

- washed with deionised water;
- abraded to remove the outer surface with a DREMEL tool mounting a 2.4 mm tipped diamond wheel point (mod. 7144);
- washed with deionised water;
- abraded with a DREMEL tool mounting a 2.4 mm diamond wheel point (mod. 7103) in order to extract a

---

[1] Samples from the Anglo-Saxon sites were provided by the Osteological Laboratory at the Department of Archaeology of the University of Southampton with kind permission of Dr. John Robb.

sufficient amount of powder that was directly collected into a sterile glass vial.

The total amount of bone ash remaining after the preparation varied according to the initial weight of the sample. For ICP-MS analysis up to 5 grams of bone powder were collected while approximately 0.05 grams of enamel were obtained from the abrasion of the crown surface. Following the collection of bone and enamel material, the samples had to be chemically processed in order to be ready for ICP-MS analysis. The method was provided by NERC laboratories (NERC ICP-MS Facility – Kingston University) and followed standard procedures (Table 3.4). The preparation was carried out in the Geochemistry Laboratory of the Southampton Oceanography Centre.

ICP-MS Analysis Protocol (NERC ICP-MS Facility – Kingston University)	
BIOLOGICAL SAMPLING	**MEASUREMENTS**
SPECIMEN: bone or enamel	**METHOD**: Inductively Coupled Plasma-Mass Spectrometry (ICP-MS)
VOLUME: 0.005 g. (bone); 0.001 g. (enamel)	**ANALYTE**: Elements in Table 5.2
CONTROLS: double reading for 5 specimens	**REAGENTS**: 18 mΩ dionised water; HNO_3 (Conc)
	DIGESTION ACID: HNO_3 (Conc)
	FINAL SOLUTION: 2% HNO in 50 ml solution 18 mΩ dionised water
	BACKGROUND CORRECTION: standard drift (every 5 readings)
	CALIBRATION: internal standard
	QUALITY CONTROL: reference material
	ESTIMATED LLD: 20/(Std20ppm-stdblk)3(StdDev ·10)
INTERFERENCES: Spectral interferences are sometimes encountered. These are minimised through background corrections (drift)	

Table 3.4 Scheme of ICP-MS analytical method for bone and enamel samples.

A total of 0.5 grams of soil samples were treated according to a procedure similar to that described for bone and enamel, the only exception being the type of reagent used for dissolution (Table 3.5).

ICP-MS Analysis Protocol (NERC ICP-MS Facility – Kingston University)	
GEOLOGICAL SAMPLING	**MEASUREMENTS**
SPECIMEN: soil	**METHOD**: Inductively Coupled Plasma-Mass Spectrometry (ICP-MS)
VOLUME: 0.5 g.	**ANALYTE**: Elements in Table 5.2
CONTROLS: none	**REAGENTS**: 18 mΩ dionised water; HF (*aristar*)
	DIGESTION ACID: HF (*aristar*)
	FINAL SOLUTION: 2% HNO_3 in 50 ml solution 18 mΩ dionised water
	BACKGROUND CORRECTION: standard drift (every 5 readings)
	CALIBRATION: internal standard
	QUALITY CONTROL: none
	ESTIMATED LLD: 20/(Std20ppm-stdblk)3(StdDev ·10)
INTERFERENCES: Spectral interferences are sometimes encountered. These are minimised through background corrections (drift)	

Table 3.5 Scheme of ICP-MS analytical method for soil samples.

Laboratory contamination occurred during preparation for ICP-MS reading. As will be explained further on, zinc contamination was caused by the use of zinc-contaminated buffers resulting in the exclusion of this element. Selenium (Se77 and Se78) and europium (particularly Eu153) showed extremely low values – systematically below the detection limit – and therefore were excluded from the analysis. Laboratory contamination in relation to sample preparation was tested and excluded (see following chapters).

ASSESSING THE RELIABILITY OF THE ANALYSIS

Several authors (*e.g.* Pate *et al.*, 1989) have argued the possibility of incomplete sample dissolution for ICP-MS method, although work by Szpunar *et al.* (1978) has indicated that residual undissolved silica do not affect final results. In order to test the repetitiveness of the analysis and to verify possible contamination during the different processes of intervention on the sample, four samples of tooth were analysed twice on different days. The samples run twice show consistent values leading to the conclusion that no contamination could have occurred during the use of ICP-MS facilities. This, however, did not eliminate the chances of contamination due to post-depositional effects and lab contamination during sample preparation procedure. For both of these aspects a detailed observation of the data had to be carried out.

The best approach to test for laboratory contamination during sample preparation was to re-run the entire process of analysis and compare the results for each individual. This was based on the idea that if laboratory contamination had occurred (in terms of use of the tools, sterility of vials, consequences of the ashing procedure), this must have affected all of the samples prepared on the same day and hence produced equally biased values. Elemental concentration for samples analysed in the same day were compared, for each element, in order to assess whether possible patterns were visible. It is difficult to translate statistically such a comparison, as normal variation in the samples cannot be controlled. Hence the simple observation of the results was considered the best way forward. A further comparison between batches of samples analysed on different days can substantiate such methods of data exploration.

Further confirmation is provided by the comparison between values from Sant'Abbondio specimens and extra-site samples. ICP-MS data from the two specimens are significantly different in a way that excludes any possible laboratory or analytical contamination that would have annulled the differences between heterogeneous compounds. In terms of post-depositional phenomena, a detailed procedure for assessment of diagenetic effects is offered in Chapter Four.

DATA PREPARATION AND ANALYSIS

Once the analysis of all samples had been completed, values were laid out on a spreadsheet that could be converted into an Excel file. Before data could be used, however, it was necessary to effect a calibration according to the limit of detection of each element considered. During each day of analysis, the spectrometer was set to read each element according to a series of blanks (prepared on the first day of the session in quantity sufficient for the entire analytical process) that are run before the samples. Under the limit set by these blanks, the spectrometer is unable to read the ion beam of the plasma correctly and hence produces unreliable data. This limit is called Lower Limit of Detection (LLD) and calculated according to the following formula (Jo Greenwood pers. com.):

$$LLD = \frac{20}{(Std20ppm-stdblk)\ 3(StdDev \cdot 10)}$$

This calculation was carried out to make sure that all data used were reliable.

Once the data were inserted in the Excel file they were compared with the LLD. If the amount (in parts per million - ppm) of an element was lower than the LLD then the data could not be used. For some of the minerals observed, Sant'Abbondio yielded numbers below the LLD. In some cases, this resulted in the total exclusion of the element (as for selenium and europium 153). In other cases it caused a 'patchy' database that brought several problems, especially in terms of statistical analysis. Elemental values obtained for bone and enamel are presented as absolute concentrations and expressed in parts per million (see Appendix).

In order to perform univariate and multivariate statistical analysis, the Excel file was ultimately imported into an SPSS (version 11.0 for Windows) database. Results of the analysis and interpretation are offered in Chapter Six, where the data are examined to assess the impact of diagenetic effect, and Chapter Seven, where the results are interpreted using the theoretical models described in Chapter Two and Three.

SUMMARY

This chapter describes the method adopted for this study, while providing a review of the different techniques available in archaeological bone chemistry. The description of bioavailability of essential and non-essential elements is provided to give an indication of their presence in the tissues as a result of dietary contribution and in support of data interpretation presented in Chapter Seven. The description of the method of preparation and analysis of bone, enamel and soil samples is provided to back up methods for the assessment of diagenesis and measures to test data reliability as presented in the following chapter.

Chapter Four
Sant'Abbondio ICP-MS Trace Element Data Analysis. Assessing Diagenesis

Introduction

A major concern in trace element studies, especially when multi-elemental, is the difficulty in assessing the extent of diagenetic effects and separating these from true, reliable data. The literature on trace element studies abounds with criteria to assess the level of diagenetic effects and correctly define the biogenic portion of hard tissues (Kyle, 1986; Nelson et al., 1986; Grupe, 1988; Lambert et al., 1989; Price, 1989; Lambert et al., 1990; Price et al., 1992; Sandford, 1993), although a reluctance to apply this type of investigation, as opposed to, for example, to stable isotope analysis, is founded on the difficulty in drawing the line – in terms of absolute concentration in the human tissues – between reliable values and possible contamination. In this chapter post-depositional effects will be tested utilising potentially useful criteria that are seldom chosen in assessing diagenesis. The first part of this chapter will outline methods, providing background information where possible. A review of the preparation procedures normally applied in bone chemistry introduces the criteria selected for this study. The following section focuses on the use of reference values from the literature for comparative purposes. Further comparison with soil, fauna, and other human samples is useful in assessing biogenic vs. diagenetic portion of the bone, as well as better defining the level of interactions between humans and the environment. Two further sections illustrate how the use of known chemical and biological processes can help us determine data reliability and offer further levels of interpretation. In the second part of the chapter these criteria are applied to assess the level of post-mortem alteration of the chemical structure of bone and enamel at Sant'Abbondio, isolating elements altered by contamination and selecting ones believed to be reliable for further analysis.

Methods for assessing diagenesis

ICP-MS trace element data are normally expressed as absolute concentrations given in parts per million (ppm) or parts per billion (ppb). Such concentrations reflect chemical uptake during life but also ion exchange with the soil of deposition after burial. This effect is normalised in isotopic analyses, as only the ratio between different isotopes of the same element is used and this is believed to be equally expressed in soil and the soft and hard tissues of plants, animals and humans. When dealing with absolute concentrations obtained in ICP-MS studies, it becomes essential to assess the level of interaction between soil and tissues, as post-mortem migration of ions from one to the others can alter original values.

Procedural criteria

The choice of the sample preparation procedure is an important phase in any spectroscopic analysis. Numerous techniques can be used and each of them has advantages and disadvantages related to the type of material investigated and the specific aim of the analysis. The main issue to consider when preparing a skeletal sample for mass spectrometry is the risk of contamination. This can derive from non-biogenic absorption in the bone during burial or from chemical contamination deriving from the use of tools, equipment, containers and anything that comes into contact with the sample in the process of its preparation. Buffers or solutions can also affect its chemical structure, influencing final results. Over the last ten years, sample preparation methods have become more standardised. A preliminary distinction between physical and chemical procedures needs to be set (Lambert et al., 1990). Among physical procedures, two different options can be considered. In the first one, by Szpunar and co-workers (1978), the sample to be analysed is rinsed with deionised water and brushed clean, dried at 90°C, cooled and weighed (W2). It is then placed in a furnace and ashed overnight at 650°C. After being weighed again (W3) the sample is then dissolved for analysis. The difference between W2 and W3 gives a measure of the loss of organic material and the remaining inorganic one. This kind of method involves minimal processing of the sample, and has been found to be ineffective for the removal of diagenetic contaminants (Lambert et al., 1990). The second physical procedure, considered more reliable than the first, by Lambert and co-workers (1989), involves the removal of the outer surface of the sample by physical abrasion (the device used in this case was an aluminium oxide abrasion disc). After a first weighing (W1) the sample is rinsed in deionised water, dried and weighed again (W2). It is then ashed, powered, weighted (W3) and dissolved for analysis. The W1/W2 ratio gives the measure of how much of the material is lost after surface abrasion, while the W1/W2 ratio indicated how much of the organic portion has been eliminated. These physical criteria have provided good results in the elimination of diagenetic contaminants in the bone, being simple and more effective than the sometimes overly aggressive chemical methods.

Among chemical standards Krueger's (1989) requires the sample to be weighed (W1), washed and scraped with a porcelain spatula. After soaking overnight in 1N acetic acid it is dried at 90°C and powdered in a shatter box. The resulting powder is then soaked in 1N acetic acid again, washed, filtered and dried overnight at 130°C. Once dried the sample is weighed (W2), ashed, weighed again (W3) and dissolved for analysis. The W2/W1 ratio gives a measure of the remaining material after the chemical procedure. In a second chemical process by Sillen (1986), the sample is weighed (W1), rinsed with deionised water, powdered in a shatter box and then washed three times with acetone. After being dried it is placed in a centrifuge tube, sonicated for one minute and centrifuged for 10 seconds. A buffer made of acetic acid and sodium acetate is added to the tube and the procedure is then repeated seven to ten times while the decanted material is saved for analysis each time. This method has demonstrated several disadvantages: the equipment has produced contamination in some cases, and the use of the acidic buffer is likely to enrich the elemental constitution of the sample.

Generally it can be argued that the use of each method is strictly related to the kind of element that needs to be detected, as not all elements are equally subject to contamination and uniformly susceptible to measures directed to the reduction of diagenetic alterations. Some broad considerations are however necessary. Surface abrasion removes around 5% of the bone and seems to leave the sample with the biogenic matrix intact (Lambert *et al.*, 1990). Chemical washing with acidic solution removes up to 18% of the bone in the Krueger method and between 35% and 60% in the Sillen one (*ibid.*). As ashing removes an additional 30% of organic material, it is clear that some chemical procedures can become extremely aggressive. According to Lambert *et al.* (1990) physical abrasion procedures have a lower risk of chemical contamination: most of the elements maintain their biogenic composition and some contaminants of a diagenetic nature, such as potassium, zinc, iron, manganese and aluminium, are easily removed, although Price argues that elements such as sodium, calcium, magnesium, strontium and barium remain unchanged (Price *et al.*, 1992). Chemical methods could cause the loss of some elements such as sodium and magnesium, or enrichment of others such as iron and zinc, as a result of the use of buffers and acidic solutions (Lambert *et al.*, 1990).

As a general rule, both physical and chemical procedures need to be applied in ideal lab conditions. Lab equipment must be sterile, and only certain material can be used to process bone and enamel (*i.e.* porcelain or agate mortar as opposed to other types, glass or polyurethane vials as opposed to normal plastic ones, aluminium oxide or diamond points and abrading tools). The preparation procedure should be recorded separately each day and crosschecked between days to test lab contamination. Buffers and chemical solutions should be the same for the entire procedure so as to reduce minimal chemical alterations.

Comparison with reference values
Comparison with reference values is the standard procedure that precedes the analysis and interpretation of any trace element study. Known standards are used to determine whether concentrations obtained from the analysis reflect expected biogenic values. Archaeological and non-archaeological literature provide several tools for this purpose: the main sources are Iyengar *et al.* (1978), Underwood (1977), and the IAEA (1982) Progress Report (H-5) on the inter-comparison of minor and trace elements in animals. Further information can also be obtained through the World Wide Web (*e.g.* www.ch.cam.ac.uk).

Iyengar *et al.* provide values for a large spectrum of elements and a considerable number of human tissues and body fluids. For either bone or enamel standards, however, the data provided derive from a limited number of works, often using different methods (including AAS, AES, and NAA), different sources (fresh, dry, or ash bone), and sometimes limited data (*i.e.* frequently n equals to 1). Moreover, the range of values for each element is sometimes rather wide and can even vary by several orders of magnitude. The large variation in the values provided gives an idea of how different analytical procedures applied to a variety of samples, normally coming from different geographical areas, and thus subject to different geochemical influence, can reflect a general variation in the elemental concentration in the hard tissues. This highlights two important factors to consider. Firstly that a variation in the chemical composition of the tissues is 'normal' and that no final number can be given as the reference value of one element in the human body. Secondly, that under different analytical conditions it is better to avoid direct inter-site comparison of elemental concentration in the hard tissues, but rather it could be advisable to appreciate the degree of variability within each sample and use that as a general reference.

This explains how, despite the importance of using reference data in trace element work, not all scholars necessarily do so. Reference values are not representative of general human elemental variation as the material used is normally modern and it may not adequately reflect past situations. Moreover, some of the sources on reference data use recent samples generated for environmental studies on pollution or for medical purposes, normally in relation to cancer research. In addition, very limited studies are available to measure homeostasis in relation to biochemical maximum (*i.e.* before toxic effects) or minimum (*i.e.* before elemental deficiency) concentrations. Regional variability in the geochemical properties of the various environments is also a major issue to consider and can result in strongly differentiated patterns of element uptake in humans within a normal biogenic variation.

All of these aspects should lead to a careful use of standards. Available literature should be used as a support to assess general data reliability and must consider a number of intrinsic biases, in particular the use of modern specimens, small sample size, and differences in analytical method. To overcome this problem it is important to achieve a good level of integration between different sources. Not least, the biochemical function and behaviour of each element should be considered.

Comparison with soil
In archaeological bone chemistry, the comparison with soil samples is essential in assessing ion substitution between skeletal remains and the soil of deposition. Two main issues are involved in the comparison of elemental concentration between ancient bone and soil. The first aspect to consider is the level of interaction between living species and the environment. Each environment has specific geological and geochemical settings that influence the local vegetation and fauna, hence influencing human occupants. Soil and groundwater can have a range of chemical properties that are taken up by living species and reflected in the chemical composition of their tissues. A well-known example of this exchange between the environment and its occupants is reflected in the scheme of the trophic pyramid as described by Radosevich (1993), on the differentiated mechanism of absorption of strontium from plant to herbivores, to carnivores, and humans. Research has shown how strontium concentration depends upon local geology, pedology and climate (Skougstad and Horr, 1960; Bohn *et al.*, 1985). This scheme of reasoning, however, does not apply to every element as not all elements are chemically mobile or, if they are, not to the same extent and in the same way. Nevertheless this provides a visible example of the chemical interaction between humans and the environment. As an example, Mertz (1985) has demonstrated how regions with low levels of specific elements can influence the health status of the living population in the so-called 'goiter belt' in the United States, characterised by iodine-poor soils. Moreover, geochemical variation can occur not only in space but also in time (Radosevich, 1993). It is therefore important to be cautious when performing comparative analyses between sites distant in time and/or space.

The level of interaction between soil and the bone under analysis, not only *in vivo* but mostly after burial needs also to be considered. Exchange between soil of deposition and bone is the most likely type of contamination to take place in an ancient contexts, and a number of studies have demonstrated the ability of some elements to fill the voids in the organic matrix of bone (Kyle, 1986; Lambert *et al.*, 1989). This is not a one-way process though, as ion substitution does not only move from the soil to the bone but also *vice versa* (Radosevich, 1993). Soil contamination may also occur if soil residues are present in the solution of bone dissolved for analysis. Post-mortem variation *per se* has been the object of different studies (cf. Lambert *et al.*, 1979; Gordon and Buikstra, 1981; Kyle, 1986; Pate *et al.*, 1989), illustrating how skeletal preservation depends on a number of factors: soil texture (*e.g.* dry and sandy soils are less aggressive), soil pH (*e.g.* alkaline soil are less contaminant), permeability and degree of water percolation, microorganism activity, bone density, age of the individuals and their life and health conditions. It is difficult to assess the degree of influence that each of these factors has, as each context is a unique setting with particular conditions. Each aspect can be used as a general indication of the contaminant potentials although not all can be precisely measured and reconstructed. Some of the studies just described (Kyle, 1986; Pate *et al.*, 1989) have demonstrated that a number of elements – normally those that are major components of the soil – seem to be more mobile than others and should be considered as less reliable for bone chemistry. Lambert *et al.* (1979) stress that metals like iron, aluminium, manganese and potassium in the bone are easily influenced by soil contamination, although a study by Pate *et al.* (1989) has shown that alkaline soils immobilise iron, aluminium, molybdenum, copper, zinc, cobalt, manganese, lead and nickel so that ion substitution rarely takes place. For this work, the comparison between the elemental concentration of the soil and that of the bone and the enamel will take into consideration the results emerged from the literature.

Comparison with fauna
Animal bone samples can be used as 'reference markers' of known dietary regime and biochemical properties against which human elemental concentration can be tested. Within specific archaeological contexts, the use of faunal specimens in combination with human ones can help in assessing the level of interaction between living species and the environment, not only through trophic position but also through comparison of absolute concentrations of different elements.

The comparison between human and animal samples is traditionally associated with strontium for which the biochemical properties and role along the food chain are well known. The ability of mammal to discriminate against strontium in favour of calcium means that the quantity of strontium accumulated in bone is inversely proportional to the position of the mammal along the trophic chain. This means that herbivores (which eat strontium-rich plants) have a higher concentration of strontium than carnivores (which eat herbivores), while humans are theoretically placed somewhere between the two.

The comparison between animals and humans could also help to reconstruct the relationship between human and the environment through the observation of the relationship between animals and the environment. In ancient communities based on animal husbandry, for example, the comparison between humans and animals can help to determine the level of residential vs. mobile habitation in a specific ecological niche.

Comparison between tissues
Of the many tissues in the human body, the ones archaeologists are left with are bone and teeth. For both, the literature provides expected elemental concentrations (Iyengar *et al.*, 1978). Bone and enamel have profoundly different matrices, the former being primarily organic and the latter mainly inorganic. This results in different absolute elemental values, as bone takes up more from the environment than teeth. The comparison between the two tissues is a valuable tool to measure data reliability, as the proportion of the same element in the two should be different. The level of post-mortem alteration must be observed taking into consideration the fact that any diagenetic phenomenon would affect bone, which is porous and chemically unstable, more significantly than teeth, which are influenced to a lesser extent.

Observation of expected chemical behaviour
Most of the tests reported in the literature that have been undertaken to assess chemical interaction between nutritional essential and non-essential elements are on animals. Some of these have successfully demonstrated that laboratory depletion or supplementation of a number of elements affects the chemical behaviour of others (Hurley *et al.*, 1988). This mechanism can lead to an enrichment of a specific element with the increase of another (synergy) or to a decrease of one element as a consequence of the increase of a different one (antagonism). Work on mice by Stoecker and Li (1988) has proved that vanadium levels tend to increase in chromium-deprived mice, while Mikkanen (1985) demonstrated how high quantities of arsenic inhibited selenium absorption in chicks. Chemical interaction is also the basis of homeostatic regulation in the human body although the causes and modalities of this interaction are still under study. The observation of elemental synergy or antagonism can help to better understand the significance of elemental concentration in human tissues, but the prevalence of single-elemental studies as opposed to multi-elemental investigations has resulted in the neglect of this line of enquiry. Sandford refers to element interaction in her extensive work on chemical analyses in archaeology (Sandford, 1993) explaining how, in humans, zinc is known to interact positively with aluminium, manganese, sodium and sulphur, while it antagonises with calcium, copper, iron, cadmium, manganese, nickel and lead (also cf. Hurley *et al.*, 1988). Iron antagonises with vanadium, chromium, manganese, aluminium, zinc and nickel (Underwood, 1977) as a result of similar mechanisms of absorption, and is chemically dependent on copper, which is responsible for its immobilisation in human tissues (Sandford, 1993).

A further type of chemically based data screening uses some elements as a probe to measure the level of chemical exchange between soil and hard tissues in the assessment of post-depositional effects, on the basis of their expected amount in the tissues. Uranium, for example, normally occurs at a very low concentration in human bone and enamel (Bumsted, 1985; Millard and Hedges, 1995) therefore unexpected high values are likely to be diagenetic. Such a method should be considered with care as not all elements participate in soil/tissue interaction in the same way, so the model of ion exchange between one element and buried bone cannot be associated with a whole spectrum of elements that have different chemical characteristics (see Chapter Three for a discussion).

Observation of expected biological behaviour
The use of elements' biochemical behaviour and the observation of homeostatic regulation in the human body is frequently too quickly dismissed in bone chemistry. Biochemical information on the human organism can be extremely useful to determine biogenic as opposed to diagenetic phenomena. Some essential and trace elements have well-known homeostatic functions that are easily identified and tested when assessing diagenesis. Particularly useful is elemental synergy and antagonism within the human organism, as partially described above. Nevertheless, many elements are unreliable in this regard. The biochemical role of strontium for example is not known, and only its position in relation to calcium has been studied. Other elements, however, follow mechanisms of absorption and excretion that are associated with biological aspects (for a detailed review see Chapter Five). Lead, for example, is normally higher in very young children because of their tendency to store abundant quantity of this element (up to 40% more than adults) and their subsequent inability to excrete it because of the incompleteness of the gastrointestinal tract (Zigler, 1978). Similarly, zinc concentration is higher in infants as a result of retention from *in utero* (Underwood, 1977), whereas strontium seems to be lower in children and gradually increases with growth (Price *et al.*, 1985b). Adults can also show age related differential metabolism: manganese requirements tend to increase with age (Spencer *et al.*, 1979) while ageing causes gradual chromium depletion (Mertz, 1969).

Homeostasis also varies in accordance with sex, and hormonal influence on biochemical mechanisms (Sandford, 1993: 38). Pregnancy and lactation can cause enhanced absorption of copper and nickel (Underwood, 1977; WHO, 1996) and loss of strontium and chromium (Hambridge, 1974; Price *et al.*, 1985b). Homeostatic processes are also regulated by metabolic factors. Price *et al.* (1985b) offer a good review of how a number of physiological or pathological conditions (such as nutritional deficiency, anaemia and osteoporosis) may influence homeostasis in the human organism. In Price *et al.*'s study (*ibid.*), porotic hyperostosis and iron-deficiency anaemia were associated with zinc deficiency following research by Gilbert (1975) and Bahou (1975), although one major aspect fails to be considered: iron-deficiency anaemia can be tested in relation to a group of elements that interact negatively with iron as illustrated in the previous section on elemental antagonism. Elements such as vanadium, chromium, manganese and nickel have a chemical mechanism during absorption similar to that of iron so are defined as iron antagonists. If anaemia reflects martial deficiency, iron antagonists should be present in relatively high concentration. The efficacy of this approach is twofold: it can help define the aetiology of multi-factorial pathologies and it can serve as a method to test data reliability. For diseases such as osteoporosis, skeletal studies can benefit from the support of elemental data; it is known, for example, that high iron level can increase the severity of this disease (Diamond *et al.*, 1989).

The use of biological data is essential for discussing trace element results, as knowing the mechanism of absorption and excretion of some elements can help infer the sex and age of skeletally indeterminable individuals, or combine chemical and anthropological information with archaeological data to investigate cultural differentiation in accordance with biological categories. Furthermore, one of the advantages it offers lies in the possibility to observe children or categories of individuals often neglected in archaeological as well as anthropological investigations (*sensu* Sofaer Derevenski, 1997).

Comparison with samples from other sites
The comparison of a given sample with specimens from different contexts should be treated with extreme care. Each living human has a level of interaction with his/her environment that is subject to a multitude of influences. Age, to some extent sex, and health conditions are the first variables to consider (Price *et al.*, 1985b). Geographical setting and geochemistry of the environment are further ones. The chronological period under study is also important to consider. All of these features render the comparison of trace element data between different contexts very problematic. In general, when dealing with absolute concentrations a direct comparison should not be attempted at all, although general observations of elemental variation can be made. The use of heterogeneous samples can be useful, however, in assessing analytical accuracy when performing spectroscopic analyses, basing on the principle that laboratory and instrumental contamination would obliterate any original differences, producing homologous patterns of elemental variation. This method is seldom used in archaeological bone chemistry as a result of the tendency to rely only on the comparison with reference values.

Intra-site comparison
The comparison of elemental concentration between people from the same context is useful to test homogeneity of trace element results. Moreover, while it is inadvisable to apply inter-site variation of elemental concentration to make cultural inferences (although it can be applied to test lab contamination in relation to expected heterogeneity of results), it can be useful to observe intra-site variablity to assess the influence of cultural phenomena on the elemental concentration of the tissues

The first level of intra-site analysis is on a purely biological/metabolic basis, as elemental concentration can vary in accordance with sex, age, health status and general life conditions of a specific population. Thus, if the sample behaves consistently with the expected biological characteristics it is possible to assume that diagenesis is not so strong as to obliterate the genuine chemical signal. The second level of investigation is invested with cultural significance, according to which a series of social, economic, political and cultural factors can be argued on a biochemical basis. Trace element analysis can be used to test whether cultural or economic differences produced differentiated chemical patterns within the same context. Post-mortem alterations are able to obliterate existing differences and homogenise elemental variation within the sample. However, when patterns of variation are observed in accordance with aspects that are not explicable through diagenetic changes it is possible to infer on a cultural basis.

ASSESSING DIAGENESIS AT SANT'ABBONDIO
Having discussed a range of criteria used to observe post-depositional effects on the elemental concentration of skeletal remains, these will be applied to the Sant'Abbondio sample to test data reliability.

For data analysis, final values in parts per million (see Appendix) were converted from Excel files into an SPSS database. Archaeological and osteological information was added to the chemical data in order to expand the range of information on the context and provide back up data to investigate diagenesis. The different variables are reported in Table 4.1.

At Sant'Abbondio, particular concern over diagenesis resulted from the state of preservation of the skeletal sample. Although the type of soil characterising the site is not acidic (mean pH 7.3), overall the skeletal remains were poorly preserved. This raised the question of possible ion exchange between soil and hard tissues and forces consideration of diagenesis. As discussed earlier, soil contamination can be eliminated by physical removal of the surface of the sample and by analysing the geochemistry of the context. The first procedure is likely to get rid of most of the contamination, while the second ensures a critical reading of the data, especially if elemental behaviour and potential chemical interaction are observed.

Variable	Description
Indiv	Individual (burial number/year of excavation)
Sex	(m=male; f=female; u=unknown; j=juvenile)
Age	(adult; juvenile; infant)
Ageclass	(0=0-10 yrs; 1=10-20 yrs;
Year	Year of excavation (1993; 1996)
Area	Area of deposition (E=east; W= west)
Category	Category of sex-area of deposition
Hypopl	Hypoplasia (0=absence; 1=presence)
Caries	Caries (0=absence; 1= presence)
Ceramic	(0=absence; 1=presence)
Metal weapon	(0=absence; 1=presence)
Lithic weapon	(0=absence; 1=presence)
Metal object	(0=absence; 1=presence)
Lithic object	(0=absence; 1=presence)
Tool	(0=absence; 1=presence)
Ornament	(0=absence; 1=presence)
Element (bone)	Value of each element in the bone (ppm)
Element (enamel)	Value of each element in the enamel (ppm)

Table 4.1 Sant'Abbondio data classification

Procedural criteria

The choice of the sample preparation procedure is the first criterion used to eliminate post-depositional contamination. Specific treatments to the bone and the enamel are directed to the removal of the diagenetic portion of the tissues. If successfully carried out, such procedures are believed to be able to isolate solely the biogenic fraction of the bone and the enamel (Lambert *et al.*, 1990).

At Sant'Abbondio, sixty-two bone and forty-eight enamel samples were collected from the 62 individuals preserved. A list of samples (by year of excavation) is shown in Table 3.3. The procedure used for collection was as described by Lambert *et al.* (1990), and is considered an adaptation of the traditional method described by Szpunar and co-workers (1978). Such method involved the physical removal of the outer surface of the bone and the collection of pure cortical bone and dental powder (a detailed description of the preparation procedure of bone, enamel and soil samples is given in Chapter Three).

Two main aspects linked with the preparation procedures were subject to the risk of contamination of the biogenic portion of the tissues under study: Laboratory contamination during the first phase of bone treatment (abrasion, cleaning, ashing, and dissolution – see Chapter Three), and contamination during the final dissolution prior to ICP-MS analysis. During these stages the samples could come into contact with contaminated equipment or solutions able to alter the chemical composition of the bone or the enamel. To overcome this risk only sterile tools and machinery were used.

To check that no contamination had taken place during the first laboratory preparation, each step was carefully recorded. The abrasion, cleaning, ashing and powdering of the bone were carried out on different days (as an example, only 12 samples could be ashed at one time, meaning that the ashing procedure alone had to take place over several days). Equally, dissolution of the powder obtained after the initial part of the first phase of the preparation required three different days, again a record of the procedure was kept (Table 3.4). Finally, the last dissolution and analysis took place with a schedule involving separate analytical procedures, once again recorded separately. As the preparation procedure and the analytical process took different days to be carried out, the comparison of results for different dates offered the chance to measure laboratory contamination and instrumental accuracy basing on the principle that any contamination would have generated patterns in accordance with the various days of the analysis.

Once ICP-MS analysis was completed, a crosschecking of the data in accordance with the different preparation schedules was performed, founded on the belief that if contamination had taken place this would have produced patterns of equally biased results matching the various laboratory procedures. For Sant'Abbondio the crosscheck produced a negative result for contamination.

Most of the elements observed have yielded reliable values either for bone or enamel. A few elements represented exceptions: zinc was found to be contaminated during ICP-MS lab preparation through the use of zinc-contaminated buffers. While this did not affect the results for other elements, it forced the exclusion of zinc from the final analysis. Selenium and Europium were considered unreliable because they occurred in very low amounts, below the threshold of instrumental accuracy – systematically below the Lower Limit of Detection (LLD) – and were both excluded from the analysis. For the remaining elements, contamination or instrumental error could be excluded, as double readings carried out for the five samples analysed repeated times to check contamination, display a shift that falls within an acceptable analytical variation.

Comparison with reference values

Having confirmed that no laboratory contamination had taken place and tested instrumental accuracy, elements could be compared with reference material in order to measure whether the range values obtained from the Sant'Abbondio specimens matched expected biochemical concentrations. Elemental concentrations from Sant'Abbondio bone and enamel specimens are expressed as parts per million (ppm), and refer to absolute concentrations. To test data reliability mean values for bone and enamel were compared with reference data provided by Iyengar *et al.* (1978), and Underwood (1977), together with a number of other sources, and provided respectively for bone and enamel in Table 4.2 and Table 4.3.

	Sant'Abbondio - bone - ppm			ref. values (Iyengar et al., 1978) ppm		ref. values (Underwood, 1977) ppm	ref. values Goodman ppm	ref. values (others) ppm
Elements	mean	std	n	mean	n	mean	mean	mean
Vanadium (V51)	65.6	21.11	57	17.6 f	1	n.a.	0.006	2.59-4.09 (3)
Chromium (Cr52)	11.6	13.38	37	33	341	n.a.	0.1 – 0.3	0.72 (3)
Manganese (Mn55)	46.9	57.00	57	13.7 a	341	n.a.	0.2 – 100	3.2 (3) – 46 (1)
Cobalt (Co59)	3.51	1.82	57	43.5/4.6	341/1	n.a.	0.01 – 0.04	n.a.
Copper (Cu63)	32.1	27.19	45	25.7	341	5.7*	1 – 26	7 (1)
Arsenic (As75)	9.5	3.87	57	4.1 a	341	n.a.	n.a.	n.a.
Nickel (Ni60)	17.4	8.15	56	110 a	341	n.a.	0.7	n.a.
Zinc (Zn66)	-	-	-	187	341	n.a.	150 – 250	n.a.
Rubidium (Rb85)	1.29	0.84	57	5.11	2	n.a.	n.a.	1.0 (3)
Strontium (Sr88)	791.7	256.2	57	237	2	160-320	36 – 140	167 (1) – 436 (3)
				172 a	734	n.a.		128 (2)
				147 a	341	n.a.		254 ng/mg (4)
Yttrium (Y89)	5.7	6.46	57	0.07	44	n.a.	n.a.	n.a.
Zirconium (Zr90)	140.1	88.81	57	0.1 a	44	n.a.	n.a.	18 (3)
Niobium (Nb93)	1.91	1.06	57	0.07	44	n.a.	n.a.	n.a.
Tin (Sn118)	5.5	7.53	29	3.9 a	44	n.a.	n.a.	n.a.
Hafnium (Hf178)	1.26	0.91	57	n.a.	n.a.	n.a.	n.a.	0.0072 (3)
Tantalum (Ta181)	0.20	0.12	63	n.a.	n.a.	n.a.	n.a.	0.040 (3)
Gold (Au197)	1.0	1.48	21	0.03 a	44	n.a.	n.a.	0.0032 (3)
Lead (Pb208)	2.6	2.29	58	43 a	258	n.a.	n.a.	37.4 (1)
REE								
Lanthanum (La139)	7.3	11.54	57	0.2 a-6.6	1	n.a.	n.a.	0.9 (3)
Cerium (Ce140)	1.6	1.98	57	n.a.	n.a.	n.a.	n.a.	0.71 (3)
Praseodymium (Pr141)	1.13	1.70	57	n.a.	n.a.	n.a.	n.a.	n.a.
Neodymium (Nd146)	4.3	5.98	57	n.a.	n.a.	n.a.	n.a.	4.7 (3)
Samarium (Sm147)	0.89	1.03	54	n.a.	n.a.	n.a.	n.a.	0.068 (3)
Europium (Eu151)	0.21	0.19	56	n.a.	n.a.	n.a.	n.a.	0.0098 (3)
Gadolinium (Gd157)	0.86	1.04	56	n.a.	n.a.	n.a.	n.a.	n.a.
Terbium (Tb159)	0.13	0.14	56	n.a.	n.a.	n.a.	n.a.	n.a.
Dysprosium (Dy163)	0.72	0.85	56	n.a.	n.a.	n.a.	n.a.	0.25 (3)
Holmium (Ho165)	0.18	0.18	53	n.a.	n.a.	n.a.	n.a.	n.a.
Erbium (Er166)	0.55	0.55	56	n.a.	n.a.	n.a.	n.a.	n.a.
Thulium (Tm169)	0.099	0.08	48	n.a.	n.a.	n.a.	n.a.	n.a.
Ytterbium (Yb172)	0.62	0.54	57	n.a.	n.a.	n.a.	n.a.	0.30 (3)
Lutetium (Lu175)	0.109	0.08	51	n.a.	n.a.	n.a.	n.a.	0.076 (3)
Thorium (Th232)	1.00	0.91	63	0.04 a	44	n.a.	n.a.	0.128 (3)
Uranium (U238)	38.2	15.50	63	0.02 a	44	n.a.	n.a.	1-3 (3)

Table 4.2 Sant'Abbondio mean values (ppm) and standard deviation for bone samples with reference values from Iyengar et al. (1978), Underwood (1977), and other sources. *(1)* (Lambert 1978); *(2)* (Grupe 1988); *(3)* Bumsted (1985); *(4)* Sillen (1981). a= ash bone; f= fresh bone. *Calculated as 2% of total Cu concentration (35 ppm) according to Underwood (1977). n.a.= not available.

Mean concentrations are compared for practical purposes, although for some of the elements considered the distribution did not display a normal curve so that the overall average may be influenced by a limited number of outlying values. It should be stressed that reference values are offered through synthetic works that are normally based on a limited number of investigations often using heterogeneous material and methods (see section above), hence comparative analysis should be carefully treated. For Sant'Abbondio most elements could be evaluated in accordance with the reference values although, in general, bone standards were more available than enamel ones.

	Sant'Abbondio - enamel - ppm			reference values (Iyengar et al., 1978) ppm		reference values (Underwood 1977) ppm	reference values (others) ppm
Elements	Mean	Std	n	Mean	n	Mean	Mean
Vanadium (V51)	17.1	15.90	51	0.01	23	0.1µg/g	n.a.
Chromium (Cr52)	6.2	12.06	51	3.2	28	n.a.	n.a.
Manganese (Mn55)	9.1	9.08	33	30/0.28	?/28	n.a.	n.a.
Cobalt (Co59)	3.1	2.04	50	00.2	28	n.a.	n.a.
Copper (Cu63)	2.9	2.23	32	4.2	28	n.a.	n.a.
Nickel (Ni60)	33.0	56.19	51	n.a.	n.a.	0.64 µg/g	n.a.
Zinc (Zn66)	-	-	-	199	28	n.a.	n.a.
Arsenic (As75)	3.2	2.43	18	0.07	75	n.a.	n.a.
Rubidium (Rb85)	1.30	0.79	51	0.39	28	n.a.	n.a.
Strontium (Sr88)	382.7	322.41	51	81	28	n.a.	n.a.
				111	7	n.a.	n.a.
				94	10	n.a.	n.a.
Yttrium (Y89)	11.9	17.65	51	0.007	28	n.a.	n.a.
Zirconium (Zr90)	28.6	34.26	51	0.1	28	n.a.	n.a.
Niobium (Nb93)	0.51	0.41	51	0.28	28	n.a.	n.a.
Tin (Sn118)	4.4	10.81	49	0.21/120	20/1	n.a.	n.a.
Hafnium (Hf178)	0.45	0.40	51	0.08	28	n.a.	n.a.
Tantalum (Ta181)	0.14	0.11	51	0.1	28	n.a.	n.a.
Gold (Au197)	1.3	5.41	31	0.02	28	n.a.	n.a.
Lead (Pb208)	3.2	2.81	44	3.6	38	n.a.	n.a.
REE							
Lanthanum (La139)	22.3	37.03	51	0.02	28	n.a.	n.a.
Cerium (Ce140)	3.0	2.65	51	0.07	28	n.a.	n.a.
Praseodymium (Pr141)	3.7	6.02	51	0.027	28	n.a.	n.a.
Neodymium (Nd146)	13.8	21.89	51	0.045	28	n.a.	n.a.
Samarium (Sm147)	2.3	3.30	51	0.08	28	n.a.	n.a.
Europium (Eu151)	0.49	0.69	51	0.04	28	n.a.	n.a.
Gadolinium (Gd157)	2.1	3.04	51	0.08	28	n.a.	n.a.
Terbium (Tb159)	0.32	0.40	49	0.02	28	n.a.	n.a.
Dysprosium (Dy163)	1.6	2.15	49	0.08	28	n.a.	n.a.
Holmium (Ho165)	0.35	0.45	48	0.02	28	n.a.	n.a.
Erbium (Er166)	0.97	1.28	49	0.09	28	n.a.	n.a.
Thulium (Tm169)	0.20	0.18	38	0.02	28	n.a.	n.a.
Ytterbium (Yb172)	0.95	1.13	47	0.007	28	n.a.	n.a.
Lutetium (Lu175)	0.16	0.16	44	0.02	28	n.a.	n.a.
Thorium (Th232)	1.40	1.10	51	n.a.	n.a.	n.a.	n.a.
Uranium (U238)	7.8	10.75	51	n.a.	n.a.	n.a.	n.a.

Table 4.3 Sant'Abbondio - mean values and standard deviation for enamel samples (in ppm) with reference values from Iyengar *et al.* 1978, Underwood 1977 and others. n.a. = not available.

For bone, all elements seem to concur with expected values, with the exception of strontium, yttrium, zirconium, gold and uranium. Strontium is found slightly above the expected concentration although this is mainly due to a number of outliers that skew the overall mean. Furthermore, previous studies (Price *et al.*, 1998) have demonstrated the great variation, in terms of absolute concentration, of this element.
For strontium, the reason for discordant values (in relation to diagenesis as opposed to biogenic differences) for individual samples is not relevant at this stage and will be discussed when observing groups of individuals according to each element (see later in this chapter and Chapter Seven). In general, however, the reason for very high or very low values in bone and in enamel is not easily explained. High concentrations may be the result of a strong reliance on low-trophic vegetables (Radosevich, 1993) and marine products. Equally, metabolic or biological conditions can influence strontium values. Both factors are suggested for strontium values in Sant'Abbondio individuals, that are considered to be reliable and only the

expression of great variation due to a series of physiological as well as cultural factors. Yttrium has chemical characteristics identical to that of lanthanides (Thompson, 1979) and together with zirconium and gold is part of the group of transitional metals. Values such as those displayed by the Sant'Abbondio set can easily be produced by incorrect reading by the spectrometer, as some metals (particularly gold) do not properly dissolve in HNO_3 so that undissolved particles may float in the plasma and enter the torch in this form and hence produce very high concentrations (Jo Greenwood pers. com.). For this reason, yttrium, zirconium, and gold were excluded from the analysis.

As regards to the lanthanides, reference values were not available for all of the elements considered, although those that were compared with reference standards seem to fit with the expected values. Taking into account the strong chemical homogeneity of Rare Earth Elements it can be argued with a certain confidence that the Rare Earths group displays reliable data. The only exception is represented by uranium (an actinide) that shows unexpectedly high values in both tissues. Uranium is known to be present in the human body in extremely low concentration (Millard and Hedges, 1995). The most likely reason for the Sant'Abbondio values is contamination either from the soil of deposition or from laboratory preparation.

In conclusion, the comparison with reference values is useful in the identification of large-scale differences, and can trace gross contamination. However, it is not a good tool for measuring diagenesis at a smaller scale, as it does not permit the interception of small signals of post-depositional effects. This is due to the approximate nature of the method itself, which is based on limited samples and different analytical methods. It is therefore little surprise that few scholars resort to it for trace element studies.

Comparison with soil samples from Sant'Abbondio and the Sarno area

Before the chemical composition of bone tissue and dental enamel can be interpreted and discussed it is important to consider the chemical nature of the soil around the area of investigation, as soil is able to interact with the human tissues *in vivo*, through the consumption of food and water, as well as after deposition, through diagenesis. At Sant'Abbondio, the examination of the geology of the Sarno region was thus directed to the identification of post-depositional effects and the control of diagenesis. Furthermore, the character of the soil in the area of the cemetery is relevant to trace element data from bone and enamel analysis as a result of chemical interaction between the Sant'Abbondio people and the surrounding environment.

The geology of the Sant'Abbondio area is closely connected with the presence of Vesuvius in the Pompeii plain. The whole region of Pompeii is characterised by lava soils – as the result of the intense activity of the volcano during prehistoric and historical times – mixed with limestone formation and riverine zones of sandy sediments (for a discussion of the geological and pedological nature of the area under study see Chapter Four). In order to test the pedological and geochemical characteristics of the area of the cemetery and its surroundings a total of 13 samples were collected. Eleven came from different sections of the Sant'Abbondio cemetery and were collected to examine ion substitution between soil and skeletal remain. For this reason most of the samples come from the burials themselves. The remaining two samples came from the Sarno valley (Castellammare), and a location within the Sorrento peninsula (Agerola). Castellammare is a costal region characterised by Pyroclastic sandstones and pumices, while Agerola is an elevated area in the Sorrento limestone Promontory. The lava deposits that cover the area of Pompeii made it very difficult to collect soil samples, and only coastal regions or highland areas (specifically Castellammare and Agerola) were suitable. Means and standard deviations of elemental concentration are shown in Table 4.4.

The importance of having a range of soil samples to compare with those from the Sant'Abbondio site has a twofold nature. Firstly, it allows the testing of contamination in relation to the expected heterogeneity the samples should show regarding the geologically different areas from which they come. Secondly, the comparison between elemental concentration in the bone and the enamel and in the soil provides a wider range of information on the pedological nature of the area under study. Given the interaction between human and the environment this could allow the inference of locality and mobility.

Some of the elements examined (vanadium, chromium, cobalt, nickel, and arsenic) are not present for all of the samples. This was not due to an insufficient amount in the soil specimen (*i.e.* values below the LLD), but rather to a procedural change over the course of the research. Some of the elements were introduced into the analysis in a later phase of the project to broaden the scope of analysis following discussion of preliminary results with staff of the NERC ICP-MS Facility. Consequently, all of the soil samples that were analysed before that date could not provide data for the more recently adopted element spectrum.

Overall, results within the Sant'Abbondio context are relatively homogeneous. The two samples external to the site, on the other hand display values that are dissimilar both to each other and in comparison with those of Sant'Abbondio soil, demonstrating that under different geological conditions trace element results produce expected variation in accordance with different geochemical configurations encountered even only a few kilometres away from the site. This also indicates that no laboratory contamination took place.

In order to test for diagenesis and to examine chemical interaction between human tissues and the environment, mean concentrations of all elements in the soil from Sant'Abbondio were compared with average values for bone and enamel samples from the site. If a soil/bone or a soil/enamel contamination occurred this would be reflected in the pattern of mean element concentrations displayed by the human tissues, generating homogeneous trends of distribution of the elemental concentration of bone and enamel. The matrix of these two tissues is profoundly different and therefore undergoes the diagenetic processes in diverse ways. Bone, being organic, is more subject to ion substitution with the soil, while enamel, being mainly inorganic, is only superficially affected by post-mortem alterations. However, if ions substitution between the soil and the tissues, took place, despite the different concentrations, it would show similar variation.

	Sant'Abbondio (n = 11)			Agerola (n =1)	Castellammare (n = 1)
Element (ppm)	mean	sd	c.v.	ppm	ppm
Vanadium (V51)	150.5	19.75	13.1	-	-
Chromium (Cr52)	65.5	17.5	26.7	-	-
Manganese (Mn55)	998.1	194.4	19.4	1123.3	431.6
Cobalt (Co59)	21.81	2.4	11	-	-
Nickel (Ni60)	43.9	2.7	6.1	-	-
Copper (Cu63)	69.0	15.2	22	36.0	10.2
Zinc (Zn60)	86.4	117.8	136.3	83.3	24.5
Arsenic (As75)	19.9	4.3	21.6	-	-
Selenium (Se77)	19.7	24.4	123.8	-6.5	-3.26
Selenium (Se 82)	7.1	5.4	76	1.22	1.6
Rubidium (Rb85)	290.3	176.1	60.6	489.3	94.3
Strontium (Sr88)	651.0	163.1	25	692.3	453.3
Yttrium (Y89)	16.7	4.3	25.7	18.2	11.7
Zirconium (Zr90)	200.5	66.9	33.3	314.6	66.9
Niobium (Nb93)	33.9	11.7	34.5	59.5	10.7
Tin (Sn118)	7.4	7.7	104	3.3	1.6
Hafnium (Hf178)	5.0	1.2	24	6.0	1.9
Tantalum (Ta181)	1.8	0.4	22.2	2.3	0.3
Gold (Au197)	0.4	0.4	100	0.3	0.4
Lead (Pb208)	33.4	10.1	30.2	58.1	9.5
REE					
Lanthanum (La139)	40.9	11.1	27.1	74.9	22.6
Cerium (Ce140)	86.4	19.6	22.6	127.6	37.6
Praseodymium (Pr141)	9.1	2.0	21.9	13.3	5.1
Neodymium (Nd146)	33.0	7.8	23.6	44.6	17.7
Samarium (Sm147)	6.5	1.4	21.5	6.7	3.4
Europium (Eu151)	1.8	0.4	22.2	2.1	1.0
Europium (Eu153)	2.1	0.5	23.8	2.1	1.0
Gadolinium (Gd157)	6.2	1.3	20.9	6.6	3.8
Terbium (Tb159)	0.8	0.1	12.5	0.7	0.5
Dysprosium (Dy163)	3.8	0.7	18.4	3.4	1.8
Holmium (Ho165)	0.6	0.1	16.6	0.6	0.3
Erbium (Er166)	1.9	0.4	21	1.6	1.1
Thulium (Tm169)	0.2	0.02	10	0.2	0.2
Ytterbium (Yb172)	1.7	0.4	23.5	1.5	1.1
Lutetium (Lu175)	0.2	0.02	10	0.2	0.1
Thorium (Th232)	16.7	5.1	30.5	35.9	6.1
Uranium (U238)	3.8	1.0	26.3	11.7	4.3

Table 4.4 Mean and standard deviation of elemental concentration for Sant'Abbondio, Agerola, and Castellammare soil samples. Values are expressed in ppm.

At Sant'Abbondio (Fig. 4.1), not only do bone and enamel display a different pattern from the soil but they also display different patterns to each other. Furthermore, we might expect high values in the soil to be reflected in similar proportion in bone and to a lesser extent in enamel, especially for mobile elements (*e.g.* manganese). This does not appear to happen for the Sant'Abbondio sample.

While the ideal way to test for diagenesis would be to compare skeletal and dental samples for each burial with soil samples taken from directly adjacent contexts, due to the circumstances of the excavation this was not possible except for burial 4(B).

For a more general comparison pooled data can be used. For individual 4(B), buried in the eastern half of the cemetery, elemental concentration in the two tissues was observed in relation to the concentration in the soil of deposition collected in the burial. No comparable trends are observable, as the individual does not display parallel patterns of variation across soil, bone and enamel, even for the group of elements (vanadium, chromium, manganese, cobalt, nickel, copper, arsenic, rubidium and strontium – all trace essentials) at higher risk of ion substitution (indicated with the dotted squares in figure 4.2).

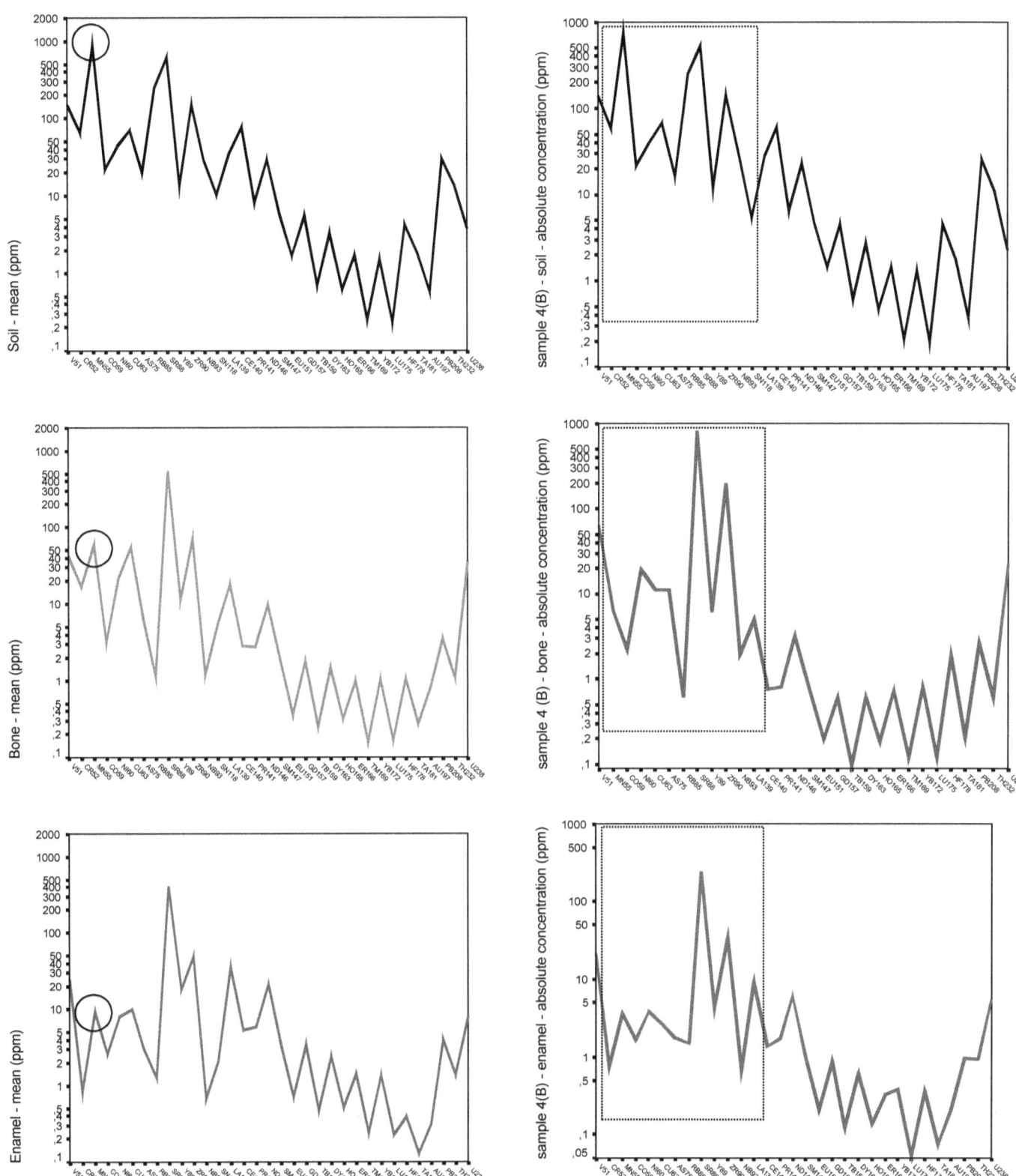

Fig. 4.1. Sant'Abbondio. Comparison of mean values (expressed on a logarithmic scale) of all the elements for soil, bone and enamel. Manganese (circled), considered to be a highly mobile element therefore indicative of diagenesis, shows heterogeneous concentration in the various samples.

Fig. 4.2 Sant'Abbondio. Individual 4(B)/96 – Eastern half of the cemetery. Comparison of absolute concentrations (on a logarithmic scale) of all the elements for soil, bone and enamel. The dotted area shows the spectrum of elements more subject to diagenesis.

In conclusion, for all elements analysed ion substitution with the soil cannot be dismissed although it is difficult to assess whether and to what extent this has occurred. The sole comparison with reference values is not a reliable criterion considering that most of the standards for bone and enamel available in the literature fail to give readings of the respective soil samples, making it problematic to measure how bone matrix is biogenetically effected by the local geochemistry. The major factor to take into account when assessing post-depositional effect though is that, overall, diagenesis cannot create new phenomena nor obliterate actual patterns but rather enhance or reduce existing situations; as Bumsted 1985 stresses "for many of our questions, we do not need to know the source of variation (…) if males and females or social classes can be grouped by their relationships of elemental concentrations, it does not matter if part of that patterning is due to contamination".

Comparison between human and animal samples

The comparison between animal and human tissues founds on the principle of the different interaction with the environment, via food and ground water consumption, these species experience. Some foodstuffs for example – especially leafy vegetables and nuts – are known to be rich in a number of elements that should be present in high concentration in animals thriving on them and to a lesser extent in humans relying on a more varied diet. It is thus interesting to select a number of elements and look at them in detail to test expected values. Among these elements, vanadium, nickel and strontium are abundant in vegetables and plants, while zinc and rubidium are richer in meat. Furthermore manganese has proven to be low in animal tissue (cf. Underwood, 1977). The comparison between animal and human tissues should thus reveal a decreasing trend, from animals to humans, for those elements known to be rich in plants and an inversed one for elements highly present in meat.

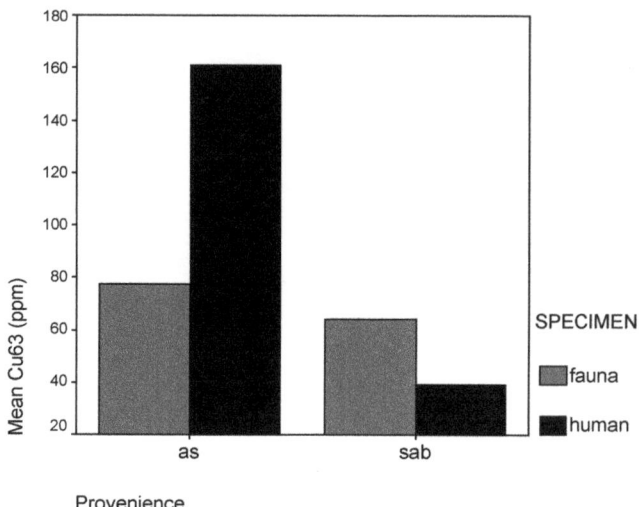

Fig. 4.4 Nickel concentration (ppm) in human and animal bone samples for Sant'Abbondio and comparative sites. as = Anglo-Saxon; sab = Sant'Abbondio.

As Sant'Abbondio is a funerary site, the presence of animals is very limited. For this analysis three faunal species were used as comparative samples. Extra-site faunal specimens (*sus scrofa*, and sheep) came from unspecified Anglo-Saxon sites, while only one sample of *bos* was available from the Bronze Age Sant'Abbondio site. Results from the comparison between human and animal concentrations at Sant'Abbondio and other sites do not meet expectations. Vanadium (Fig. 4.3), nickel (4.4) and strontium (4.5), are higher in human samples as opposed to animal ones. However, for strontium these values are surprisingly low both in Sant'Abbondio and extra-site fauna. In contrast, manganese (Fig. 4.6) values follow expectations at Sant'Abbondio as fauna samples show lower values than human samples. Values are however extremely high in the Anglo-Saxon animal specimens and again they reach numbers that are not consistent with reference material. Zinc values could not be tested because of zinc contamination (see above). Beside contamination of a number of samples, other hypotheses can be suggested for such a scenario. For vanadium and nickel, for example, high values in the human specimens could be related to the contribution of vanadium-rich (*i.e.* fish) or nickel-rich (grains) foodstuffs to the diet.

In general, a wider faunal sample would be auspicable in order to be able to compare mean values from highly variable human samples (often including outliers) and animals.

Comparison between tissues

The comparison of elemental concentration in bone and enamel revealed that the two tissues display expected values for all elements and concentrations in the bone are higher than that in teeth for most essentials and non-essentials (Table 4.6), as expected. However, for a group of elements (manganese, cobalt, copper and all Rare Earths), enamel shows higher values. When observing patterns of variation for single individuals, it is clear that enamel has a number of outliers for all elements that skew the overall mean. This seems to be confirmed by the coefficient of variation for this tissue (Table 4.6). Not surprisingly, for manganese the outliers are primarily

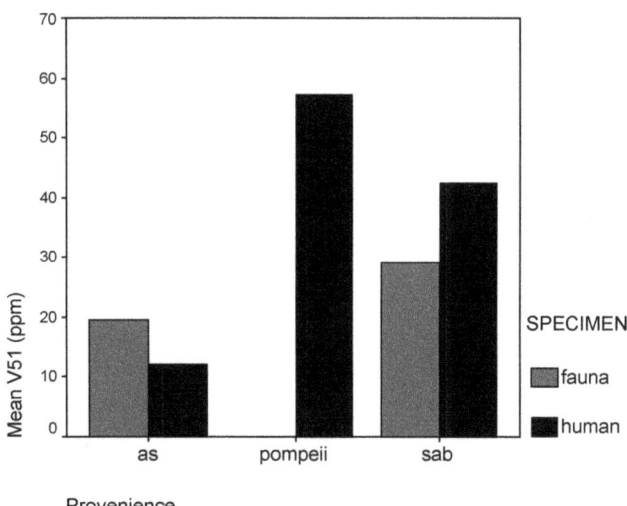

Fig. 4.3 Vanadium concentration (ppm) in human and animal bone sample for Sant'Abbondio and comparative sites. as= Anglo-Saxon; pompeii = Roman Pompeii; sab= Sant'Abbondio.

infants and juveniles, a pattern expected when considering metabolic differences between adults and children. For the other elements, the origin of such high concentration can only be attributed to a higher degree of variation in enamel values as opposed to bone ones.

This phenomenon will be discussed in Chapter Five, in relation to female outliers along the bone axis as indicative of different environmental stimuli during childhood.

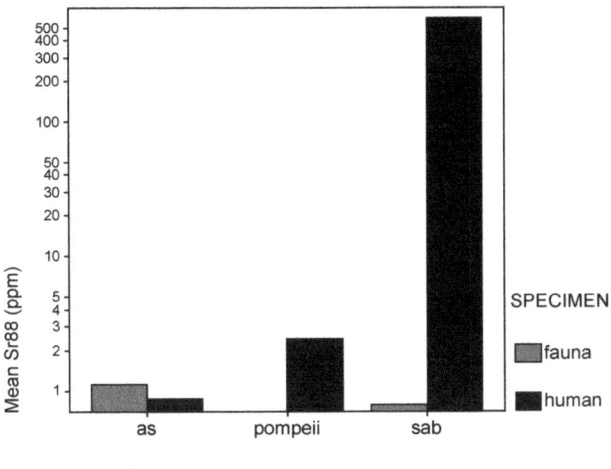

Fig. 4.5 Strontium concentration (ppm) in human and animal bone samples for Sant'Abbondio and comparative sites (values are expressed on a logarithmic scale). as = Anglo-Saxon; pompeii = Roman Pompeii; sab = Sant'Abbondio.

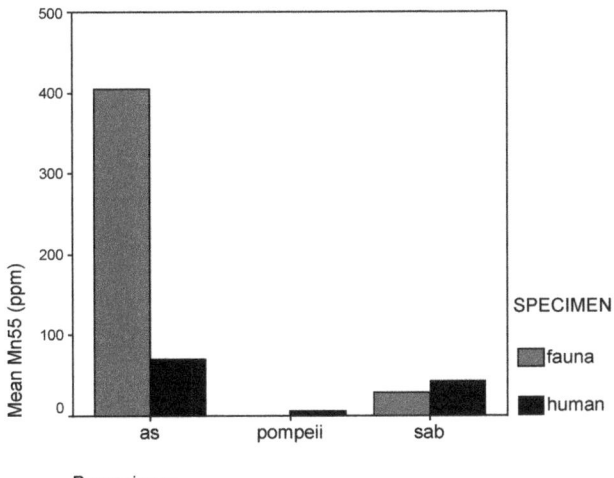

Fig. 4.6 Manganese concentration (ppm) in human and animal bone samples for Sant'Abbondio and comparative sites. as= Anglo-Saxon; pompeii= Roman Pompeii; sab= Sant'Abbondio.

Testing expected chemical behaviour

The observation of elemental concentration in relation to chemical interaction between elements is useful to assess diagenesis. If elemental variation follows expected patterns it is in fact possible to infer that no post-depositional phenomena have altered the biogenic nature of concentrations in the tissues, which still behave according to chemical expectations. At Sant'Abbondio, expected chemical behaviour of elements in relation to human homeostasis was examined through a number of elements known to interact with iron. Being a major element, iron it is not included in the spectrum of elements observed in this study but iron antagonists were examined to assess if, as expected, they show a similar pattern of variation. Iron antagonists observable at Sant'Abbondio are vanadium, chromium, manganese and nickel. Given their chemical properties, they should show similar trend or variation in relation to their similar reaction to iron values in the tissues. The relationship between antagonists can be tested through linear regression, for both bone and enamel, for pairs of antagonists. The graphs in the following pages display elemental concentrations for single individuals divided by sex, tested through linear regression with a 95% confidence interval. While it would be prohibitive to compare all 32 elements with each other it was felt that data exploration should cross boundaries between chemical groups and methodological criteria and hence a range of combinations of elements were cross-plotted to represent varying sequences. The bone samples reveal no correlation in the distribution of vanadium and manganese or between chromium and nickel bone, or in enamel values for vanadium and manganese. However, there does seem to be a correlation for chromium and nickel in bone (Fig. 4.7). The lack of correlation for pairs of iron antagonists in the bone could be due to post-mortem alterations, although it should be stressed that all of the elements considered are highly nutritional and could therefore reflect dietary consumption rather than diagenesis. From this analysis it is not possible to distinguish between the two.

A general examination has revealed no correlation between iron antagonists in the elemental concentration of bone. However, it seems to suggest a level of correlation in the enamel (reflective of childhood), perhaps confirming a general tendency to suffer from iron depletion during early life as opposed to adulthood. This result seems to suggest no diagenetic effect for the enamel.

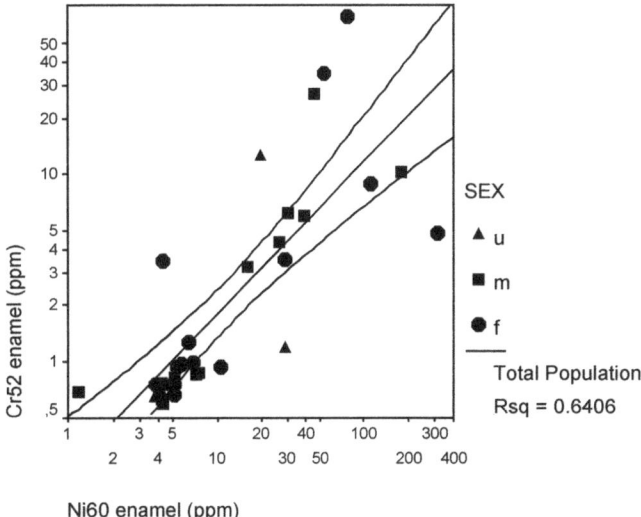

Fig. 4.7 Linear regression analysis for chromium and nickel concentration in enamel samples. Regression line is displayed together with confidence interval bands (95%). Individuals are divided by sex. A slight correlation is observable (Rsq = 0.6406).

Testing expected biological behaviour

Earlier it has been described how biological and metabolic factors are able to influence elemental concentration in the tissues. At Sant'Abbondio we should therefore expect a number of elements to vary in accordance with age, sex, and general health conditions of the individuals.

Elemental variation in accordance with age can be examined through lead concentrations, for which juveniles display slightly higher values than adults (cf. Table 4.7 and 4.8). Young children would be expected to store higher quantities of this element in the tissues as the natural consequence of the immaturity of the organs of the stomach. The category of younger subadults (0-6 yrs) shows higher concentration of lead in bone and enamel than older ones (7-12), and are, therefore, in agreement with expectations (Fig. 4.7).

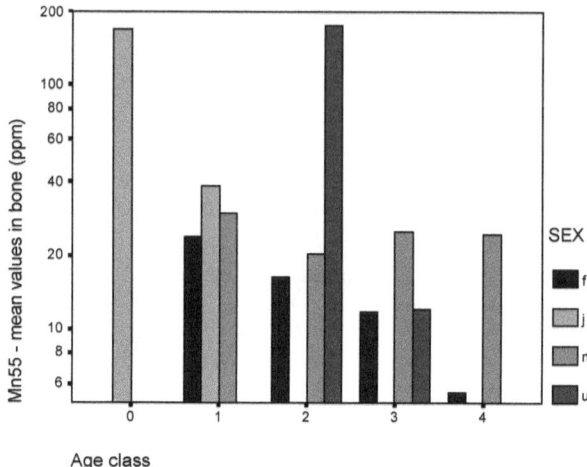

Fig. 4.8 Manganese mean concentration in the bone according to age classes (0= 0-10 yrs; 1=11-20 yrs; 2=21-30 yrs; 3=31-40 yrs; 4=40+ yrs), divided by sex.

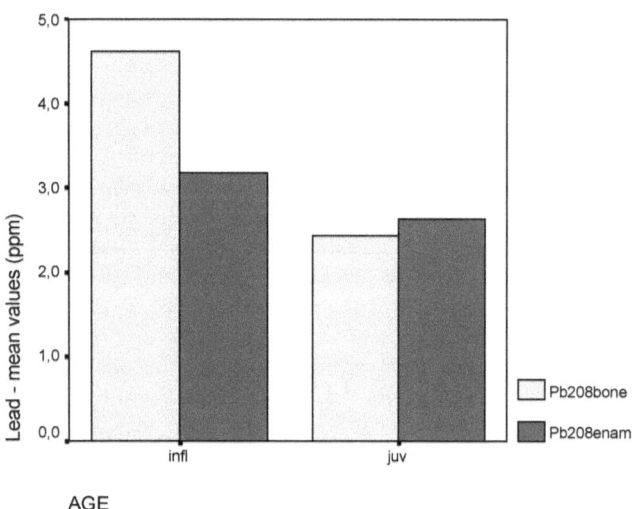

Fig. 4.7 Mean concentration of lead in bone and enamel in accordance with categories of subadults (infl=0-6 yrs; juv=7-12 yrs).

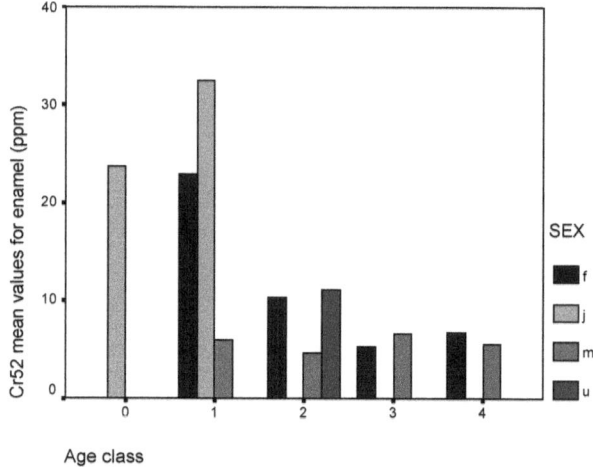

Fig. 4.9 Chromium mean concentration in the bone according to age classes (0= 0-10 yrs; 1=11-20 yrs; 2=21-30 yrs; 3=31-40 yrs; 4=40+ yrs), pooled by sex.

Manganese should also display mean values that tend to increase with the age of the individuals as a consequence of higher manganese requirements during mature life. In contrast, chromium values should be inversely proportional to age as a result of metabolic depletion of chromium during older age. However, for bone, the tissue related to adulthood, manganese concentration does not fit with the expected scenario (Fig. 4.8), while chromium values seem to follow the normal homeostatic mode (Fig. 4.9).

Variation of homeostatic processes in relation to sex can be investigated through the well-known biochemical behaviour of strontium during pregnancy and lactation, as gestation and breastfeeding are known to cause strontium loss in the bone (Blakely, 1989). Biogenic patterning in strontium metabolism has already discussed in Chapter Three. Here it is worth recalling that Blakely (*ibid.*) has demonstrated that gestation and breast-feeding cause strontium depletion in bone due to differential uptake and fractionation. This provides and important baseline for interpreting the Sant'Abbondio data. Elemental concentration in the bone of Sant'Abbondio females was plotted according to age categories and results meet expectations (Fig. 4.10).

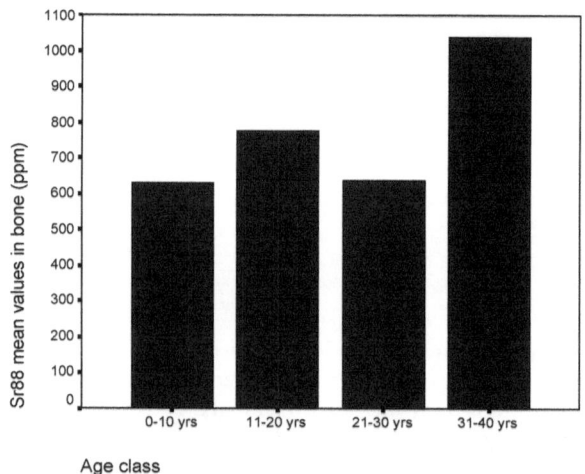

Fig. 4.10 Strontium mean concentration in Sant'Abbondio females in accordance with age classes.

Trends in element variation can also be examined in accordance with specific physiological conditions that are likely to modify homeostatic processes. Some of these, as discussed above, are particularly related to elemental concentration in the tissues (*i.e.* iron-deficiency diseases) and will be further discussed in the following chapter.

The lowest values are reported for juveniles (which normally have lower strontium values as this elements builds up with age) and for females of reproductive age, while older women show the highest numbers in the sample.

Comparison with other humans

As well as the human samples from Sant'Abbondio a total of five extra-site samples were analysed using ICP-MS in order to have a comparative set to test variation between samples. According to expectations, samples of different origin should reveal different concentration as a result of different interaction with the environment. Through comparison, groups of mobile elements should show similar variation. The comparative material consisted solely of bone specimens, as no enamel specimens were available. Bone came from two adults from a Romano-British cemetery (Huntsman's Quarry, Gloucestershire, U.K.), one adult from an Anglo-Saxon cemetery (with no indication of the site of provenience), one juvenile from a Bronze Age site (Huntsman's Quarry, Gloucestershire, U.K.) and one adult from the Roman excavations at Pompeii. Sex and age of all the individuals are unknown, although this does not affect the outcome of a general comparison. Mean values and standard deviation for bone samples are shown in Table 4.5.

The comparison between Sant'Abbondio and extra-site specimens shows heterogeneity between samples, thereby excluding laboratory contamination and instrumental error as sources of post-mortem alteration. For vanadium, manganese, cobalt, niobium, tin, gold, thorium, and uranium, values from the Anglo-Saxon sites, Roman Pompeii and Sant'Abbondio are dissimilar from one another (Table 4.5). The comparison with reference material has also revealed how Anglo-Saxon and Roman Pompeii bone samples show doubtful values for such elements as arsenic, strontium and yttrium. Test on laboratory procedures and data history suggest possible post-depositional contamination.

Element (ppm)	Sant'Abbondio			Pompeii		Anglo-Saxon		
	n	mean	sd	n	absolute conc.	n	mean	sd
Vanadium (V51)	57	65.6	21.11	1	57.4	4	12.1	3.6
Chromium (Cr52)	37	11.6	13.38	1	--	4	22.7	6.7
Manganese (Mn55)	57	46.9	95.18	1	7.1	4	71.0	44.6
Cobalt (Co59)	57	3.51	1.82	1	4.3	4	4.1	0.7
Nickel (Ni60)	56	17.4	8.15	1	--	4	19.0	4.9
Copper (Cu63)	45	32.1	27.19	1	--	1	16	
Arsenic (As75)	57	9.5	3.87	1	--	1	65.1	
Rubidium (Rb85)	57	1.29	0.84	1	--	0	--	
Strontium (Sr88)	57	791.7	256.28	1	2.4	4	0.8	0.3
Yttrium (Y89)	57	5.7	6.46	1	1031.3	4	376.1	25.6
Zirconium (Zr90)	57	140.1	88.81	1	0.3	4	2.1	0.8
Niobium (Nb93)	57	1.91	1.06	1	14.6	4	3.0	0.7
Tin (Sn118)	29	5.5	7.53	1	1.2	4	0.3	0.3
Hafnium (Hf178)	57	1.26	0.91	1	--	2	0.1	0.04
Tantalum (Ta181)	63	0.20	0.12	1	--	1	0.02	
Gold (Au197)	21	1.0	1.48	1	0.7	3	0.6	0.2
Lead (Pb208)	58	2.6	2.29	1	0.2	3	0.2	02
REE								
Lanthanum (La139)	57	7.3	11.54	1	0.5	1	2.7	
Cerium (Ce140)	57	1.6	1.98	1	0.6	4	1.7	0.2
Praseodymium (Pr141)	57	1.13	1.70	1	1.0	4	1.1	0.4
Neodymium (Nd146)	57	4.3	5.98	1	0.2	4	0.3	2.3
Samarium (Sm147)	54	0.89	1.03	1	0.5	4	1.5	0.2
Europium (Eu151)	56	0.21	0.19	1	--	2	0.3	0.01
Gadolinium (Gd157)	56	0.86	1.04	1	--	3	0.1	0.01
Terbium (Tb159)	56	0.13	0.14	1	--	4	0.1	0.03
Dysprosium (Dy163)	56	0.72	0.85	1	0.2	4	0.3	0.1
Holmium (Ho165)	53	0.18	0.18	1	4.7	4	0.06	0.01
Erbium (Er166)	56	0.5	0.5	1	0.1	4	0.3	0.1
Thulium (Tm169)	48	0.099	0.08	1	0.04	4	0.07	0.01
Ytterbium (Yb172)	57	0.62	0.54	1	--	4	0.1	0.05
Lutetium (Lu175)	51	0.109	0.08	1	--	1	0.04	
Thorium (Th232)	63	1.00	0.91	1	--	1	1.4	
Uranium (U238)	63	38.2	15.50	1	158.6	2	2.3	1.3

Table 4.5 Mean and standard deviation (ppm) of the elemental concentration (bone only) for Sant'Abbondio and Roman Pompeii and Anglo-Saxon sites. Values from Pompeii are absolute concentrations.

Intra-site comparison of individuals from Sant'Abbondio

Values between individuals from Sant'Abbondio were compared to examine whether variation in the bone and the enamel could be due to phenomena other than biological in order to infer the cultural influence of elemental intake. The mean, standard deviation, and coefficient of variation were calculated separately for bone and enamel (Table 4.6). The large standard deviation for the mean of each element shows that elemental concentration is rather variable.

To measure the differences in bone and enamel values in accordance with categories of age and sex, bar graphs showing the elemental concentration were produced for each element. The main drawback of this kind of analysis is that for each element the use of the mean values implies that individuals showing extremely high concentrations may influence the general outcome of the whole variable. When observing the distribution of each element for each individual it is observable how variation has a different origin.

This is evident for lead, for which juveniles shows extremely high values for all individuals, whereas the females' higher enamel concentrations are due to few individuals having high values that skew the overall mean. Hence, mean values and standard deviation were calculated separately for adults – divided in accordance with estimated sex – (Table 4.7), and for infants and juveniles (Table 4.8).

Among adults, overall, there seems to be a greater variation in the elemental concentration of enamel as opposed to that of bone; this is evident when observing the coefficient of variation for the single elements in the two tissues. Within enamel variation, females show a greater degree of inconsistency. Bone, on the other hand, seems to vary more for males. In general, the high degree of variation may also be due to internal shifts determined by the variable nature of the samples; bone fragments and enamel transects selected for analysis may be heterogeneous and reflect different histological periods, resulting in a large variation within an overall consistency.

As discussed, children display visibly higher values for elements with known age-related differential homeostasis (chromium, manganese, cobalt – see above). Higher values of lead in children are expected, although enhanced absorption and reduced excretion of this element tends to normalise after the second year of age. On a detailed level), the only two infants of the site (5 n.2 and 17/93) show high lead levels although these values are normalised in the overall mean of elemental concentration for children displayed in Table 4.8.

Element (ppm)	n	Bone mean	sd	c.v	n	Enamel Mean	sd	c.v.
Vanadium (V51)	57	65.6	21.11	32.2%	51	17.1	15.90	93%
Chromium (Cr52)	37	11.6	13.38	115%	51	6.2	12.06	194%
Manganese (Mn55)	57	46.9	95.18	203%	51	41.6	225.84	542%
Cobalt (Co59)	57	3.51	1.82	51.8%	50	3.1	2.04	65%
Copper (Cu63)	45	32.1	27.19	84.7%	31	51.2	209.43	409%
Arsenic (As75)	57	9.5	3.87	40.7%	18	3.2	2.43	76%
Rubidium (Rb85)	57	1.29	0.84	65.1%	51	1.30	0.79	60%
Strontium (Sr88)	57	791.7	256.28	32.3%	51	382.7	322.41	84%
Nickel (Ni60)	56	17.4	8.15	46.8%	51	33.0	56.19	170%
Yttrium (Y89)	57	5.7	6.46	113%	51	11.9	17.6	148%
Zirconium (Zr90)	57	140.1	88.81	63.3%	51	28.6	34.26	119%
Niobium (Nb93)	57	1.91	1.06	55%	51	0.51	0.41	80%
Tin (Sn118)	29	5.5	7.53	137%	49	4.4	10.81	245%
Hafnium (Hf178)	57	1.26	0.91	72.2	51	0.45	0.40	88%
Tantalum (Ta181)	63	0.20	0.12	60%	51	0.14	0.11	275%
Gold (Au197)	21	1.0	1.48	148%	31	1.3	5.41	416%
Lead (Pb208)	58	2.6	2.29	88%	44	3.2	2.81	88%
REE								
Lanthanum (La139)	57	7.3	11.54	158%	51	22.3	37.03	166%
Cerium (Ce140)	57	1.6	1.98	123%	51	3	2.56	85%
Praseodymium (Pr141)	57	1.13	1.70	150%	51	3.7	6.02	162%
Neodymium (Nd146)	57	4.3	5.98	139%	51	13.8	21.89	158%
Samarium (Sm147)	54	0.89	1.03	115%	51	2.3	3.30	143%
Europium (Eu151)	56	0.21	0.19	90%	51	0.49	0.69	140%
Gadolinium (Gd157)	56	0.86	1.04	121%	51	2.1	3.04	144%
Terbium (Tb159)	56	0.13	0.14	107%	49	0.32	0.40	125%
Dysprosium (Dy163)	56	0.72	0.85	118%	49	1.6	2.15	134%
Holmium (Ho165)	53	0.18	0.18	100%	48	0.35	0.45	128%
Erbium (Er166)	56	0.5	0.5	100%	49	0.97	1.28	131%
Thulium (Tm169)	48	0.099	0.08	8%	38	0.20	0.18	90%
Ytterbium (Yb172)	57	0.62	0.54	87%	47	0.95	1.13	118%
Lutetium (Lu175)	51	0.109	0.08	73%	44	0.16	0.16	100%
Thorium (Th232)	63	1.00	0.91	91%	51	1.40	1.10	78%
Uranium (U238)	63	38.2	15.50	40%	51	7.8	10.75	137%

Table 4.6 Mean, standard deviation (in ppm) and coefficient of variation (in %) of the element concentration of bone and enamel samples from Sant'Abbondio.

	Bone								Enamel							
	males				females				males				females			
Element (ppm)	n	mean	sd	c.v (%)	n	mean	sd	c.v.	n	mean	sd	c.v.	n	mean	sd	c.v. (%)
Vanadium (V51)	16	67.7	18.6	27.4	18	61.2	17.2	28.1	16	17.4	13.8	79.3	16	10.6	5.5	51.8
Chromium (Cr52)	12	5.8	1.3	22.4	12	11.0	7.8	70.9	16	4.2	6.7	23.8	16	8.7	18.2	209
Manganese (Mn55)	16	24.7	14.8	59.9	18	14.4	8.6	59.7	16	8.4	6.8	80.9	17	7.9	4.4	31.0
Cobalt (Co59)	16	3.3	1.2	36.3	18	2.7	0.7	25.9	15	2.8	1.6	57.1	17	2.7	1.5	55.5
Nickel (Ni60)	16	16.3	4.2	25.7	18	17.6	5.3	30.1	16	24.5	43.6	188	17	45.8	77.5	169
Copper (Cu63)	14	27.2	17.0	62.5	14	28.2	17.9	63.4	9	5.9	3.8	64.4	12	19.6	27.1	138
Arsenic (As75)	16	9.5	2.8	29.4	18	9.8	4.7	47.9	5	2.9	1.4	48.2	6	1.6	0.7	43.7
Rubidium (Rb85)	16	1.6	0.9	56.2	18	0.9	0.3	33.3	16	1.0	0.4	40	17	1.2	0.6	50
Strontium (Sr88)	16	839.7	254.2	30.2	18	760.3	293.7	38.5	16	339.7	165.3	48.7	17	298.5	180.8	60.3
Yttrium (Y89)	16	2.9	2.1	72.4	18	5.6	6.9	123	16	10.7	11.1	103.7	17	16.2	26.9	166
Zirconium (Zr90)	16	143.9	71.7	49.8	18	112.1	82.3	73.4	16	19.6	13.5	68.8	17	25.2	19.4	76.9
Niobium (Nb93)	16	2.2	0.9	40.9	18	1.5	0.9	60	16	0.4	0.2	50	17	0.4	0.3	75
Tin (Sn118)	7	2.0	1.9	95	11	5.3	6.7	126	16	1.9	1.8	94.7	16	8.1	18.1	223
Hafnium (Hf178)	16	1.3	0.8	61.5	18	1.0	0.8	80	16	0.4	0.4	100	17	0.4	0.2	50
Tantalum (Ta181)	16	0.2	0.1	50	18	0.2	0.1	50	16	0.1	0.1	100	17	0.1	0.1	100
Gold (Au197)	5	0.8	0.4	50	7	0.6	0.7	116	11	3.0	9.0	300	12	0.3	0.3	100
Lead (Pb208)	15	3.0	3.0	100	16	1.8	0.7	38.8	13	1.9	1.6	84.2	16	4.1	3.0	73.1
REE																
Lanthanum (La139)	16	3.2	3.1	96.8	18	6.7	11.2	167	16	19.7	19.7	100	17	31.4	58.4	185
Cerium (Ce140)	16	1.5	1.3	86.6	18	0.9	0.5	55.5	16	2.2	1.6	72.7	17	3.3	2.3	71.8
Praseodymium (Pr141)	16	0.5	0.5	100	18	1.0	1.6	160	16	3.2	2.9	90	17	5.2	9.5	182
Neodymium (Nd146)	16	2.1	1.7	80.9	18	3.8	6.0	157	16	12.0	11.1	92.5	17	19.2	34.6	180
Samarium (Sm147)	14	0.4	0.3	75	17	0.8	0.9	112	16	1.9	1.7	89.4	17	3.0	5.1	170
Europium (Eu151)	16	0.1	0.06	60	17	0.2	0.2	100	16	0.4	0.3	75	17	0.6	1.1	183
Gadolinium (Gd157)	16	0.4	0.2	50	18	0.8	1.0	12.5	16	1.9	1.7	89.4	17	2.9	4.6	158
Terbium (Tb159)	15	0.08	0.04	50	18	0.1	0.1	100	16	0.2	0.2	100	17	0.4	0.6	150
Dysprosium (Dy163)	16	0.4	0.2	50	18	0.6	0.7	116	16	1.4	1.3	92.8	17	2.0	3.2	160
Holmium (Ho165)	15	0.1	0.05	50	16	0.1	0.1	100	16	0.3	0.2	66.6	17	0.4	0.6	150
Erbium (Er166)	16	0.3	0.2	66.6	17	0.5	0.5	100	16	0.8	0.8	100	17	1.2	1.9	158
Thulium (Tm169)	9	0.06	0.05	83.3	17	0.09	0.07	77.7	13	0.1	0.1	100	15	0.2	0.2	100
Ytterbium (Yb172)	16	0.4	0.2	50	18	0.6	0.5	83.3	16	0.7	0.7	100	17	1.1	1.6	14.5
Lutetium (Lu175)	12	0.07	0.03	42.8	17	0.1	0.07	70	15	0.1	0.1	100	17	0.1	0.2	200
Thorium (Th232)	16	1.0	0.7	70	18	0.7	0.7	100	16	1.3	1.0	76.9	17	1.4	1.2	85.7
Uranium (U238)	16	40.8	13.9	34	18	35.8	13.8	38.5	16	6.3	5.7	90.4	17	3.0	3.4	113

Table 4.7 Sant'Abbondio mean and standard deviation (ppm) of bone and enamel elemental concentration for adults divided by sex.

	Bone			Enamel		
Element (ppm)	n	mean	sd	n	mean	sd
Vanadium (V51)	9	72.9	30.7	12	16.4	8.9
Chromium (Cr52)	7	21.0	27.2	12	3.4	3.0
Manganese (Mn55)	9	128.2	159.4	12	144.1	465.2
Cobalt (Co59)	9	5.1	2.3	12	2.9	1.6
Nickel (Ni60)	9	21.5	15.8	12	28.8	47.5
Copper (Cu63)	7	47.0	54.2	7	11.4	9.6
Arsenic (As75)	9	11.2	4.5	4	4.6	1.7
Rubidium (Rb85)	9	1.4	0.9	12	1.4	1.2
Strontium (Sr88)	8	868.1	217.7	12	378.2	259.5
Yttrium (Y89)	9	11.4	9.5	12	8.1	7.5
Zirconium (Zr90)	9	200.1	114.5	12	30.9	29.2
Niobium (Nb93)	9	2.44	1.2	12	0.6	0.4
Tin (Sn118)	5	9.7	14.7	11	5.3	6.5
Hafnium (Hf178)	9	1.8	1.4	12	0.5	0.4
Tantalum (Ta181)	9	0.2	0.1	12	0.1	0.09
Gold (Au197)	3	0.4	0.04	7	0.3	0.3
Lead (Pb208)	9	3.7	3.3	11	2.7	1.8
REE						
Lanthanum (La139)	9	15.4	18.1	12	13.7	12.6
Cerium (Ce140)	9	3.6	3.9	12	2.5	2.1
Praseodymium (Pr141)	9	2.4	2.9	12	2.3	2.0
Neodymium (Nd146)	9	9.1	9.8	12	8.7	7.5
Samarium (Sm147)	9	1.8	1.7	12	1.4	1.2
Europium (Eu151)	0	0.3	0.2	11	0.3	0.2
Gadolinium (Gd157)	9	1.7	1.6	12	1.4	1.2
Terbium (Tb159)	9	0.2	0.2	10	0.2	0.1
Dysprosium (Dy163)	9	1.5	1.5	10	1.2	0.8
Holmium (Ho165)	9	0.3	0.2	9	0.2	0.2
Erbium (Er166)	9	1.0	0.8	10	0.7	0.5
Thulium (Tm169)	9	0.2	0.1	6	0.2	0.06
Ytterbium (Yb172)	9	1.2	0.8	9	0.8	0.5
Lutetium (Lu175)	9	0.2	0.1	8	0.1	0.07
Thorium (Th232)	9	1.7	1.4	12	1.4	1.1
Uranium (U238)	9	44.8	21.2	12	12.3	15.0

Table 4.8 Sant'Abbondio, mean and standard deviation (ppm) of bone and enamel elemental concentration for juveniles (0-12 years).

DISCUSSION

The purpose of this chapter has been to recognise the range of methods useful in assessing post-depositional effects and determining data reliability in trace element studies. Most of these techniques are described in the literature and are normally applied singularly. Rarely have all of these procedures been employed at the same time, either because of a lack of reliance on a multidimensional approach or, perhaps, as a result of excessive confidence in 'traditional' methods. The simultaneous application of the criteria described in this chapter has proven to be successful. Not only has it allowed us to test for diagenesis but it has helped determine the eliminate laboratory contamination and has revealed how reliable data could be considered. Moreover it has demonstrated that several factors can differently affect trace element concentration in the bone and that corrupted results not only originate from post-mortem variation in the tissues, but also from procedural inaccuracies that are often disregarded. The possibility to examine post-depositional changes in the tissues through a range of criteria, as for example the use of biological and chemical expectations, has also allowed the ascertaining of the reliability of the data.

Diagenesis is multi-factorial, which is why trace element analysis cannot be based on the assessment of post-mortem alterations according to a selected spectrum of elements of known homeostatic properties, but must rely on all chemical and biological information available. The human organism is regulated by different biochemical mechanisms, and the observation of diagenesis should consider as many of them as possible.

Overall assessment of diagenesis and taphonomic phenomena at Sant'Abbondio can be summarised as follows (Table 4.9):

- Selenium (Se77 and Se82) and europium (Eu151 and Eu153) were not taken up by the ICP-MS apparatus and were found to be below the limit of detection. Hence the elements were excluded from the analysis.
- The use of a zinc-contaminated solution resulted in laboratory zinc (Zn66) contamination. Extreme readings for zinc were revealed to be suspect and tests performed in the lab demonstrated that a zinc-enriched solution was used, affecting final data.

- Instrumental error is likely to have caused incorrect reading of yttrium (Y89), zirconium (Zr90) and gold (Au197). The chemical characteristics of these elements may have resulted in undissolved particles taken up by the spectrum with consequent high readings.
- High values of uranium (U238) – an element present in extremely low quantities in the human body – in the tissues might be the result of post-mortem alteration.

All of these elements have been excluded from the analysis. In addition to this the following should be considered:
- Strontium values are slightly higher than the mean concentration indicated by reference material, however, the comparison with available literature on strontium studies has demonstrated for this element a great variation in absolute concentration in accordance with the provenience of sample treated. All test criteria for data reliability and consistency suggest that there is no reason not to use the strontium data in this study. It must be stressed however that concentration of strontium in the human tissues is particularly variable and a number of previous studies have revealed that results from Sant'Abbondio fall within the normal range (cf. absolute concentrations from Price *et al.*, 1998).

The observation of some elements in bone and enamel in relation to expected homeostatic patterns in groups of individual from Sant'Abbondio revealed that elements vary in accordance with chemical interaction (synergy and antagonism between elements), biological factors (sex and age), and physiological conditions (pathologies or metabolic alterations). Data history was carefully recorded and no laboratory contamination (tested through the analysis of batches of samples per day of analysis) seems to have occurred.

Overall, the examination of data permitted the identification of diagenesis (either in relation to post-mortem alteration or laboratory contamination) for a number of elements but also evidenced patterns of variation in relation to the tissue or the category of individuals observed. Enamel, as opposed to bone, reveals a higher degree of variation (see the coefficient of variation – Table 4.7). The significance of such difference will be explored and discussed in the following chapter. Such variation is, however, already associable with adult females or children, as opposed to males. These and other patterns are discussed in Chapter Seven.

CRITERION	EXPECTATIONS	METHOD/TEST	RESULTS
♦ Procedural criteria	Removal of the diagenetic portion on hard tissues	Physical abrasion of outer surface of bone (ca. 3 mm) and enamel (ca. 1 mm) (Lambert et al. 1990)	<ul><li>Laboratory contamination of zinc</li><li>Instrumental error for: yttrium, zirconium, gold</li><li>Post-mortem variation of uranium</li></ul>
♦ Comparison with reference values	Homogeneity in absolute concentrations of different elements in the tissues	Underwood, 1977; Iyengar et al., 1978; WHO, 1996; ww.ch.cam.ac.uk	Unreliable values for zinc, yttrium, zirconium, gold and uranium
♦ Comparison with soil	Chemical interaction (via food and ground water) between human and the environment	<ul><li>Soil samples from Sant'Abbondio</li><li>Soil samples from the Sarno area</li></ul>	No evident signs of contamination, although variation in the values shown
♦ Comparison with fauna	Different dietary regimes between humans and animals	<ul><li>Anglo-Saxon samples (*sus scrofa*, sheep)</li><li>Sant'Abbondio (*bos*)</li></ul>	<ul><li>Non-testable values from extra-site specimens</li><li>Consistency between Sant'Abbondio human and fauna</li></ul>
♦ Comparison between tissues	Differences in absolute concentrations	Direct comparison and comparison with reference values	Reliable difference in absolute concentration between the tissues
♦ Comparison with expected chemical behaviours	Mineral variation and chemical interaction between elements in accordance to synergy or antagonism Iron-antagonists (vanadium, chromium, manganese, nickel) are expected to have similarly high values in general and in iron-deficient individuals in particular	Tentative correlation between iron-antagonists	Linear regression for between iron antagonists shows positive correlation
♦ Comparison with expected biological behaviour	Mineral variation in accordance to biological and metabolic factors o **Age** Lead and manganese are expected to by high in children and low in older people Strontium is expected to be low in children o **Sex** Strontium values are expected to be low in female of reproductive age because of pregnancy and lactation o **Physiological conditions** Elemental variation in accordance with pathologies and metabolic stress	*Comparison between categories of individuals*	■ **Age** Children with higher values; Lead and manganese show high values in younger children while strontium is lower in children as opposed to adults Chromium is lower in older adults in relation to age-related Cr depletion ■ **Sex** Strontium depletion in young and young-adult females ■ **Physiological conditions** Possible correlation between iron-antagonists and aenemia
♦ Comparison with humans from other contexts	o Adequate homogeneity to assure reliability of data o Sufficient heterogeneity to exclude instrumental error	Direct comparison	Unreliable values from extra-site specimens
♦ Comparison between individuals from the same context	o Differences on biological and metabolic bases o Possible differences in accordance with archaeological data	Comparison of mean values in the bone and the enamel. Adults and children-juveniles were kept separate.	<ul><li>Greater variation in the enamel for females</li><li>Greater variation in the bone for males</li><li>Difference between eastern and western area of the cemetery not explicable through post-depositional effects/soil contamination. Such a difference applies differently to females and males.</li></ul>

Table 4.9 Summary of the results from the different criteria used to assess diagenesis and data reliability at Sant'Abbondio.

Chapter Five
Sant'Abbondio ICP-MS Trace Element Data Analysis and Interpretation

Introduction

Having assessed diagenesis and discussed the reliability of values obtained, the results from ICP-MS multi-elemental analysis on the skeletal sample from Sant'Abbondio is used to explore the theoretical assumptions presented in the early part of this work. The potential of the multi-elemental approach, through the different chemical (diagenetic) and biochemical (biogenic) properties of particular elements, makes it possible to set a range of questions that can be examined through the use of a specific combination of elements. The intention is to use trace element data not only in relation to paleonutritional queries, but rather to discuss wider scenarios that scholars dealing with Italian recent prehistory are normally confronted with. Particular attention will be given to the idea of gender-specific mobility at Sant'Abbondio, as proposed by Puglisi's work (1959) (see Chapter One for a discussion). Puglisi's assumption of patrilineal and pastoral communities involved in differentiated mobility in relation to economic needs (transhumant male herders) or social constructions (bride exchange) will be tested using bone and enamel values in the diachronic sequence these tissues represent (Table 1.1).

The first part of the chapter is devoted to data presentation and explorative univariate analysis, while the second part uses bivariate statistics to test elemental variation in light of archaeological and skeletal data. In particular, the bivariate approach examines the influence of biological and metabolic factors in the chemical composition of hard tissues in relation to specific physiological conditions (metabolic stresses and pathologies) recorded in the sample. Furthermore the comparison between bone and enamel values can be used to expose gender-specific patterns of elemental concentration differentiated per tissue.

A reconstruction of Sant'Abbondio's cultural scenario is offered as a reconsideration of the traditional depiction of Bronze Age groups of Central and Southern Italy.

Data preparation and exploration – preliminary analysis

The analysis of trace element data proceeded on different levels. Differences in central tendency, patterns of variation and specific outliers were recorded. To measure the level of dispersion of data for each element, mean, standard deviation, and coefficient of variation were calculated for all individuals for the two tissues (Table 4.6). As the standard deviation suggests, most elements are highly variable and sample is seldom normally distributed. This derives mainly from the fact that most of the children tend to be skewed towards higher values in the elements relating to metabolic factors.

As described in the previous chapter, variation seems to display differentiated patterns in accordance with sex and age. This is confirmed by mean values calculated separately for adults (Table 4.7) and children (Table 4.8). The overall picture emerging from a preliminary data exploration is of a possible relationship between tissue variation and sex: greater variation expressed in the enamel mainly affects females, while where it is expressed in the bone it seems to be primarily related to males. To observe more closely how sex may have influenced the chemical composition of the tissues, z-scores were calculated for bone and enamel values separately, using only those elements (trace essentials and non-essentials) with known biochemical behaviour. The purpose of z-scores is to reduce the variation in the concentration of the different elements for each tissue and measure the extent to which a given individual deviates from the mean. Once z-scores were calculated a t-test was performed on the z-scores in accordance with estimated sex of adult individuals. Results are reported in table 5.1.

No significant sex-related difference seems to occur in overall bone and enamel values although it is evident that the mean values for the two categories are rather different.

Z-scores bone – all elements (no REE)						Z-scores enamel – all elements (no REE)					
males (n=16)		females (n=18)		T-Test		males (n=16)		females (n=17)		T-Test	
mean	sd	mean	sd	P		mean	sd	Mean	sd	P	
-0.02	0.4	-0.2	0.3	0.134		-0.1	0.4	-0.01	0.4	0.547	

Table 5.1 T-test of the z-scores of bone and enamel values divided by sex. Rare Earth Elements are excluded.

A T-test, divided by sex, for each element was performed for bone and enamel of adult individuals. Because the distribution of the two tissues was not always normal, T-Test, Kolgomorov-Smirnov, and Mann-Whitney U-test for adult individuals divided were carried out, element by element, for the two tissues. None of the three tests shows significant differences between elemental concentration of males and females. The only exception to this is rubidium, for which sex-related differences may be connected with the dietary regime of Sant'Abbondio individuals and will be discussed later in this chapter.

Results at this level of analysis reflect little differentiation in central tendency, however they do not offer a detailed perspective. Principal Component Analysis (PCA) was carried out to measure the relationship between elements, which grouped together by chemical properties in accordance with categories of age and sex. This confirms the results from the initial data exploration discussed in Chapter Four, which revealed that, when performing an internal comparison of elemental concentration in the tissues at Sant'Abbondio, major differentiation occurs on a biological level between groups of individuals according to sex and age. A more in-depth level of exploration, of how single individuals differ from the rest of the group, needs to be performed through the observation of specific outliers and is presented in the following sections.

BIVARIATE ANALYSIS

Bivariate analsysis was carried out to reach a more detailed examination of the variation of elemental concentration in the bone and the enamel for single individuals at Sant'Abbondio. The use of scatterplots is a useful strategy, as it allows the singling out of specific individuals that can be referred back to anthropological as well as archaeological data. Single or groups of people can be identified as outlying from general patterns and inferences in relation to the type of individual involved and the nature of its outlying position can be made. On the diagram, y-axis reflects element concentration in the bone while x-axis indicates enamel. The two are the visual representation of the 'dynamic relationship with the environment' described by Sandford (1992) created through elemental absorption in the tissues via food and ground water. Bearing in mind the differences in terms of chemical development between the two tissues, the bone axis represents on-going life (or better, the last 7-10 years of life), while enamel depicts childhood.

Several factors are involved in elemental uptake by human tissues from food, groundwater, and other sources, otherwise known as biogenic processes. Some of them can be of a nature that is extraneous to normal dietary intake, such as absorption via air, through cooking vessels, or through contact. Independently from the way elemental absorption is achieved, mechanisms of biogenic processes and elemental homeostasis have been extensively studied and are associated with biological factors such as growth, sex, health status, pregnancy and lactation, and pathological conditions (Sandford, 1993). Some of these aspects (for which a preliminary discussion is provided in chapters Five and Six) are reflected in patterns of elemental concentration shown by the Sant'Abbondio population. They will be further explored and discussed in the following section through bivariate scatterplots and parametric and non-parametric tests.

In order to better assess who and how is an outlier within Sant'Abbondio group it is essential to consider how to determine the cut-off point between individuals falling within the normal range of variation and proper outliers. There is no general rule to do so. According to Price *et al.* (1998 and following), the standard deviation can be used. The mean value ±2 standard deviations is considered the cut-off value that measures normal distribution as opposed to outlying results. Such method has been applied to this work although it shows to be not entirely appropriate. In Price *et al*'s work, where strontium ratios are used, the range of variation between ratios is rather limited, therefore the use of the standard deviation reveals to be an appropriate method. The concentration of each element at Sant'Abbondio is highly variable making the standard deviation rather high (Table 4.6) and difficult to use to assess the cut-off point. Absolute values are thus used taking into account the order of magnitude of each element. In the data analysis outliers were retained as an integral part of the dataset. As shown in the previous chapter, only elements considered reliable following a wide range of methodological testes were included in the analysis and hence there is no *a priori* reason to suspect that outliers represent bad data. Moreover, some of the social patterns of variation outlined in Table 1.1 would be expected to result in very different chemical values and hence outliers could prove the most informative aspect of the data.

Biogenic processes and biological factors

To explore how biological factors can influence the chemical composition of the tissues several analytical avenues were taken. A first data exploration expressed differentiation only on the basis of categories such as 'sex' and 'age' (the latter only distinguishing between sexed adults and juveniles). A bivariate comparison – through scatterplots – between bone and enamel tissue was therefore carried out for each element in order to have a measure of the variation of single individuals within the sample.

A primary distinction in terms of the biochemical nature of the elements involved is revealed by the fact that, once again, essential and non-essential elements show a different pattern of behaviour from Rare Earths. All lanthanides displayed extremely similar patterns, with a cluster of individuals showing similar values and few individuals outlying both along the enamel and the bone axes. Enamel outliers are nearly systematically infants and juveniles, suggesting an age-related biological interpretation of this pattern. Bone outliers, on the other hand, are not always recurring and would benefit from further analysis once more information on the biochemical role of Rare Earth elements in the human organism is available in order to interpret this result. One individual – 37/93 – is a repeated outlier along both axes, for all Rare Earths. Its extreme difference to other individuals can only be explained with a profound different geochemical characterisation of the environment in which the individual in question lived. On a chemical basis, lanthanides are extremely stable elements that show clear differentiation only in terms of pedological and geological variation (Kym Jarvis, pers. com.), this well explains the nearly systematic repetition of patterns of distribution of the elemental concentration of Sant'Abbondio individuals for most of the Rare Earths.

Within the categories of essential and non-essential elements, two major considerations emerge from the bivariate analysis. Firstly, multiple factors seem to affect the patterns of distribution between individuals: these are either of possible biological or metabolic significance or biologically and metabolically unrelated, hence of possible cultural origin.

Cultural aspects will be discussed later in the chapter, together with non-biological patterns which seem to suggest the association of bone and enamel concentration with archaeological evidence (*i.e.* area of deposition within the cemetery).

Subadult metabolism

The most evident biological aspect influencing elemental concentrations in the tissues observed is related to the age of the individuals. Among infants and juveniles, two main factors are involved in differentiated patterns:

1. the incomplete development of the gastrointestinal tract (the one mainly responsible for element absorption and excretion);
2. elemental retention from neonatal life.

Both aspects cause a tendency to retain elements absorbed via the placenta and through food/fluids, particularly in regime of liquid diet (WHO, 1996) as a result of accumulation and subsequent inability to excrete elements. This feature is normally persistent in the first two years of life, after which elemental homeostasis tends to 'normalise' (for a discussion of subadult element metabolism see Underwood, 1977).

One of the elements primarily involved in retention due to the incompleteness of the gastrointestinal tract is lead. Results from the Sant'Abbondio sample (Fig. 5.1) are extremely coherent with expectations as the only two infants in the group (namely, 5 n.2 and 17/93) show considerably higher values in bone – although not in the enamel - when compared with other children and adults.

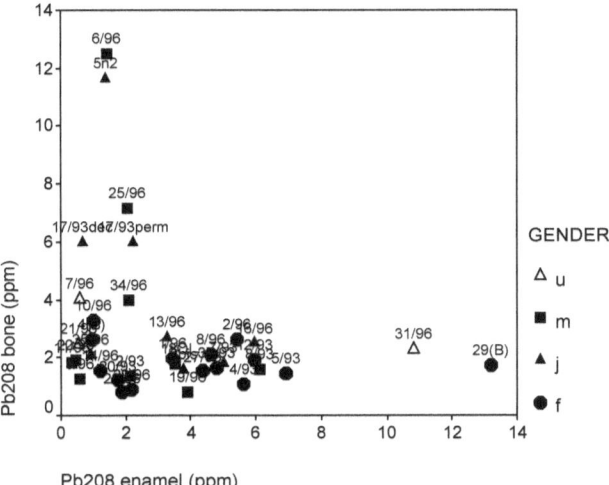

Fig. 5.1 Scatterplot of lead concentration in bone and enamel. u= indeterminate; m= males; j= juveniles; f= females.

Retention from neonatal life also occurs to overcome low quantities of nutritional elements found in human milk (Underwood, 1977). Looking at the results for copper (Fig. 5.2), individual 5n.2, estimated age 1 year, appears isolated from other infants and juveniles of the group. This can be attributed to his/her young age. When individual 5 n.2 is observed in comparison to 17/93, a clear difference in the concentration of lead in the bone is observable.

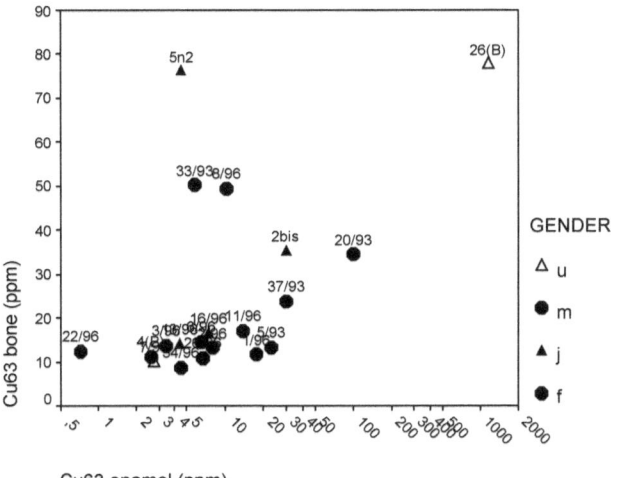

Fig. 5.2 Scatterplot of copper concentration in bone and enamel (values on the x axis are expressed on a logarithmic scale). u= indeterminate; m= males; j= juveniles; f= females.

This suggests that individual 17/93, estimated aged 2 years, must have already changed his/her metabolism in terms of element retention from *in utero*. Low values in the teeth, for both infants cannot be explained if not through the collection of the enamel sample from an area of the buccal surface corresponding to a later age, when the metabolic normalisation of elemental uptake had already taken place.

Elemental homeostasis in relation to the metabolism of children deserves further attention in relation to the evidence of iron-related variation emerged in the previous chapter. As described earlier, the mechanism of iron absorption in the bone is similar to that of a number of other trace elements (*i.e.* vanadium, manganese, cobalt, arsenic, and nickel). This results in a biochemical antagonism between them that leads to a reciprocal discrimination during absorption, therefore, it should be possible to make inferences regarding the metabolism of Sant'Abbondio juveniles using the concentration of antagonists as indicative of iron levels in the hard tissues.

The trend of vanadium is not clearly defined among subadults, as children are distributed together with adults. However, all of the other iron antagonists show similar patterns to each other. As an example, a cluster of infants and young children (2bis, 5n.2, 17/93, 13/96) shows extremely high values of manganese (Fig. 5.3), not only for bone but also for enamel. Cobalt, likewise, shows a clear distinction in concentration in relation to age (Fig. 5.4). For these elements, the pattern could derive from systematic iron-deficiency experienced by children who might have been more susceptible to insufficient or inadequate nutrition.

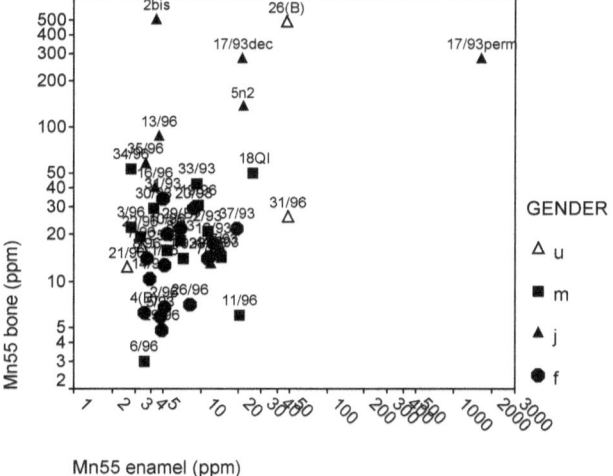

Fig. 5.3 Scatterplot of manganese concentration in bone and enamel (values for both axes are expressed on a logarithmic scale). u= indeterminate; m= males; j= juveniles; f= females.

Elemental variation in accordance with pathological conditions

The occurrence of a number of skeletal and dental pathologies in the Sant'Abbondio population offer the potential to examine whether changes in the elemental concentration of the bone or the enamel could be related to pathological conditions.

Cribra orbitalia is the most immediate pathology that could have this kind of potential. This a multi-factoral condition although it is traditionally associated with iron-deficiency anemia (Stuart-Macadam, 1998). When considering the antagonistic relationship between iron and a number of trace elements in the human organism, we should be confronted with a scenario where iron-deficient individuals (*i.e.* those showing signs of cribra orbitalia) display high concentrations of iron-antagonists (*i.e.* vanadium, chromium, manganese, arsenic and nickel).

interesting results. In this perspective, levels of vanadium, manganese, nickel, and strontium – all elements largely associated with diets based on vegetables and grains – in the enamel in relation to the presence or absence of hypoplasia could be associated with the presence of hypoplasia and, conversely, low values should coincide with an absence of such pathology however, for both bone (Fig. 5.7) and enamel (Fig. 5.8) no association between hypoplasia and elemental concentration is evident.

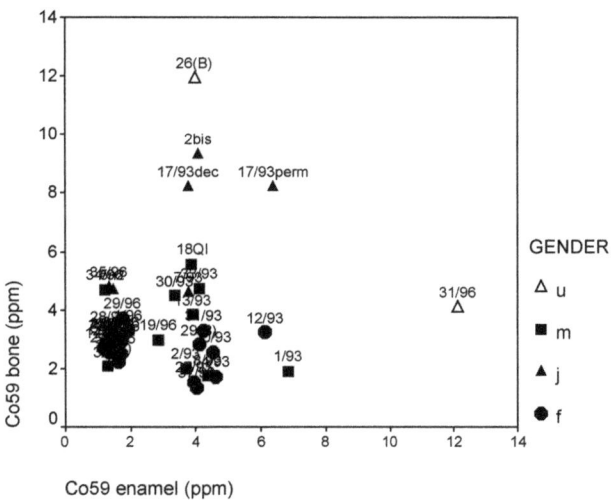

Fig. 5.4 Scatterplot of cobalt concentration in bone and enamel. u= indeterminate; m= males; j= juveniles; f= females.

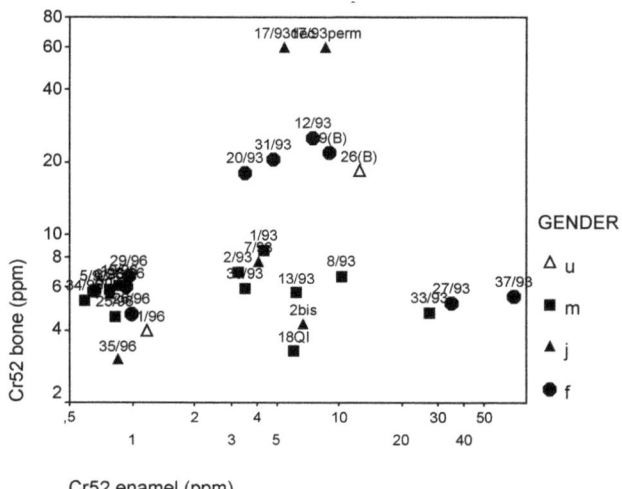

Fig. 5.5 Scatterplot of chromium concentration in bone and in enamel (values on the x axis are expressed on a logarithmic scale). u= indeterminate; m= males; j= juveniles; f= females.

As suggested earlier, data on cribra orbitalia would substantiate the explanation for iron-deficiency in children however, no data on cribra orbitalia are available for the juveniles. Among adults, four individuals (three females and one male) had sign of cribra. According to Stuart-Macadam (1985), anemia acquired during adulthood does not affect the bone and if present in adults is indicative of the development of the pathology during childhood and can be regarded as a consequence of iron-deficiency suffered during early life.

Results from both bone (as reflective of ongoing life) and enamel (as reflective of childhood) of the adults from the cemetery, allow the examination of a diachronic picture of these individuals' metabolism and the testing of Stuart-Macadam's statement.

In terms of chemical behaviour according to iron antagonism – either for bone or enamel, individual 12/93, a young (16-20 yrs.) female showing the most severe case of cribra, is systematically skewed towards high values of iron antagonists (except for arsenic for which no values were available) for both bone and enamel. In particular chromium (Fig. 5.5) and nickel (Fig. 5.6) could reflect repeated episodes of iron depletion perhaps in relation to malnutrition suffered during childhood. The other individuals affected (2/96, 10/96 and 25/96) do not show as high values as 12/93 although, especially for enamel concentration, they seem to reveal high numbers within the subgroup of individuals they cluster with.

The observation of enamel hypoplasia in relation to elemental concentration can be indicative of the influence of pathological conditions in elemental uptake. Hypoplasia is normally associated with systemic metabolic stress suffered during childhood (Goodman and Rose, 1991), therefore the observation of this pathology in relation to diet could produce

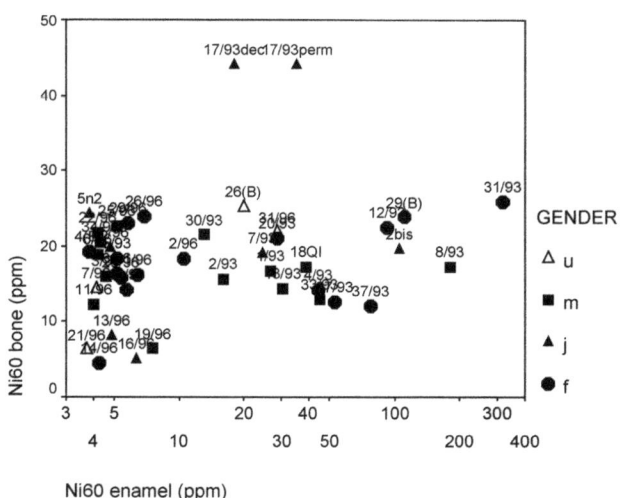

Fig. 5.6 Scatterplot of nickel concentration in bone and enamel (values on the x axis are expressed on a logarithmic scale). u= indeterminate; m= males; j= juveniles; f= females.

Adult metabolism – sex and age differences

Differential metabolism reflected in elemental absorption and excretion is not expressed solely for sub-adults. Among adults, sex and age can also be causes of discrepancies in element concentrations. Research by Schroeder and Nason (1969) showed that nickel, copper and cobalt undergo sex-related homeostasis; nickel absorption is enhanced during breastfeeding, while copper concentration in women is normally up to 10% higher than in men and during pregnancy can reach values 3 times greater (WHO, 1996). If, again, we observe values for copper (Fig. 5.2), the three female outliers along the bone axis could represent the result of women's higher retention of the element during pregnancy. The three females (8/96, 20/93, 37/93) all fall within the age range of 20-30 years, leading to idea that in this case such a correlation could be pertinent. For strontium, low levels associated with women, especially in relation to pregnancy and lactation, have been reported in the literature (see for example Blakely, 1989). Within the Sant'Abbondio sample no clear-cut differentiation in the concentration of strontium is evident between the sexes (Fig. 5.9) however a group of younger females clusters in the lower section of the diagram, as would be expected if they were pregnant or breast-feeding.

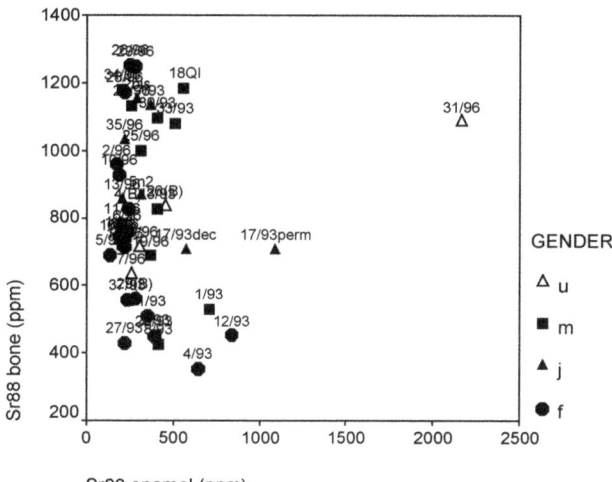

Fig. 5.9 Scatterplot of Strontium concentration in bone and enamel. u= indeterminate; m= males; j= juveniles; f= females.

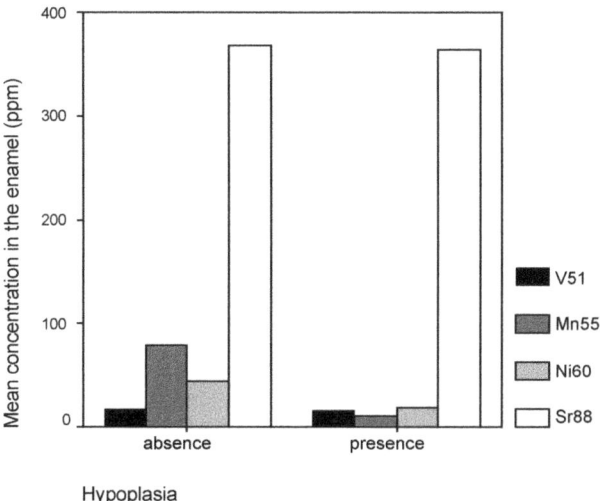

Fig. 5.7 Bar chart depicting mean concentrations of vanadium, manganese, nickel and strontium in enamel in relation to presence or absence of enamel hypoplasia.

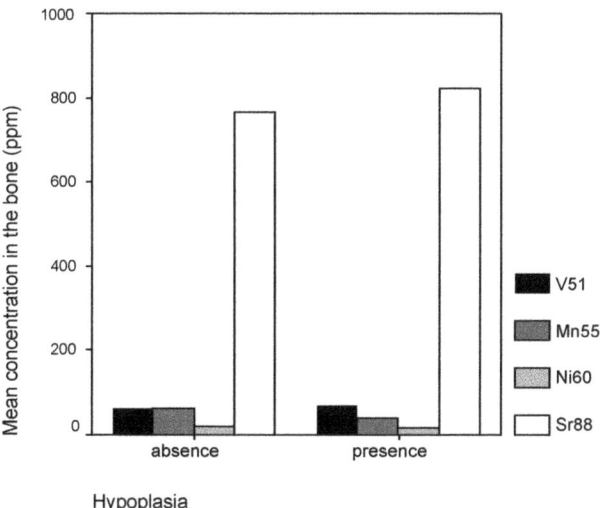

Fig. 5.8 Bar chart depicting mean concentrations of vanadium, manganese, nickel and strontium in bone in relation to presence or absence of enamel hypoplasia.

Differentiated patterns among adults could reflect metabolic differentiation connected to age, just as for juveniles. As already described, manganese storage is likely to increase with age (cf. Wenlock et al., 1979). Manganese concentration in the two tissues (Fig. 5.3) shows a distinct difference between males (with higher values) and females (with lower ones) expressed along the bone axis. This pattern could reflect the demographic background of the community rather than sex-differentiated diet or gender-based cultural influences. Paleodemographic analysis on the Sant'Abbondio population, reveals a higher frequency of adult/mature men as opposed to young/adult females (Fig. 2.5). If an age/manganese concentration correlation exists, for Sant'Abbondio this would be expected to display exactly the kind of pattern shown in the graph. Furthermore, the few males showing low manganese concentrations are of young-adult age. Strontium concentrations, like for manganese, tend to increase with age (Sandford, 1993). It is interesting to observe that the lower part of the diagram in figure 5.9 is mainly occupied by females, overall younger at Sant'Abbondio, while higher values are mainly related to males, generally older in this population.

NON-BIOLOGICAL FACTORS

In trying to interpret patterns of elemental variation not explainable in a biological perspective, a series of possible implications can be proposed Very few similar studies are present in the literature (cf. Schoeninger, 1979; Price et al., 1994; 1998; 2000) so any interpretative attempt is in need of theoretical and methodological back-up.

Three features, which will be discussed below, deserve particular attention:

1. the presence of differentiated patterns of elemental concentration in accordance with sex, which cannot be explained in a biological/metabolic perspective;
2. the presence of outliers along the bone and enamel axes as to suggest cultural implications, especially in terms of social mobility;
3. the presence of separate clusters of individuals reflecting separate areas of deposition within the cemetery, leading again to further cultural inferences, possibly in terms of social identity.

Sex and differentiated diet

Trace elements are mainly introduced into the human organism via food and water, hence the chemical concentration of hard tissues is connected with dietary habits. The main aims of this work, however, go beyond paleonutrition as the reconstruction of diet alone, therefore dietary factors need to be put in social context. The intent of this section is to discuss a number of patterns suggesting more complex interpretation of the social and economic dynamics of the Sant'Abbondio community, expressed through the ways that Sant'Abbondio people ate. What proposed here is one of the many possible explanations, which considers elements with a strong nutritional role.

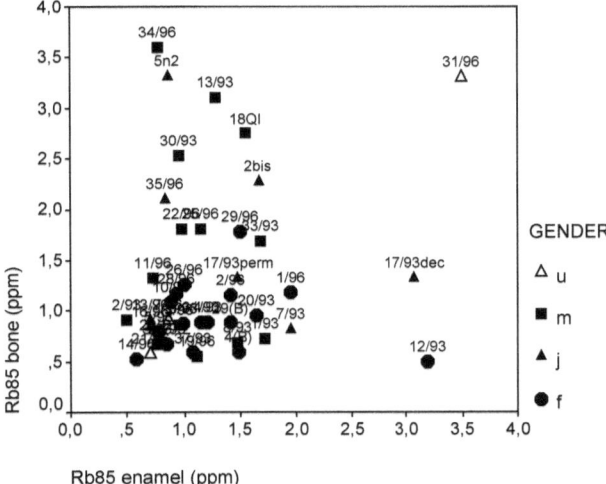

Figure 5.10 Scatterplot of rubidium concentration in bone and enamel. u= indeterminate; m= males; j= juveniles; f= females.

A t-test (Table 5.2) carried out for males and females shows significant differences in the concentration of rubidium in the bone, confirming the initial impression given by the scatterplot (Fig. 5.10). Although I am not basing this argument upon significance testing (and is questionable whether conventional inferential statistics based on comparing central tendencies would do justice to other kinds of patterns of difference), we do need to remember the possibility of apparent differences arising through random chance when one carries out a large number of comparisons. However, this would result in random or unpatterned extreme differences; as shown below, there is a consistent pattern in how difference between males an female occur.

T-test for rubidium – males vs. females					
males (n =16)		females (n = 15)		T-Test	
mean	std	mean	std	p	
1.6	0.9	0.9	0.3	0.005	

Table 5.2 T-test on the concentration of Rubidium in the bone divided by sex.

Underwood (1977) argues that human diets that are rich in cereals would supply less rubidium than ones rich in meat or dairy products. This poses the question as to whether the Sant'Abbondio females had a lower meat or dairy contribution to their diet than the men, possibly already at relatively young age, as high nickel (a low-contributor in meat, milk and other dairy products and inhibited by iron uptake) values in the enamel seems to suggest. In the scatterplot depicting nickel (Fig. 5.6), along the enamel axis, within the two distinct clusters of people corresponding to the two areas of the cemetery, males normally group in the lower segment of the diagram.

Other elements such as strontium (Fig. 5.9) or vanadium (Fig. 5.11) traditionally believed to be nutritionally relevant – although in relation to meat rather than fish – also seem to confirm a male/female opposition that could substantiate the interpretation of a sex-related differentiation in the diet. In order to further discuss dietary influences on elemental concentration it is useful to use the frequency of carious lesions at Sant'Abbondio as an indicator of carbohydrate assumption.

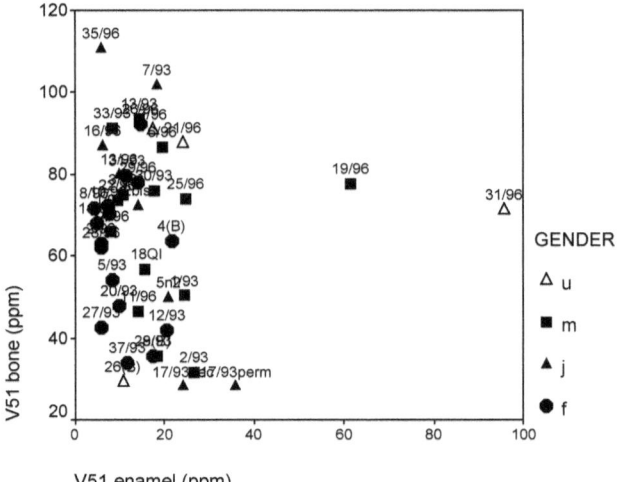

Figure 5.11 Scatterplot of vanadium concentration in bone and enamel. u= indeterminate; m= males; j= juveniles; f= females. The ellipses show the male/female clustering

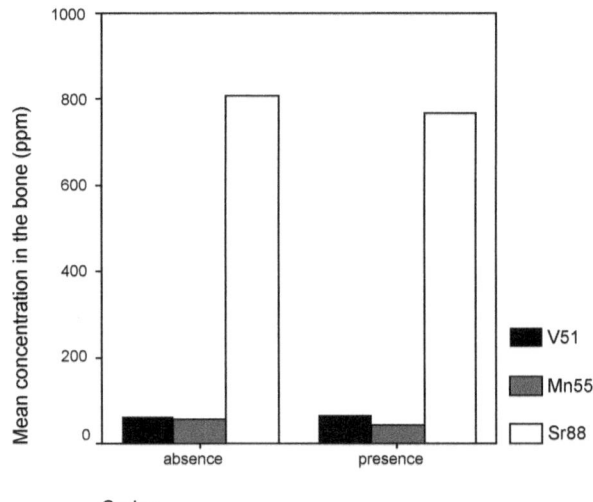

Figure 5.12 Bar chart depicting the mean concentration of vanadium, manganese and strontium in bone in relation to presence/absence of caries.

Caries can be observed in relation to elements found abundant in grains such as vanadium, manganese, and strontium (Fig. 5.12), which should show high concentrations in individuals showing this pathology. Vanadium mean values are in line with expected results. Individual affected with carious lesions show high levels of vanadium in the bone, possibly in relation to vanadium-rich diet based on cereals. Manganese and strontium, however, show no clear relationship between the presence of the pathology and values in the bone. The explanation for such a pattern could lie in the occurrence of metabolic changes – in relation to the age of the individuals – that affected similarly people with and without caries.

Geochemistry and mobility. Marrying in and eating out
Scatterplots depicting bone and enamel values show outliers for a number of elements for which elemental differences cannot be explained on a purely biological or metabolic basis. Patterns along the bone or the enamel axis may entail different implications in terms of interpretative processes involved since – as already stressed – the two axes reflect two distinct moments of life. More specifically, outliers along the bone axis should be seen as the result of processes occurring during adult life. This suggests mobility, although factors such as the particular role of the individual within the community or a different social status or identity could also be involved. Enamel axis, on the other hand, is representative of childhood and therefore differences in concentration between bone and enamel can be connected with mobility and different residence between early and late life. Despite possible metabolic factors, outliers along the enamel axis could represent outsiders within the community displaying the different chemical significance of their tissue as a result of differences in food and water intake during childhood (cf. Schneider and Blakeslee, 1990). One of the major questions in this work is the investigation of economic strategies – normally involving males – and marriage exchange and post-marital residence – mainly involving females – in Puglisi's model of Italian Bronze Age society. Given Puglisi's interpretation, in male dominated pastoral communities the system of social organisation should have involved the predominance of male practising transhumant pastoralism. Furthermore, descent along the male line and exogamic marriage system could have involved male residence within the group of origin and female movement out of natal community and into the marital one (see the discussion of the reconstruction of Bronze Age kinship system and economic strategies in Chapter Three).

Bone variation and male mobility in life
Individuals outlying along the bone axis seem to be recurrently males or juveniles. The main elements involved are manganese (Fig. 5.3), rubidium (Fig. 5.10), niobium (Fig. 5.13) and lead (Fig. 5.1), and for most of them biochemical role is known. Other elements (i.e. cobalt – Fig. 5.4, strontium – Fig. 5.9, vanadium – Fig. 5.11) suggest a similar pattern although less clearly.
Unlike for the enamel axis, along which female outliers are only a selected group of recurring individuals; for the bone axis males show a dual pattern. For lead (Fig. 5.1), a few male adults (6/96, 25/96, 34/96) show different concentrations from the rest of the group, while for manganese, rubidium and niobium all of male individuals cluster in high values contrarily to the rest of the population. This may suggest different implications for Sant'Abbondio males. Human dietary absorption of lead ranges between 5 and 10% (Underwood, 1977), rising to over 40% if water contribution is included (WHO, 1996). The presence of a few individuals showing elevated concentration of lead in the bone could suggest a different dietary regime in relation to water rather than other foodstuffs. This could suggest the residence – of a selected group of male individuals – in a different environment presumably characterised by soft (Underwood, 1977) lead-rich waters. Such a scenario fits well with the idea of selected mobility within the Sant'Abbondio group, possibly in relation to economic activity (i.e. transhumant pastoralism, trade, social exchange) that mainly involved men.

For the group of elements manganese rubidium and niobium, males are normally placed in a large group in the higher section of the diagram. For manganese and rubidium in particular it seems that almost all the men, with the exception of a few individuals, show high concentrations in bone. The reason for this could be either nutritional or metabolic. Both factors could explain why most, if not all, males seem so show higher values. The role of niobium in human organism is poorly studied, nonetheless both manganese and rubidium have been demonstrated to have known homeostatic behaviour and nutritional relevance as described in the previous chapter.

Other than the outliers for lead and the group of males with high concentrations of manganese, rubidium and niobium, most of the remaining outliers along the bone axis are infant and juvenile individuals for which patterns biological reasons have been suggested earlier in this chapter. It is tempting to suggest that an elemental relationship between adult males and juveniles can be related to descent systems that required the residence of offspring in the male group, but it is extremely difficult to discuss children's elemental concentration in these terms, particularly in the light of the profound differences between infant and adult metabolism.

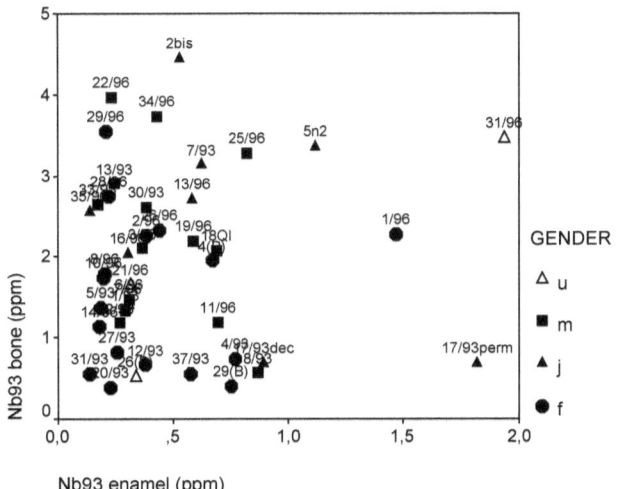

Figure 5.13 Scatterplot of niobium concentration in the bone and the enamel. u= indeterminate; m= males; j= juveniles; f= females.

Enamel outliers and female exogamy
Puglisi's implication of female movement in relation to exogamic marriage exchanges cannot be excluded and could be substantiated by the recurrence of female outliers along the enamel axis (as in relation to childhood), showing values highly

discordant from the ones displayed by the rest of the group, therefore manifesting a different chemical uptake during early life. A good number of elements such as chromium (Fig 5.5) nickel (Fig. 5.6), copper (Fig. 5.2), and tin (Fig. 5.14), display several outlying females (6/93, 12/93, 20/93, 29B, 27/93, 31/93, 37/93), while other elements, such as rubidium (Fig. 5.10), lead (Fig. 5.1), and thorium (Fig. 5.15), the number of female outliers is smaller but nevertheless coherent (in terms of individuals involved) with this pattern.

According to Price *et al.* (1998), an outlier can be defined by calculating a variability of 2 times the standard deviation as a cut-off point. Despite the attempt to apply this method for this study (Table 5.3), it is evident that it does not represent a good indicator of outlying individuals. The elemental concentration in the tissues is rather variable in relation to the analytical method used (Price and colleagues used strontium ratios as opposed to trace element analysis) and the standard deviation does not represent a good tool to measure variation. This will have to be observed for each element using absolute concentrations in the enamel. Such observation seems to confirm that the most of the western females showing higher or lower values for the enamel can be considered as outliers, especially when comparing concentrations with the overall mean for the categories of females (see Table 4.7). Rubidium and tin are the only two elements that show values that line with the average concentration.

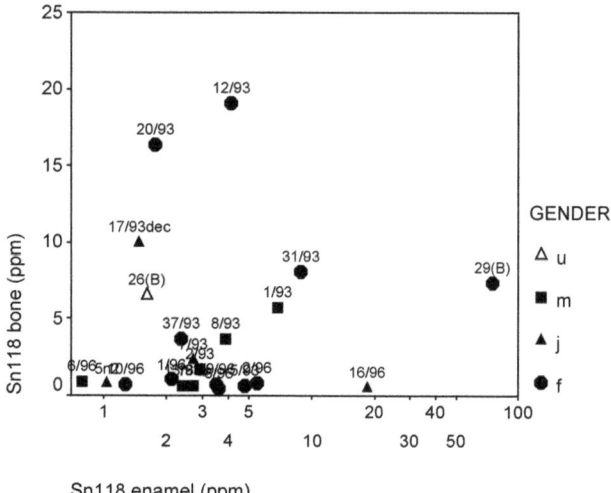

Figure 5.14 Scatterplot of tin concentration in bone and enamel. u= indeterminate; m= males; j= juveniles; f= females.

The T-test performed earlier (Table 5.1) on the z-score for all trace essential and non-essential elements as well as the t-tests carried out separately for each element did not reveal a significant difference between the two sexes although the mean values for males and females are frequently diverse. This may also be due to the limited number of females outlying and to the relatively small degree of this variation. Although biological and metabolic processes cannot be excluded *a priori*, it is interesting to note how, while the bone concentrations of these females seem to be fairly coherent with those displayed by the rest of the group – as to suggest that during adult life, diet and geochemical environment were not particularly dissimilar from that experienced by the rest of the community

– enamel values – and therefore childhood diet and geochemical interaction with the environment – are strongly discordant. These females may be differently displaying an allochthonous origin, as suggested by the strong divergence in elemental concentrations from the rest of the group. All of the elements showing such a pattern (with the only exception of thorium for which biochemical mechanisms are still unstudied) are considered nutritionally essential and can be seen as strongly related to the local environment (both in terms of the contribution of resources and the geochemistry).

By and large, the Sant'Abondio skeletons resemble, in terms of chemical concentration, the local soil more than that sampled from the two narby localities (see Tables 4.5 and 4.7); this suggests that most of the population is local in origin (for a discussion excluding diagenetic causes for this similarity, see Chapter Four). However, some of the enamel samples from outlying females have points of resemblance with the Agerola sample. This does not necessarily imply that this is the place of origin for females (especially as no soil data is available for most of the regions surrounding Sant'Abbondio), but rather it may suggest that they originated from this general type of environment, a limestone area.

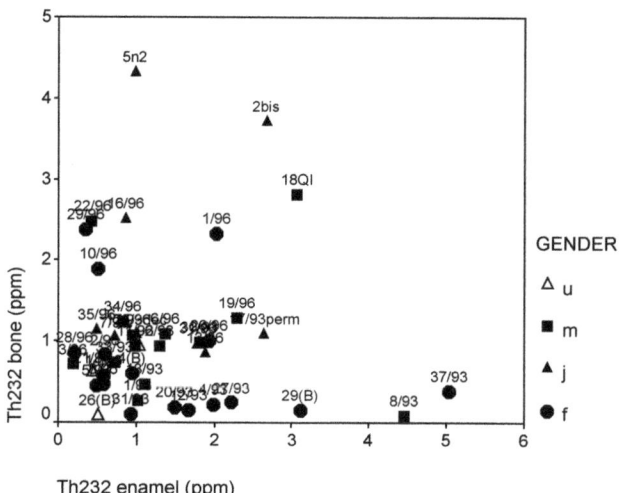

Figure 5.15 Scatterplot of thorium concentration in bone and enamel. u= indeterminate; m= males; j= juveniles; f= females.

Interestingly, the outlying females are buried in the western half of the cemetery. Four out of eight of them (4/93, 5/93, 12/93, 20/93) were buried with a good number of grave goods, normally consisting of one or two pots together with a flint or metal object, while two were part of a double burial (29/93 is a young adult female buried with an indeterminate adult and 31/93 is a juvenile/young female buried with a young male). It is noteworthy that most of the individuals in question are associated either with a particular feature (the two footed vessels for 4/93 or the elaborate pit for 20/93) or with another person. The nature of the different elemental concentration in the enamel for these females is heterogeneous, outlying females are a recurrent feature (12/92, 29B, 27/93, 31/93, 37/93) but the individuals in question differently diverge for a different range of elements. As will be discussed later in this chapter, most, if not all, of the 'western' females seem to carry a dissimilar elemental background from the rest of the group, expressed through higher values in the dental enamel and lower concentrations in the bone tissue. Excluding metabolic or biological phenomena, such a scenario could be the result of the different origin of these females, buried in the western section of the cemetery. These women may have grown up in a different geochemical environment from that characterising the rest of the individuals forming the residential community – thereby explaining the enamel differences – and subsequently moved into the Sant'Abbondio group – thereby explaining the general bone homogeneity. This may have been in relation to post-marital residence or social exchange. On a metabolic basis, no clear evidence seems to explain such a pattern and biological implications should be reflected for more than a limited number of individuals. Movement might have been the cause for chemical diversity, especially as this is expressed as discordance between infant and adult chemical life.

Within the variation of the enamel concentrations of western females a further difference characterises the elemental concentration of the bone of this group of the Sant'Abbondio population. As will be discussed later, low values of a number of elements suggest a difference in food consumption for the western females that can reflect cultural aspects.

ENAMEL VALUES								
Individual	sex	area	Cr52	cut-off	Ni60	cut-off	Cu63	cut-off
4/93	f	West	-	31.4	44.2	145.7	-	470
5/93	f	West	0.66	31.4	5.2	145.7	23.2	470
12/93	f	West	7.45	31.4	0.9	145.7	-	470
20/93	f	West	3.5	31.4	28.8	145.7	102	470
27/93	f	West	34.57	31.4	52.5	145.7	-	470
29(B)	f	West	8.96	31.4	110.3	145.7	-	470
31/93	f	West	4.84	31.4	315.3	145.7	-	470
37/93	f	West	69.7	31.4	77.4	145.7	30.4	470
Individual	sex	area	Rb85	cut-off	Sn118	cut-off	Pb208	cut-off
4/93	f	West	1.2	2.9	3.7	26	5.6	8.8
5/93	f	West	0.8	2.9	4.7	26	6.9	8.8
12/93	f	West	3.2	2.9	4.1	26	5.9	8.8
20/93	f	West	1.6	2.9	1.7	26	1.7	8.8
27/93	f	West	0.9	2.9	4.3	26	4.3	8.8
29(B)	f	West	1.4	2.9	75.7	26	13.2	8.8
31/93	f	West	0.9	2.9	8.8	26	-	8.8
37/93	f	West	0.6	2.9	2.3	26	4.8	8.8

Table 5.3 Absolute concentrations (in ppm) of relevant elements for the group of outlying females with indication of the cut-off limit in accordance with Price *et al.*'s (1998) method.

Organisation within the group: the eastern half of the cemetery vs. the western.
Patterns of distribution of trace element concentration from Sant'Abbondio individuals can also be related to a repeated difference in the composition of enamel between people buried in the eastern and western areas of the cemetery. The two areas of deposition correspond to the two seasons of excavation of the cemetery. This could immediately lead to the idea that such changes between the seasons caused the contamination of the human remains. However, if this were the case, contamination would have influenced many or most of the elemental values and not only a number of them. This in turn would have originated a clustering of individuals in relation to the year of excavation for all of the elements considered for analysis and not for some of them. More significantly, it would have affected all of the individuals buried in one area of the cemetery as opposed to the other and not a part of them, as seems to be the case for a number of elements displaying diverging values for all western females but not for western males (see below). Moreover, the excavators report no difference in the excavation technique or post-excavation treatment of the bones from the two parts of the cemetery. Chemical preservative were not used for either (Marisa Mastroroberto pers. com.).

Laboratory contamination, either in relation to the preparation of the samples or to the procedure of analysi, has been tested and can be excluded (see Chapter Three), measures of control of non-biogenic factors are also provided (Chapter Four). As a general observation, it is therefore reasonable to think that any post-mortem alteration would have equally affected all individuals and not only some of them.

A further test fo post-depositional phenomena is performed through the analysis of soil samples collected from the two halves of the cemetery. Trace element data from the two areas, are extremely homogeneous – especially for those elements displaying diverging patterns in the skeleton – and sometimes divergent for elements that do not show such an East/West dichotomy in the bone (Fig. 5.16). Statistical analysis to measure the difference between the mean values from the two areas has been carried out element by element, and appears to exclude diagenesis. It is also important to stress that the elements displaying the east/west clustering of individuals are considered reliable. As an example, manganese, one of the elements believed to be more subject to ionic exchange between soil and buried bones, does not show the East/West patterning. The distribution of females, males, and juveniles in the two halves of the cemetery is equal (see Chapter Two), so demographic biases can be excluded. The archaeological record shows no clear differentiation in the composition of grave goods (Table 2.7) and excludes possible chronological differences.

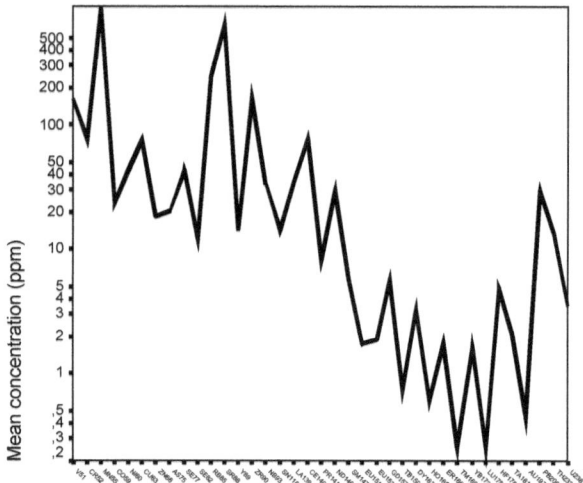

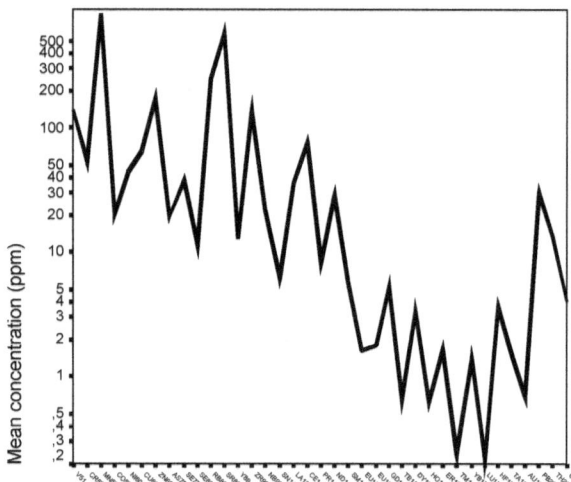

Figure 5.16 Mean values of each element considered for ICP-MS analysis in the soil samples in accordance with the two sections of the cemetery.

Elements showing contrasting patterns fall, once again, within the category of essentials and non-essentials. This is visible primarily in the enamel. Elements such as cobalt (Fig. 5.4), chromium (Fig. 5.5), and nickel (Fig. 5.6) show a clear binary division (the East/West dichotomy is readable through the individual number: individuals labelled with '93' are from the western section, while individuals labelled with '96' are from the eastern section). In order to obtain a more detailed examination, a further bivariate analysis of all elements was undertaken at a deeper level of characterisation of the individuals. The variables "category" and "age class" were added to the analysis, revealing some interesting patterns. For elements such as cobalt (Fig. 5.17), the East/West opposition showed no particular differentiation in terms of sex and age range and simply reflected the different area of the cemetery for all of the categories indicated. For vanadium (Fig. 5.18), strontium (Fig. 5.19), and niobium (Fig. 5.20) a clear relationship between area of deposition and sex and age at death was instead displayed. Western females are systematically clustered in the lower area of the diagram, along the bone axis, and are all of young/young-adult age (Fig. 5.21 – Fig. 5.22 – Fig. 5.23). Results from the T-test comparing mean elemental concentration for western and eastern females are significant (Table 5.4).

Individuals divided per area of deposition – females only					
	East (n=9)		West (n=9)		T-Test
Element (ppm)	mean	sd	mean	sd	p
Vanadium	71.2	9.3	51.0	17.7	0.008
Strontium	953.1	220.7	567.6	225.8	0.002
Niobium	2.1	0.6	0.7	0.3	0.000

Table 5.4 T-Tests for elements showing East/West patterning. Only females are considered.

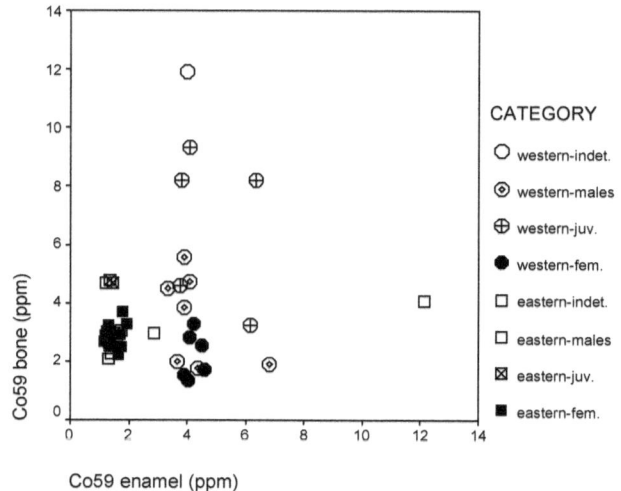

Figure 5.17 Cobalt – Clusters of western females along the bone axis.

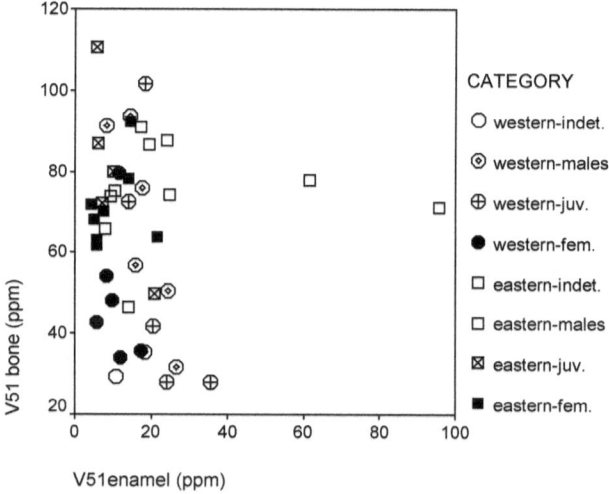

Figure 5.18 Vanadium – Clusters of western females along the bone axis. The ellipse shows the western females.

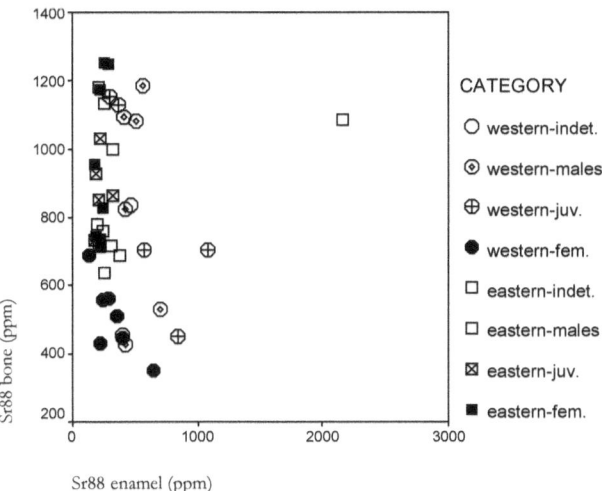

Figure 5.19 Strontium – Clusters of western females along the bone axis. The ellipse shows the western females.

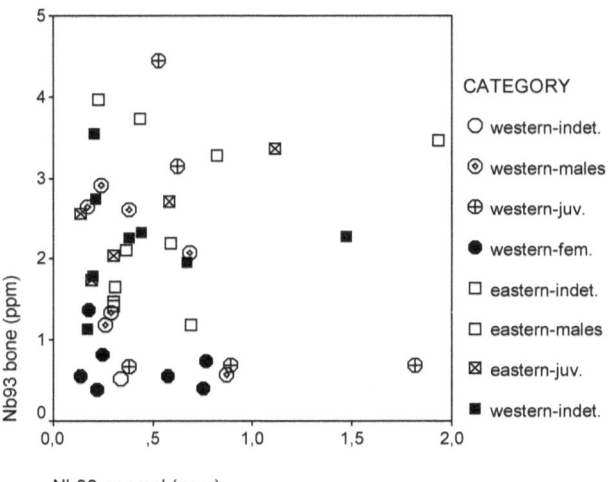

Figure 5.20 Niobium – Cluster of western females along the bone axis. The ellipse shows the western females.

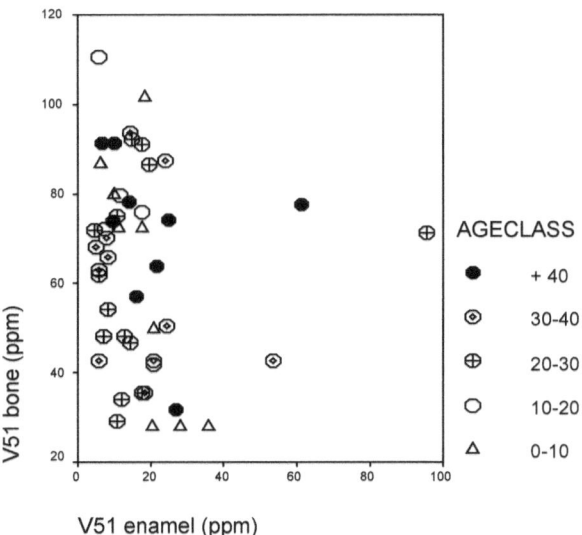

Figure 5.21 Vanadium – distribution of the individuals according to age categories. Age classes are express in years.

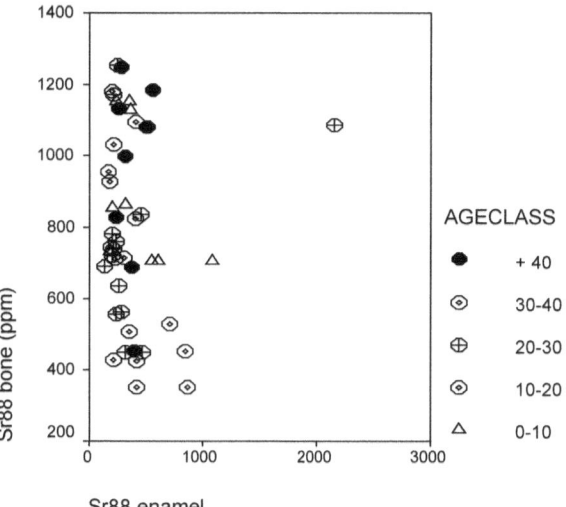

Figure 5.22 Strontium – distribution of the individuals according to age categories. Age classes are expressed in years. The ellipse shows the western females.

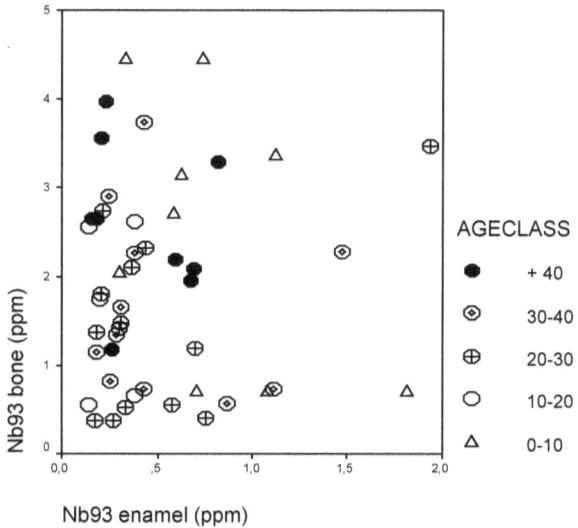

Figure 5.23 Niobium – distribution of the individuals according to age categories. Age classes are expressed in years.

It must be stressed that the predominance of young/young-adult females in the western group might not be significant. The paleodemographic scenario of the Sant'Abbondio group is generally characterised by young and young/adult females (in very few cases were women recorded as older than 40) and hence the demographic framework of the known section of the population might bias the overall picture. It is nevertheless interesting to note that the group clustering away from the rest of the sample *is* mainly composed of females, all of whom were buried in the western area of the necropolis. This leads to the following considerations:

- clusters of individuals may be formed in accordance with biological factors, and
- for clusters of biological significance there might be a relation with non-biological features.

Therefore, results emerged can be summarised as follows:
- some young and young-adult females show low values for a number of elements in the bone;
- some of the elements involved are characterised by sex-specific homeostasis;
- all the females involved are buried in the western area of the cemetery.

The archaeological evidence of a binary division between groups of individuals in accordance with possible biological features can be discussed through a number of different, although often contrasting, avenues.

Strontium is one of the elements involved in the western-females pattern immediately suggests a biological explanation for the clustering of the western women. It is possible that all of these females showed low strontium levels because – as their age would suggest – they were pregnant or lactating. This, however, does not explain the similar patterning of vanadium and niobium for which sex-related homeostatic differences are not known. A second interpretation can be given for the subgroup of western females in terms of a difference in the dietary regime, especially when considering the high contribution shellfish and marine products in general give in terms of strontium and vanadium uptake. Conversely, for terrestrial products, the nature of this difference does not necessarily relate to the type of resources consumed but rather to the environmental influence these resources were subject to. Strontium and vanadium are particularly linked to the chemical properties of rocks, soils and waters and can be contained in different amounts in plants and grains (that are particularly rich in these elements) in accordance with their area of growth.

The patterning of western females in the lower section of the diagrams for strontium, vanadium and niobium, could be explained if this subgroup of females were gathering specific resources in areas geochemically different from that used by the rest of the community. It is likely that not all of the food resources these women consumed were procured in a different zone but, presumably, only a selection of them, possibly in relation to a habitual practice or long-standing tradition maintained by this subgroup of the community. Conversely, low values of these elements in the bone of western females could also be explained through an exclusion of this subgroup from the consumption of a specific foodstuff eaten by the rest of the Sant'Abbondio people.

Whether the explanation of such a pattern is biological (young females in their reproductive age suffering from physiological elemental depletion) or non-biological (young females subject to a geochemically different dietary regime) both explanations relate to a main cultural differentiation as all of the females involved were buried in a specific area of the cemetery. The western half of the necropolis is clearly differentiated from the eastern one. It represents the lower portion of the Sant'Abbondio hill, and consisted of a strip of land sloping towards the Sarno River. This difference cannot be overlooked and it must have carried significance for Sant'Abbondio people when choosing where to bury their dead.

The western females show contrasting patterns for bone and enamel, as to suggest that the dietary and geochemical conditions they were subject to in their childhood were different from those they experienced during adult life. Moreover, during adult life they were likely to have practiced a partially different dietary regime from the rest of the Sant'Abbondio people. The combination of trace element data seems to suggest a different origin for the western females. This would explain why their teeth do not show the same elemental composition as the rest of the community and it could clarify why they show a further differentiation in their bone, maybe as the result of a 'culturally-driven' subsistence activity (perhaps a particular habit) that brought them to consume a specific type of food or to gather their resources in a different area from the rest of the community. It could be that the western female were maintaining a tradition they carried with them once they moved out of their village, a particular tradition that left a trace in their bone and differentiated them from the rest of the Sant'Abbondio people.

It could further illuminate why this subgroup of women were buried in a specific section of the cemetery, sometimes in association with particular objects or in direct association with other individuals.

To better assess the level of dietary contribution to the elemental concentration of human tissues, the ratio of carbon and nitrogen were observed. Eleven individuals from the two sections of the cemetery were selected. Due to poor preservation, collagen samples were obtained for only few of the selected individuals. The little results obtain did not reveal differences in C and N isotope ratio.

Summary

This Chapter has shown that the use of trace element analysis in a non-paleonutritional approach represents a new, tangible method of investigating the social dynamics of past communities, offering a level of reliability and consistency that not always may be found in material culture. At this level of analysis the major considerations that emerged from this work are of a complex nature.

1. Multi-element studies are extremely informative on past diet and behaviour, especially for the type and extent of data they offer in terms of interaction between elements.
2. Both biological and non-biological factors are involved in the interpretation of trace element results. Particular attention should be given to the foundations of cultural inferences in terms of the exclusion of biological explanation.
3. Multiple levels of interpretation can be reached through the observation of trace element data, often extending from the initial theoretical question and developing into new avenues of investigations. A number of inferences (*i.e.* short-term mobility) are impossible to reach through ICP-MS analysis and should be investigated through other methods.

Bearing in mind the scheme proposed in Chapter One (Table 1.1), it is possible to associate the different patters emerging from this analysis with aspects causing social dynamics, either in terms of mobility (*i.e.* economic strategies, social exchange) or in accordance with gender ideology and individual and social identity (Table 4.9). These will be discussed in the conclusive chapter of this work.

Chapter Six
Mobility food and praxis

Introduction

In this work, ICP-MS trace element analysis on human bone and dental enamel has been directed towards the identification of patterns of mobility and food consumption within the Middle Bronze Age group of Sant'Abbondio. The theoretical background proposed by Puglisi regarding the socio-economic setting of Bronze Age communities of Central and Southern Italy, is of patrilineal groups characterised by nomadic pastoralism. These premises were explored through the identification of patterns of mobility in relation to post-marital residence and movement associated with a transhumant herding economy. Past mobility was observed through the reconstruction of diet, not only in its specific characteristics but mostly for what it reflects in terms of the relationship between resources and the environment, being thus indicative of locality. Food consumption was explored through trace element analysis of bone and dental enamel and interpreted in relation to the two moments of life they represent: respectively, ongoing life and childhood.

The application of trace element analysis on both tissues allowed the exploration of Puglisi's idea, while the interpretation of the data combined with the archaeological evidence brought the identification of several levels of complexity within Puglisi's original theoretical question, allowing further inferences of the cultural scenario of the Sant'Abbondio group. Patterns of variability of the elemental concentration of bone and enamel reveal how food is able to define ontological concepts, and be used as a form of expressing the self. Food and ground water, as reflected in the elemental concentration of bone and enamel, appear to be the means through which the *habitus* (*sensu* Bourdieu, 1977) of the people of Sant'Abbondio is expressed. Through habitual practices of eating and drinking, conceived as a formal expression of culture, ideological concepts can be explored, especially in relation to the perception of the self and the other expressed by past communities. Mobility and food despite being conceptually independent, both contribute to the understanding of social dynamics and can be linked, through the use of trace element analysis of skeletal remains, to create a deep understanding of prehistoric Italy.

Sant'Abbondio trace element data explained through a cultural perspective

Data arising from the multi-elemental ICP-MS method have revealed the multidimensional potentials of trace element data for human bone and enamel and have demonstrated that a number of factors, both biological and cultural, can contribute to the creation of specific patterns of variation in the chemical concentration of these tissues within the same population. For Sant'Abbondio biological factors determining different chemical concentrations in children as opposed to adults, and young adults as opposed to mature individuals, have been described and need not be further discussed. Sex-related differences have also been argued in the previous chapters and hence will not be treated here. What deserves further analysis is the presence, as introduced in Chapter Five, of patterns of variation that cannot be explained either through post-mortem alteration of the chemical structure of bone and enamel, or through biological causes affecting the homeostatic process.

These patterns can therefore be attributed to cultural factors and can be directed towards the study of dynamics of gender and identity.

In the discussion of patterns of elemental variation, the presence of male outliers along the bone axis for lead, which is mostly connected to the chemical properties of ground water, suggests the residence of a group of Sant'Abbondio men in areas characterised by water with different elemental composition from that available near the site. Soft water is particularly rich in lead and could have well been the type consumed by the few Sant'Abbondio male outliers. In line with Puglisi's idea, the observation of lead concentration in the bone of these individuals suggests the practice of seasonal transhumant pastoralism, which is likely to force a section of the community to reside away from the main village for few months during the year. It is however difficult to determine the role of the Sant'Abbondio outliers within the community using trace element data alone. One alternative interpretation might see these individuals as newcomers, moving to Sant'Abbondio in relation to a specialised activity such as metallurgy (Bietti Sestieri, 1981). It is also possible that such specialised activity was carried out within the site and caused an enhanced absorption of lead. High dietary intake of lead cannot be excluded, although the quantity of lead in foodstuffs is relatively low and hardly exceeds determined limits.

Given Puglisi's interpretation, the most suitable explanation for the chemical composition of the bone for the male outliers at Sant'Abbondio, is differentiated water intake from areas external to the site. If these men were using different water sources, it is likely that were residing away from Sant'Abbondio, perhaps to tend their herd during the summer months (Fig. 8.1). Ethnographically, the system according to which a few people take care of the herd, moving it to faraway pastures, while the rest of the community remains in the village is known as "herdsman husbandry" or "distant pastures husbandry" (Khazanov, 1983: 22) and is known to be adopted by semi-nomadic groups of Northern Africa, Arabia and the Near East. Semi-nomadic pastoralism represents a favourable measure to rely on animal resources without having to carry out a fully nomadic way of life and maintaining the opportunity to practice other forms of food production (*i.e.* agriculture), as part of a sedentary lifestyle. Mixed economy is particularly favoured in the Mediterranean, where the climate does not require a constant movement of animals, but rather a seasonal one, and transhumance is vertical rather than horizontal. Middle latitudes also offer the opportunity to practice a productive agriculture. A scenario of mixed economy characterised by a significant pastoral input along with the contribution of farming and/or gardening is exactly that described by Puglisi and later supported by Barker (1986) and could apply to the Sant'Abbondio group.

It is difficult however to discuss the specific economic scenario of Sant'Abbondio. Archaeological data from cemeteries generally offer little insight on subsistence strategies. Sant'Abbondio does not provide faunal data;

furthermore there is no evidence of nearby villages associated with the necropolis. Material culture, is equally non informative in this perspective, none of the typical milk boilers frequently found in Middle Bronze Age settlements are present and other evidence of the type of subsistence activity is also absent. Nonetheless, the anthropological analysis confirms the picture of a mixed economy through the relatively high prevalence of caries as to suggest a good contribution of carbohydrates to the diet, with subsequent low prevalence of porotic hyperostosis, as an indication of limited metabolic stress. Such a combination of factors seems to reveal the reliance, for Sant'Abbondio group, on a mixed system of subsistence, which generally prevents physiological stress.

A further dimension of variability in the Sant'Abbondio data refers to the presence of female outliers along the enamel axis, reflecting the different geochemical background to which such females were subject during childhood. Elements such as chromium, nickel, copper and tin, together with other essential and non-essential elements, show a constant group of women outlying on the enamel axis, which suggests a different elemental uptake during growth. The influence of biological and metabolic processes in the production of these results cannot be excluded, although it is worth noting that bone concentrations for the same females are fairly coherent with those displayed by the rest of the group, indicating that during adult life, diet and geochemical environment were not dissimilar from that experienced by the whole community. In accordance with Puglisi's interpretation, the outlying females may be displaying their allochthonous origin, materialised in the discrepancy between the elemental uptake (reflective of geochemical background) relative to childhood and that of adult life. Interestingly, all of the elements involved are considered nutritionally essential and are closely related to soil geochemistry (Fig. 8.1).

The interpretation of trace element data in connection with archaeological evidence revealed that all of the female outliers were buried in the western half of the cemetery – a sloping stretch of land that parts from the small hill of Sant'Abbondio where the rest of the (eastern) inhumations are placed. This suggests for Sant'Abbondio women the spatial manifestation of a cultural differentiation between groups of females of different origin. The architecture of the various tombs is overall similar, although it is interesting to observe how two of the females involved in such differentiated patterns (specifically 29/93 and 31/93) were part of a double burial. All of these aspects could be indicative of a formal differentiation of western female identity as marked through the presence of particular objects (*e.g.* the beautiful footed vessel associated with individual 4/93) or the association with another individual (a spouse?).

Further analyses have revealed how the western females also display bone differences for a selected spectrum of elements. For vanadium and strontium, bone values are significantly lower than those of the rest of the community. Post-depositional phenomena differently affecting the two areas of the cemetery can be excluded by the alignment of western male values with those of the rest of the group. The East/West divide within the cemetery, in terms of trace element data, is also unlikely to be due to chronological features, being material culture as well as funerary practices homogeneous. It would not be possible, of course, to distinguish small-scale chronological gaps, i.e. 50-100 years, there is no reason, however to expect that one generation would differ from the previous one in a way that affected males and females differentially. It is more likely that a cultural significance is expressed in the topographic differentiation on the tombs; a plausibly similar cultural significance could be given to the chemical data obtained from the analysis. Coming to such specific cultural significance, although low levels of strontium could be associated with pregnancy or lactation, it is unlikely that *all* of the western females were either pregnant or breast-feeding. Furthermore, this would not explain low levels of vanadium and niobium for which sex-related homeostatic differences are not known. A more likely interpretation suggests a cultural-specific difference in the dietary regime for the subgroup of western females. The nature of such difference does not necessarily relate to the *type* of resources assumed but rather to the *environmental influence* these resources were subject to. Strontium and vanadium are particularly linked to the chemical properties of rocks, soils and waters and could be contained in different amounts in plants and grains (which are particularly rich in these elements) in accordance with the area of growth. The subgroup of western females could have been gathering specific resources in areas geochemically different from those used by the rest of the community. It is likely that not all of the food resources they consumed were procured in a different zone but, most probably, only a selection of them, possibly in relation to a habitual practice or a long-standing tradition maintained by this subgroup of the community (Fig. 8.1).

Such a scenario poses the question of who were the eastern females, as to say the ones that did now show patterns of variation in enamel and bone concentration from the main group. The most direct answer explains their role as women that did not move out from the group of origin, the sisters or cousins of Sant'Abbondio men, who married inside the group. This could be the case if Sant'Abbondio group adopted a paired intermarrying system as that of the moiety system. This would outcome in marriage between pairs of lineage reseading in the same village, therefore in exogamy within a single residence unit (Chagnon, 1983). An alternative social system, could that the eastern females were coming from an area geochemically similar to that of Sant'Abbondio, so that their enamel values did not reveal their different origin. Moreover, they well integrated with the group, adopting Sant'Abbondio dietary regime, especially for what concerns the area of food procurement used, so to reveal homogeneous bone concentration and no variation from the main group's bone values. Within Puglisi's reconstruction, if Sant'Abbondio women were mobile by virtue of the matrimonial system adopted by their community, they must have changed their dietary regime if not in terms of type of resources consumed, then surely in terms of chemical properties of the same. This would have caused a difference in the chemical composition of their tissues as seen in the pattern of variation of elemental concentration in the enamel of some of the Sant'Abbondio women buried in the western area of the cemetery. The comparison between trace element and archaeological data however, seems to suggest a more complex scenario for the western females that moves away from a simplistic identification of their possible different origin and forces us to reconsider Puglisi's interpretation, if not for its plausibility, then for the nature of its complexity.

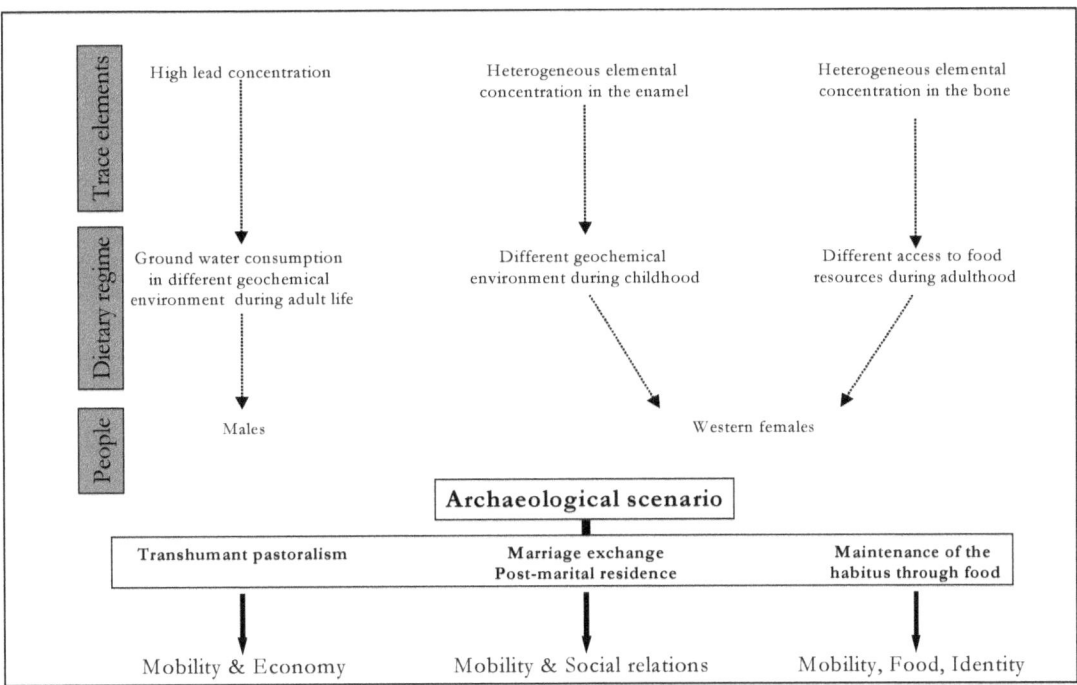

Fig. 6.1 Scheme of the interpretation of trace element data from Sant'Abbondio.

The difference in the chemical composition of bone for Sant'Abbondio western females could be the result of a cultural difference manifested in their subsistence. Such a difference could have involved this subgroup of women in the consumption of a particular type of food or brought them to gather their resources in specific areas, differently from the rest of the community. For Sant'Abbondio females, the record of a different origin could be registered in the teeth, and specifically in the diachronic comparison of the composition of enamel and bone. However the significance of such a different origin, its cultural value, might be reflected in the bones.

Sant'Abbondio women, buried in the western section of the cemetery might have had a different origin and in adulthood moved into a new group. Despite this movement however, they might have kept their natal tradition and reproduced known practices in their new household. Moving to a new environment and a new community didn't necessarily mean they had to abdicate part of their *habitus* and they could have maintained it throughout a new residence. In this perspective, Bourdieu's (1990) idea of the *transportability* of the *habitus*, and its *objective* application within practical relations is useful. In giving up their group to live in a new one, Sant'Abbondio women would have affirmed their husband's descent (cf. Strathern, 1987) but maintained their identity through 'secondary' cultural-specifics (*i.e.* food). Food might have acted as a carrier of memory and identity as reflected in the maintenance of 'difference' in the spatial organisation of the Sant'Abbondio burials.

In this scenario, it is not excluded that a differentiation in dietary habits could have also been expressed on a negative basis. Western females could have refrained from the consumption of specific foodstuffs, perhaps in relation to food restrictions or taboos.

In this perspective, the elemental composition of the bone from the Sant'Abbondio population could suggest the habitual consumption of fish and shellfish for the main group, easily procurable either from the Sarno River or from the nearby sea, and reflected in the high values of elements such as strontium and vanadium. The low values of the same elements for the western females could derive from an abstention from the consumption of marine resources.

The variability and availability of resources in the Sarno Valley supports the hypothesis of different dietary regimes practised by the Sant'Abbondio group. Within a limited environment, several ecological units are assured. Land is fertile and highly productive especially given the volcanic nature of the sediment. River courses are rich while highland areas are only few kilometres away and assure productive land during the dry season. The presence of the sea is an unquestionable resource. Finally, it is of particular interest to consider the presence of the Vesuvius in the study area. A volcano is an unavoidable presence; it rules and changes the environment in a way that forces humans to reconsider their perception of the external world and shift their landmarks, be they physical or ideological. In an unpredictable environment, the relationship between humans and resources can be played out in the predictability, or better the stability, of dietary sources especially in terms of the perception of food itself, which remains embedded in the *habitus* of an individual as well as that of group and perpetuates across individual biographical boundaries and life changes.

The use of food, and mainly of the *provenience* of food, in terms of the place from where the latter is produced or gathered has been studied ethnographically by Andrew Strathern (1973) and Marilyn Strathern (1987) in their work on Highland groups of Papua New Guinea. The two anthropologists have observed how residence in the place where the food comes from is one of the conditions to assure (in this case agnatic) descent.

If one would want to expand arguments relating to the use of food as expressive of kin and identity and assume that, for the Sant'Abbondio females, who consumes is also who gathers, then we should hypothesise that the western females gathered some resources in areas different from those accessed by the rest of the community. Western females might have preserved their habitual practice by moving to places that were part of their *habitus*, however it is *locality* rather than *mobility* that describes such *habitus*.

Whether western females consumed or procured different resources or refrained from the intake of specific foodstuffs, they might have deliberately chosen to affirm their identity through the maintenance of a practice that would have confirmed their old *habitus*. In Marilyn Strathern's words "people shed as well as acquire kinship identity, at crucial developmental junctures what may be stressed becomes not their connection to a set of persons but rather their disconnection from that set" (Strathern, 1987: 275-276). Furthermore, "in highlands and lowlands systems disconnection may instead be part of people's effort to maintain differentiation between categories of kin (cf. Wagner, 1977) to ensure that maternity and paternity make a difference in the constitution of a person. The end result of this second activity is the sustaining of difference itself and the conceptual entities thus generated must refer back to the underlying kinship connections. Gender as a source of difference plays a central role" (Strathern 1987: 276-277). In this perspective, Sorensen's idea (2000, chapter one) of women's negotiating individual identity that was disentangled from social fixed schemes is particularly useful.

The main outcome in the study of food consumption at Sant'Abbondio is thus strongly connected with the issues of gender and kin identity. Food seems to be used by Sant'Abbondio western females as a way of expressing their identity through social practices. The shift in aspects of dietary regime shown by Sant'Abbondio women, indicative of their movement to a new post-marital residence, could be read in a 'patriarchal' perspective, as the female natural subjection in a male dominated society. However, Sant'Abbondio women moved, perhaps to habitual places, also to consume specific resource from specific locations as a way to affirm their identity. In an engendered perspective, this movement can be interpreted as an essential contribution of females in the affirmation of culture. If the movement of women to a new household is a way of creating kin ties, the consumption of portable resources from a specific place could be a way of re-affirming the *habitus* and their original kinship bonds. This appears to be indicative of a specific cultural role of the women in the group, as poignant and socially relevant as that of men in providing descent.

MOBILITY FOOD AND PRAXIS

Mobility is better analysed if divorced from its conception of movement *per se* but rather investigated for the evidence it offers on locality in terms of place of residence and use of resources rather than of place from which or to which people travel. Locality furthermore, is perceived as the means by which culture, ideas and beliefs are conveyed. In the Italian Bronze Age, the lived space, the lived-in environment, was inevitably connected with subsistence resources, so that eating was the tangible trace of the exploitation of such a lived-in environment. Food is one of the primary means of expression of the self and the collective. Thus eating represents the ideal praxis that moves across experiences both material and ideological.

In creating the link between place and resources, between living and eating, the essence of individual and social identity can be re-created. The identification of outliers displaying differentiated concentrations in the chemistry of bone and enamel isolates groups of individuals plausibly characterised by a differentiated experience of life within the community, be it economical or social. Whether these people were forced through expediencies or chose to eat differently from the rest of the group, they tangibly express the complexity of the *habitus* they practiced and preserved.

Mobility, movement and action, all represent the physical expression, the praxis, through which material, as well as ideological, experiences are expressed. Food is the vehicle of such expression, an agent itself, which acts as a link between humans (as 'primary' agents) and culture. If food has the ability to express culture, if it does stand between the inside and the outside (Lupton, 1996), then it is able to express different levels of complexity any culture inevitably carries. If we are what we eat, we then are 'where' we eat, but also 'when' and 'how' we eat. Archaeology, in a multidisciplinary approach, has the ability to explore each one of these levels of complexity.

REFERENCES CITED

Acsàdi, G. Y. and J. Nemeskéri 1970. *History of Human Life Span and Mortality*. Budapest, Kiadò.

Albore Livadie, C. 1994. *Territorio e insediamenti nell'agro Nolano durante il Bronzo antico (facies di Palma Campania): Nota preliminare*. L'eruzione vusuviana delle "Pomici di Avellino" e la facies di Palma Campania (Bronzo Antico), Ravello, Edipuglia.

Albore Livadie, C., G. D'alessio, G. Mastrolorenzo and G. Rolandi 1986. Le eruzioni del Somma-Vesuvio in epoca protostorica. *Trémblements de terre, éruptions volcaniques et vie des hommes dans la Campanie Antique*. Naples, Publications du Centre Jean Bérard. VII: 55-66.

Albore Livadie, C. and A. Marzocchella 1999. Riflessioni sulla tipologia funeraria in Campania fra Bronzo Antico e Bronzo Medio. *19° Convegno sulla Preistoria-Protostoria e Storia della Daunia*: 117-134.

Albore Livadie, C., G. Mastrolorenzo and G. Vecchio 1998. *Eruzioni pliniane del Somma Vesuvio e siti archeologici dell'area Nolana*. Archeologia e Vulcanologia in Campania, Pomei, Arte Tipografica Napoli.

Anderson, R. A. 1988. *Dietary Chromium intake*. Abstract of the 14th International Congress of Nutrition, Seoul.

Andrews, A. D. 1960. Cobalt. *New Zeland Journal of Agricultural Research*, 2: 364.

Asling, C. W. and L. S. Hurley 1963. The influence of trace elements on the skeleton. *Clinical Orthopedics*, 27: 213-264.

Aufderheide, A. C., F. D. Neiman, L. E. J. Wittmers and G. Rapp 1981. Lead in bones II: skeletal lead content as an indicator of lifetime lead ingestion and the social correlates in an archaeological population. *American Journal of Physical Anthropology*, 55: 285-291.

Bahou, W. F. 1975. *The relationships of particular trace elements to various bone pathologies in the Dickson Mounds skeletal population*. Unpublished Senior Honours thesis. Department of Anthropology. Amherst, University of Massachusetts.

Barfield, L. 1986. Chalcolitic burials in Northern Italy: problems of social interpretation. *Dialoghi di Archeologia*, 3: 241-248.

Barfield, L. 1998. Gender issues in north Italian prehistory. R. Withehouse. *Gender and Italian Archaeology: challanging the stereotypes*. London, Accordia Research Institute UCL. 7: 142-156.

Barker, G. 1981. *Landscape and Society: Prehistoric Central Italy*. London, Academic Press.

Barker, G. 1984. *Ambiente e società nella preistoria dell'Italia Centrale*. Roma, Nuova Italia Scientifica.

Barker, G. 1986. Un'indagine sulla sussistenza e sulle economie delle società preistoriche. *Dialoghi di Archeologia*, I: 51-60.

Bayrabar, J. P. and C. de la Rua 1997. Reconstruction of diet with trace elements of bone at the Chalcolitic site of Pico Ramos, Basque County, Spain. *Journal of Archaeological Science*, 24: 355-364.

Beck, L. A. 1985. Bivariate Analysis of trace element in bone. *Journal of Human Evolution*, 14: 493-502.

Bietti Sestieri, A. M. 1981. Produzione e scambio nell'Italia protostorica. Alcune ipotesi sul ruolo dell'industria metallurgica nell'Etruria mineraria alla fine dell'età del Bronzo. *L'Etruria mineraria. Atti del XII Convegno di studi etruschi e italici*: 223-264.

Bietti Sestieri, A. M. 1992. *The Iron Age community of Osteria dell'Osa. A study of socio-political development in Central Tyrrhenian Italy*. Cambridge, Cambridge University Press.

Bietti Sestieri, A. M. 1996. *Protostoria. Teoria e pratica*. Rome, Nuova Italia Scientifica.

Binford, L. 1982. The archaeology of place. *Journal of Anthropological Archaeology*, 1: 5-31.

Blakely, R. I. 1989. Bone Strontium in pregnant and lactating females from archaeological samples. *American Journal of Physical Anthropology*, 80: 173-185.

Blakely, R. I. and L. A. Beck 1981. Trace elements, nutritional status and social stratification at Etowah, Georgia. *Academic Science*, 376: 416-431.

Bloomer, L. C. and G. R. Lee 1978. Normal hepatic copper metabolism. L. W. Powell. *Metals and the Liver*. New York, Marcel Dekker: 179.

Bocquet, J. P. and C. Masset 1982. Farewell to paleodemography. *Journal of Human Evolution*, 11: 321-333.

References cited

Bohn, E. L., B. L. McNeal and G. A. O'Connor (Eds.) 1985. *Soil Chemistry*. New York, John Wiley & Sons.

Borgognini Tarli, S. and E. Pacciani 1993. *I resti umani nello scavo archeologico. Metodi di recupero e studio*. Rome, Bulzoni Editore.

Borgognini Tarli, S. M. 1992. Aspetti antropologici e paleodemografici dal Paleolitico superiore alla prima età del ferro. A. Guidi and M. Piperno. *Italia Preistorica*. Roma, Laterza: 238-273.

Bourdieu, P. 1977. *Outline of a Theory of Practice*. Cambridge, Cambridge University Press.

Bourdieu, P. 1990. *The logic of practice*. Cambridge, Polity Press.

Boyde, A. 1989. Enamel. B. K. B. Berkovitz, A. Boyde, R. M. Frank, H. J. Holing, B. J. Moxham, J. Nalbandian and C. H. Tonge. *Teeth, Handbook of Microscopic Anatomy*. New York, Springer Verlag. V: 309-473.

Braun, R. D. 1987. *Introduction to Instrumental Analysis*. Singapore, McGraw-Hill International Edition.

Brothwell, D. R. 1981. *Digging up bones*. Ithaca, New York, Cornell University Press.

Buikstra, J. E. and D. H. Ubelaker 1994. *Standards for data collection from human skeletal remains*, Arkansas Archaeological Survey Research Series.

Bumsted, M. P. 1985. Past Human Behaviour from Bone Chemical Analysis - Respects and Prospects. *Journal of Human Evolution*, 14: 539-551.

Carlstrom, D. and A. Engstrom 1956. Biophysiscs of Bone. G. H. Bourne. *The Biochemistry and Physiology of Bone*. New York, Academic Press Inc.: 149-178.

Cazzella, A. 1984. Età del Bronzo: forme incipienti di stratificazione sociale nel II millennio a.C. S. M. Cassano, A. Cazzella, A. Manfredini and M. Moscoloni. *Paletnologia. Metodi e strumenti per l'analisi delle società preistoriche*. Roma, Nuova Italia Scientifica: 275-309.

Cazzella, A. 1994a. *La facies di Palma Campania e le culture dell'Italia sud-occidentale*. L'eruzione vesuviana delle "Pomici di Avellino" e la facies di Palma Campania. Ricerche sul Bronzo Antico in Campania, Ravello, Edipuglia.

Cazzella, A. and M. Moscoloni 1995. Modelli di organizzazione spaziale in alcune necropoli eneolitiche del del Bonzo della preistoria italiana. *Preistoria e Protostoria in Etruria. Atti del Secondo Incontro di Studi*: 35-41.

Chagnon, N. 1983. *Yanomamo: The Fierce People*. New York, Rhinehart and Winston.

Childe, V. G. 1957. *The Dawn of European Civilisation*, Bungay.

Close, A. 2000. Reconstructing movement in prehistory. *Journal of Archaeological Method and Theory*, 7(1): 49-77.

Counihan, C. M. 1999. *The anthropology of food and body: gender, meaning and power*. New York, Routledge.

Delibrias, G., G. Di Paola, M. Rosi and R. Santacroce 1979. La storia eruttiva del complesso vulcanico Somma-Vesuvio ricostruita dalle successioni piroclastiche del Monte Somma. *Rendiconti della Società Italiana di Mineralogia e Petrologia*, 35(1): 411-438.

Diamond, E. G., J. Caravaca and A. Benchimor 1963. Vanadium: excretion, toxicity, lipid effecting man. *American Journal of Clinical Nutrition*, 12: 49-53.

Diamond, T., D. Stiel and S. Posen 1989. Osteoporosis in hemochromatosis: iron excess, gonadal deficiency, or other factors. *Annual of International Medicine*, 110(6): 430-436.

Douglas, M. 1983. Culture and Food. F. Morris. *The Pleasures of Anthropology*. New York, New American Library: 74-101.

Ezzo, J. A. 1994. Zinc as a paleodietary indicator: an issue of theoretical validity in bone-chemistry analysis. *American Antiquity*, 59: 606-621.

Ezzo, J. A. 1997. Analytical perspective on Prehistoric migration: a case study from East-Central Arizona. *Journal of Archaeological Science*, 24: 447-466.

Fischer, P. W. F., A. Giroux and M. R. L'Abbé 1984. Effect of Zinc supplementation on copper status in adult man. *American Journal of Clinical Nutrition*, 40: 734-746.

Fischler, C. 1988. Food, self and identity. *Social Science Information*, 27(2): 275-292.

Fornaciari, G., F. Mallegni, D. Bertini and Y. Nuti 1983. Cribra orbitalia and elemental bone iron in the Punics or Carthage. *Ossa*, 8: 63-77.

References cited

Francalacci, P. and S. Borgognini Tarli 1987. Multielementary analysis of trace elements and preliminary results on stable isotopes in two Italian prehistoric sites. Methodological aspects. G. Groupe and B. Herrman. *Trace Element in Environmental History.* Gottingen, Springer-Verlag: 41-52.

Friedman, B. J. 1987. Manganese balance and clinical observations in young men fed a manganese-deficient diet. *Journal of Nutrition*, 117: 133-143.

Gamble, C. S. and W. A. Boismier (Eds.) 1991. *Ethnoarchaeological Approaches to Mobile Campsites. Hunter-Gatherer and Pastoralist Case Studies.* International Monographs in Prehistory. Ethnoarchaeological Series 1. Ann Arbor.

Gero, J. M. 2000. Troubled travels in agency and feminism. M. A. Dobres and J. Robb. *Agency in Archaeology.* London, Routledge: 34-39.

Gilbert, R. 1975. *Trace element analyses of three skeletal Amerindian populations at Dickson Mounds. Unpublished Ph.D. dissertation. Department of Anthropology.* Amherst, University of Massachusetts.

Goodman, A. H. 1989. Dental enamel hypoplasia in prehistoric populations. *Advancese in Dental Research*, 3: 265-271.

Goodman, A. H. and G. J. Armelagos 1985. The chronological distribution of enamel hypoplasia in human permanent incisor and canine teeth. *Archives of Oral Biology*, 30: 503-507.

Goodman, A. H., G. J. Armelagos and J. C. Rose 1980. Enamel hypoplasia as indicators of stress in three prehistoric populations from Illinois. *Human Biology*, 52: 515-528.

Goodman, A. H. and J. C. Rose 1990. Assessment of Systemic Physiological Pertubations from Dental Enamel Hypoplasia and Associated Histological Structures. *Yearbook of Physical Anthropology*, 33: 59-110.

Goodman, A. H. and J. C. Rose 1991. Dental enamel hypoplasia as indicators of nutritional status. M. A. Kelley and C. S. Larsen. *Advances in Dental Anthropology.* New York, Wiley Liss: 279-293.

Goodman, J. M. 2001. www.ch.cam.ac.uk, Cambridge University.

Gordon, C. C. and J. E. Buikstra 1981. Soil pH, bone preservation and sampling bias at mortuary sites. *American Antiquity*, 46: 566-571.

Grupe, G. 1988. Impact of the choice of bone sample on trace element data in excavated human skeletons. *Journal of Archaeological Science*, 15: 123-129.

Grupe, G. 1998. "Archives of Childhood" - The Research Potential of Trace Element Analyses of Ancient Human Dental Enamel. K. W. Alt, F. W. Rosing and M. Teschler-Nicola. *Dental Anthropology. Fundamentals, Limits, and Prospects.* Wien, Springer: 337-347.

Grupe, G. and H. Pieperbrink 1988. Trace element contaminations in excavated bones by micro-organism. G. G. H. B. *Trace Elements in Environmental History.* Heidelberg, Springler-Verlag: 103-112.

Hambridge, K. M. 1974. Chromium nutrition in man. *American Journal of Clinical Nutrition*, 26: 988-991.

Hamilakis, Y. 1999. Food technologies/technologies of the body: the social context of wine and oil production and consumption in Bronze Age Crete. *World Archaeology*, 31(1): 38-54.

Hancock, R. G. V., M. D. Grinpas and B. Alpert 1987. Are archaeological bones similar to modern bones? An archaeological assessment. *Journal of Radioanalitical Nuclear Chemistry*, 110: 283-291.

Harris, M. 1986. *Good to eat: riddles of food and culture.* London, Allen & Unwin.

Hart, E. B., H. Steenbock, J. Waddell and C. A. Elvehjem 1928. Iron in nutrition. VII. Copper as a supplement to iron for hemoglobin building in the rat. *Journal of Biological Chemistry*, 77: 797.

Hastorf, C. A. 1991. Gender, Space, and Food in Prehistory. J. M. Gero and M. W. Conkey. *Engendering Archaeology. Women and Prehistory.* Oxford, Blackwell: 132-159.

Hatcher, H., M. S. Tite and J. N. Walsh 1995. A comparison of inductively-coupled plasma emission spectrometry and atomic absorption spectrometry analysis on standard reference silicate materials and ceramics. *Archaeometry*, 37: 83-94.

Heidegger, M. 1969. *Identity and difference.* London, University of Chicago Press.

Hillson, S. 1996. *Dental Anthropology.* Cambridge, Cambridge University Press.

References cited

Hurley, L. S., C. L. Keen, B. Lonnerdal and R. B. Rucker (Eds.) 1988. *Trace Elements in Man and Animals*. Davis, California, University of California.

IAEA 1982. *Inter comparison of minor and trace element in animal. Progress Report 1 (H-5)*. Vienna, International Atomic Energy Association.

Ingold, T. 2000. "Evolving Skills". H. Rose and S. Rose. *Alas, Poor Darwin: Arguments Against Evolutionary Psychology*. London, Jonathan Cape: 225-246.

Iyengar, G. V., W. E. Kollmer and H. J. M. Bowen 1978. *The Elemental Composition of Human Tissues and Body Fluids. A compilation of values for adults*. New York, Verlag Chemie.

Jarvis, K. 1997. Inductively coupled plasma-mass spectrometry (ICP-MS). R. Gill. *Modern Analytical Geochemistry. An introduction to quantitative chemical analysis for earth, environmental and material scientists*. London, Longman: 171-187.

Johnson, M. A. and J. L. Greger 1982. Effects of dietary tin on tin and calcium metabolism of adult males. *American Journal of Clinical Nutrition*, 35: 655-660.

Katzenberg, M. A. 1984. Chemical analysis of prehistoric human bone from five temporally distinct populations in Southern Ontario. *National Museum of Man, Mercury Series. Archaeological Survey of Canada*, 129.

Kelly, R. L. 1992. Mobility/Sedentism: concepts, archaeological measures and effects. *Annual Review of Anthropology*, 21: 43-66.

Kent, G. N., T. D. Price, D. H. Gutteridge, M. Smith, J. R. Allen, C. I. Bhagat, M. P. Barnes, C. J. Hickling, R. W. Retallack, S. G. Wilson, R. D. Devlin and S. St John 1990. Human lactation: forearm trabecular bone loss, increased bone turnover and renal conservation of calcium and organic phosphate with recovery of bone mass following weaning. *Journal of Bone Mineral Research*, 5: 361-369.

Khazanov, A. M. 1983. *Nomads and the outside world*. Cambridge, Cambridge University Press.

Klauder, D. S., L. Murthy and H. G. Petering 1972. *Trace substances and environmental health*. 6th Proceedings of the University of Montana Annual Conference.

Klevay, L. M. 1974. Trace substances in the environment. *Health*, 8: 9.

Krueger, H. W. 1989. *Exchange of Carbon and Strontium with hydroxyapatite: results of laboratory and natural expreriments*. Proceedings of the Second Advanced Seminar on Paleodietary Research, Cape Town.

Kruger, B. J. 1958. *Journal of Autrian Dental Association*, 3: 298.

Kyle, J. H. 1986. Effect of post-depositional contamination on the concentrations of major and trace elements in human bones and teeth - the implications for palaeodietary research. *Journal of Archaeological Science*, 13: 403-416.

Lambert, J. B., S. V. Simpson, C. B. Szpunar and J. E. Buikstra 1984. Ancient human diet from inorganic analysis of bone. *Accounts of Chemical Research*, 17: 298-305.

Lambert, J. B., C. B. Szpunar and J. E. Buikstra 1979. Chemical Analysis of excavated human bone from Middle and Late Woodland sites. *Archaeometry*, 21: 115-129.

Lambert, J. B., S. M. Vlasak, A. C. Thometz and J. E. Buikstra 1982. A comparative study of the chemical analysis of ribs and femurs in Woodland populations. *American Journal of Physical Anthropology*, 59: 289-294.

Lambert, J. B., J. M. Weydert, S. R. Williams and J. E. Buikstra 1990. Comparison of Methods for the Removal of Diagenetic Material in Buried Bone. *Journal of Archaeological Science*, 17: 453-468.

Lambert, J. B., L. Xue and J. E. Buikstra 1989. Physical removal of contaminative inorganic material from buried human bone. *Journal of Archaeological Science*, 16: 427-436.

Larsen, C. S. 1997. *Bioarchaeology. Interpreting behavior from the human skeleton*. Cambridge, Cambridge University Press.

Lévi-Strauss, C. 1966. The culinary triangle. *New Sociology*: 937-940.

Lévi-Strauss, C. 1969. *The elementary structure of kinship*. Boston, Beacon Press.

Lévi-Strauss, C. 1970. *The raw and the cooked*. London, Cape.

Lovejoy, C. O. 1985. Dental wear in the Libben population: its functional pattern and role in the determination of adult skeletal age at death. *American Journal of Physical Anthropology*, 68: 47-56.

Lovell, N. C. 1989. Test of Phenice's technique for determining sex from the os pubis. *American Journal of Physical Anthropology*, 79: 117-120.

References cited

Lupton, D. 1996. *Food the body and the self*. London, Sage Publications.

Malone, C., S. Stoddart and R. Withehouse 1994. The Bronze Age of Southern Italy, Sicily and Malta. *Sheffield Archaeological Report*, 8: 167-194.

Martin, D. L., A. H. Goodman and G. J. Armelagos 1985. Skeletal pathologies as indicators of quality and quantity of diet. J. H. Mielke. *The analysis of prehistoric diets*. Orlando, Academic Press.

Mastroroberto, M. 1998. La necropoli di Sant'Abbondio: una comunità dell'età del Bronzo a Pompei. P. G. Guzzo and R. Peroni. *Archeologia e Vulcanologia in Campania*. Pompei, Arte Tipografica: 135-149.

Mays, S. 1998. *The Archaeology of human bones*. London, Routledge.

Mays, S. and M. Cox 2000. Sex determination in skeletal remains. M. Cox and S. Mays. *Human Osteology in Archaeology and Forensic Science*.

Meindle, R. S., C. O. Lovejoy, R. P. Mensforth and L. D. Carlos 1985. Accuracy and determination of error in sexing of the skeleton. *American Journal of Physical Anthropology*, 68: 79-85.

Mertz, W. 1969. Chromium occurrence and function in biological systems. *Physiological Review*, 49(2): 163-239.

Mertz, W. 1982. Clinical and Public Health Significance of Chromium. A. S. Prasad. *Clinical, Biochemical, and Nutritional Aspects of Trace Elements*. New York, Alan R. Liss, Inc. 6: 315-323.

Mertz, W. 1985. Metabolism and metabolic effects of trace elements. R. K. Chandra. *Trace elements in nutrition of children*. New York, Raven Press: 107-119.

Metz, J., D. Hart and H. C. Harpending 1971. Iron, folate, and vitamin B12 nutrition in a hunter-gatherer poeple: a study of the !Kung Bushmen. *American Journal of Clinical Nutrition*, 24: 229-242.

Mikkanen, H. 1985. Effects of arsenic in the intestinal absorption of Se75 compounds in chicks. L. S. Hurley, C. L. Keen, B. Lonnerdal and R. B. Rucker. *Trace Elements in Man and Animals*. Davis, California, University of California: 551-552.

Millard, A. R. and R. E. M. Hedges 1995. The Role of Environment in Uranium Uptake by Buried Bone. *Journal of Archaeological Science*, 22: 239-250.

Minozzi, S., A. Canci, S. M. Borgognini Tarli and E. Repetto 1994. Stress e stato di salute in serie scheletriche dell'età del Bronzo. *Bullettino di Paletnologia Italiana*, 85: 333-348.

Minozzi, S., A. Canci, V. Scattarella and S. Borgognini Tarli 1999. Studio antropologico dei resti scheletrici umani. A. M. Tunzi Sisto. *Ipogei della Daunia. Preistoria di un territorio*. Foggia, Claudio Gerenzi Editore: 295-302.

Molleson, T. I. and M. Cox (Eds.) 1993. *The Spitafield Project, vol. 2: The Anthropology - The Middling Sort*. Research Report 86. York, Council for British Archaeology.

Moore, J. and M. E. Corbett 1971. The distribution of dental caries in ancient British populations: Anglo-Saxon period. *Caries Research*, 5: 151-161.

Moores, C. F. A., E. A. Fanning and E. E. Hunt 1963. Age formation by stages for ten permanent teeth in children. *Journal of Dental Research*, 42: 1490-1502.

Nelson, B. K., M. J. De Niro, M. J. Schoeninger, D. J. De Paolo and P. E. Hare 1986. Effects of diagenesis on Strontium, Carbon, Nitrogen, and Oxygen concentration and isotopic composition of bone. *Geochimica et Cosmochimica Acta*, 50: 1941-1949.

O'Dell, B. K. 1985. Bioavailability of and interaction among trace elements. R. K. Chandra. *Trace elements in nutrition and children*. New York, Raven Press: 41-62.

Pate, D. F. and K. Brown 1985. The stability of bone Strontium in the geochemical environment. *Journal of Human Evolution*, 14: 483-491.

Pate, D. F., J. T. Hutton and K. Norrish 1989. Ionic exchange between soil solution and bone: toward a predictive model. *Applied Geochemistry*, 4: 303-316.

Pellegrini, E. 1992. Le età dei metalli nell'Italia meridionale e in Sicilia. A. Guidi and M. Piperno. *Italia Preistorica*. Roma, Laterza: 471-516.

Phenice, T. 1969. A newly developed visual method of sexing in the Os Pubis. *American Journal of Physical Anthropology*, 30: 297-301.

Price, T. D. 1989. Multi-elemental studies of diagenesis in prehistoric bone. T. D. Price. *The Chemistry of Prehistoric Human Bone*. Cambridge, Cambridge University Press: 126-154.

Price, T. D., J. Blitz, J. H. Burton and J. A. Ezzo 1992. Diagenesis in prehistoric bone: problems and solutions. *Journal of Archaeological Science*, 19: 513-529.

References cited

Price, T. D., M. Connor and J. D. Parsen 1985a. Bone strontium and prehistoric diet: strontium discrimination in white-tailed deer. *Journal of Archaeological Science*, 12: 419-442.

Price, T. D., G. Grupe and P. Schroter 1998. Migration in the Bell Beaker period of central Europe. *Antiquity*, 72: 405-411.

Price, T. D., C. M. Johnson, J. A. Ezzo, J. Ericson and J. H. Burton 1994. Residential mobility in the Prehistoric Southwest United States: a preliminary study using Strontium Isotopes analysis. *Journal of Archaeological Science*, 21: 315-330.

Price, T. D., L. Manzanilla and W. D. Middleton 2000. Immigration and the ancient city of Teotihuacan in Mexico: a study using Strontium Isotope Ratios in human bone and teeth. *Journal of Archaeological Science*, 27: 903-913.

Price, T. D., M. J. Schoeninger and G. J. Armelagos 1985b. Bone chemistry and past behavior: an overview. *Journal of Human Evolution*, 14: 419-447.

Puglisi, S. M. 1959. *La Civiltà Appenninica. Origine delle comunità pastorali in Italia*. Firenze, Sansoni.

Quarterman, J., J. N. Morrison and L. F. Carey 1974. *Trace substitution in environmental health*. University of Montana 7th Annual Conference.

Radosevich, S. C. 1993. The six deadly sins of trace element analysis: a case of wishful thinking in science. M. K. Sandford. *Investigation of Ancient Human Tissue. Chemical Analyses in Anthropology*. Langhorne, Gordon and Breach Science Publisher. 10: 269-332.

Rellini, U. 1932. Le Stazioni Enee delle Marche di fase seriore e la civiltà Italica. *Monumenti Antichi dei Lincei*, 34.

Robb, J. 1994. Gender contradictions, moral coalitions and inequality in prehistoric Italy. *Journal of European Archaeology*, 2(1): 20-49.

Robb, J. 1997. Violence and gender in early Italy. D. L. Martin and D. W. Frayer. *Troubled times: violence and warfare in the past*. New York, Gordon and Breach: 111-143.

Robb, J. 2002. Time and biography. Osteobiography of the Italian Neolithic lifespan. Y. Hamilakis, M. Pluciennik and S. Tarlow. *Thinking through the body archaeologies of corporeality edited by*. New York, Kluwer Academic/Plenum: 153-171.

Rosi, M. and R. Santacroce 1986. L'attività del Somma-Vesuvio precedente l'eruzione del 1631: dati stratigrafici e vulcanologici. C. Albore Livadie. *Tremblements de Terre, Eruptions Volcaniques et Vie des Hommes dans la Campanie Antique*. Naples, Publications du Centre Jean Bérard. VII: 15-33.

Rubini, M., L. Andreini and A. Coppa 1990. Gli inumati della Grotta Vittorio Vecchi di Monte Fulcino (Sezze, Latina; media Età del Bronzo, XVII-XV sec a.C. *Rivista di Antropologia*, 68: 141-163.

Ruff, C. 1987. Sexual dimorphism in human limb bone structure: relationship to subsistence strategy and sexual division of labor. *Journal of Human Evolution*, 16: 391-416.

Sandford, M. K. 1992. A Reconsideration of Trace Element Analysis in Prehistoric Bone. R. S. Saunders and M. A. Katzenberg. *Skeletal Biology of Past People: Research Methods*. New York, Wiley-Liss: 79-103.

Sandford, M. K. 1993. Understanding the biogenic-diagenetic continuum: interpreting elemental concentrations of archaeological bone. K. M. Sandford. *Investigation of ancient human tissue*. Langhorne, Gordon & Breach Science Publisher. 10: 3-57.

Scheinberg, I. H. 1961. *Federal Proceedings of the American Society of Experimental Biology*, Supplement 10: 179.

Schneider, K. M. and D. J. Blakeslee 1990. Evaluating residence patterns among prehistoric populations: clues from dental enamel composition. *Human Biology*, 62: 71-83.

Schoeninger, M. J. 1979. Diet as a status at Chalcatzingo: some empirical and technological aspects of Strontium analysis. *American Journal of Physical Anthropology*, 51: 295-310.

Schoeninger, M. J. 1981. The Agriculture "Revolution": its effects on human diet in Prehistoric Iran and Israel. *Paleorient*, 7: 73-92.

Schour, I. and M. M. Hoffman 1939. Studies in tooth development. II. The rate of apposition of enamel and dentin in man and other animals. *Journal of Dental Research*, 18: 161-175.

Schroeder, H. A. 1973. *Trace Elements and Man*. Old Greenwich, Devin-Adair.

Schroeder, H. A. and J. J. Balassa 1966. *Journal of Chronic Disease*, 19: 573.

Schroeder, H. A. and A. P. Nason 1969. *Journal Invest. Dermatology*, 53: 71.

Schroeder, H. A. and I. H. Tipton 1968. *Archaeology and Environmental Health*, 17: 965.

Scott, E. C. 1979. Dental wear scoring technique. *American Journal of Physical Anthropology*, 51: 213-218.

Shroeder, H. A. 1966. Chromium deficiency in rats: a syndrome simulating diabetes mellitus with retarded growth. *Journal of Nutrition*, 88: 439-445.

Sillen, A. 1981. Strontium and diet at Hayonim Cave. *American Journal of Physical Anthropology*, 56: 131-137.

Sillen, A. 1986. Biogenetic and diagenetic Sr/Ca in Plio-Pleistocene fossils of the Omo Shangura Formation. *Paleobiology*, 12: 311-323.

Sillen, A. and M. Kavanagh 1982. Strontium and paleodietary research: a review. *Yearbook of Physical Anthropology*, 63: 39-56.

Skougstad, M. W. and C. A. Horr 1960. Occurrence and distribution of strontium in natural water. *United States Geological Survey*., 420.

Smith, B. H. 1984. Patterns of molar wear in hunther-gatherers and agriculturalists. *American Journal of Physical Anthropology*, 63: 39-56.

Sofaer Derevenski, J. 1997. Engendering children, engendering archaeology. J. Moore and E. Scott. *Invisible people and processes. Writing gender and childhood into European archaeology.* Leicester, Leicester University Press: 192-202.

Sofaer Derevenski, J. 2000a. *Age, Ageing and Human Osteoarchaeology*. Paper presented at TAG 2000.

Sofaer Derevenski, J. 2000b. Rings of life. The role of early metalwork in mediating the gender life course. *World Archaeology*, 31(3): 389-406.

Sorensen, M. L. 2000. *Gender Archaeology*. Cambridge, Polity Press.

Spencer, H., C. R. Asmussen, R. B. Holtzman and L. Kramer 1979. Metabolic balances of cadmium, copper, manganese, and zinc in man. *American Journal of Clinical Nutrition*, 32: 1867-1875.

St Hoyme, L. E. and M. Y. Iscan 1989. Determination of sex and race: accuracy and assumptions. M. Y. Iscan and K. A. R. Kennedy. *Reconstruction of Life from the Skeleton.* New York, Alan Liss: 53-93.

Stoecker, B. J. and Y. C. Li 1988. Chromium and Vanadate supplementation. L. S. Hurley, C. L. Keen, B. Lonnerdal and R. B. Rucker. *Trace Elements in Man and Animals.* Davis, California, University of California. 6: 553-554.

Strasia, C. A. 1971. *Ph.D. Thesis. University Microfilms.* Ann Arbor, Michigan University.

Strathern, A. 1973. Kinship, Descent and Locality: Some New Guinea Examples. J. Goody. *The Character of Kinship.* London, Cambridge University Press: 21-33.

Strathern, M. 1987. Two New Guinea Highlands Kinship Systems. J. Fishbourne Collier and S. J. Yanagisako. *Gender and Kinship. Essays Toward a Unified Analysis.* Stanford, Stanford University Press: 271-300.

Stuart-Macadam, P. L. 1985. Porotic Hyperostosis: representative of a childhood condition. *American Journal of Physical Anthropology*, 66: 391-398.

Stuart-Macadam, P. L. 1989. Nutritional deficiency diseases: a survey of scurvy, rickets and iron-deficiency anemia. M. Y. Iscan and A. R. Kennedy. *Reconstruction of life from the skeleton.* New York, Alan R. Liss.

Stuart-Macadam, P. L. 1998. Iron deficiency anemia: exploring the difference. A. L. Grauer and P. L. Stuart-Macadam. *Sex and gender in paleopathological perspective.* Cambridge, Cambridge University Press: 45-63.

Sutherland, L. D. and J. M. Suchey 1991. Use of the ventral arc in pubic sex determination. *Journal of Forensic Sciences*, 36: 501-511.

Szpunar, C. B., J. B. Lambert and J. E. Buikstra 1978. Analysis of excavated bones by atomic absorption. *American Journal of Physical Anthropology*, 48: 199-202.

Tafuri, M., M. Mastroroberto and G. Manzi 2003. Human skeletal remains from the Middle Bronze Age cemetery of Sant'Abbondio (Pompei, Italy). *Rivista di Antropologia*, 81: 79-106.

Thomas, J. 1996. *Time, Culture and Identity. An interpretative archaeology.* London, Routledge.

Thompson, L. C. 1979. Complexes. K. A. J. Gschneidner and L. Eyring. *Handbook of the Physics and Chemistry of Rare Earths.* New York, North-Holland: 209-297.

Todd, T. W. 1921a. Age change in the Pubic Bone. I: the male white pubis. *American Journal of Physical Anthropology*, 3: 285-334.

Todd, T. W. 1921b. Age changes in the Pubic Bone. III: the pubis of the white female. *American Journal of Physical Anthropology*, 4: 1-70.

Toots, H. and M. R. Voorhies 1965. Strontium in fossil bones and reconstructions of food chains. *Science*, 149: 854-855.

Turner, C. G., C. Nichol and G. R. Scott 1991. Scoring Procedures for Key Morphological Traits of the Permanent Dentition: The Arizona State University Dental Anthropological System. M. Kelley and C. S. Larsen. *Advances in Dental Anthropology*. New York, Wiley-Liss: 13-31.

Turner, C. G. and G. R. Scott 1977. Dentition of Easter Inlanders. A. A. Dahlberg and T. M. Graber. *Orofacial Growth and Development*. Mounton, The Hauge: 229-249.

Ubelaker, D. H. 1989. The Estimation of Age at Death from Immature Human Bone. M. Y. Iscan. *Age Markers in the Human Skeleton*. Spriengfield, Illinois, Charles C. Thomas: 55-70.

Underwood, E. J. 1977. *Trace elements in human and animal nutrition*. London, Academic Press.

Wagner, R. 1977. "Analogic Kinship: a Dairibi example". *American Ethnologist*, 4(4): 623-642.

Weinberg, E. 1992. Iron withholding in prevention of disease. P. L. Stuart-Macadam and S. Kent. *Demography, Diet and Disease: Changing Perspectives on Anemia*. New York, Aldine de Gruyter: 105-150.

Wenlock, R. W., D. H. Buss and E. J. Dixon 1979. Trace nutrients 2. Manganese in British food. *British Journal of Nutrition*, 41: 253-261.

Whitehouse, R. 2001. Exploring gender in prehistoric Italy. *Papers of the British School at Rome*, 69: 49-96.

Whitehouse, R. D. (Ed.) 1998. *Gender and Italian Archaeology. Challenging the stereotypes*. Accordia Specialist Studies on Italy. London, Accordia Research Institute UCL.

WHO 1996. *Gli oligoelementi nella nutrizione e nella salute dell'uomo*. Ginevra, Istituto Scotti Bassani.

Williams, C. T. 1988. Alteration of chemical compositions of fossil bones by soil processes and groundwater. G. Grupe and E. Herrmann. *Trace Elements in Environmental History*. Berlin, Springer-Verlag: 27-40.

Wylie, A. 1997. Good Science, Bad Science or Science as Usual?; Feminist Critiques of Science. L. Hager. *Women in Human Evolution*. New York, Routledge: 29-55.

Zhou, L. 1995. *Dental enamel defects related to famine stress in contemporary Chinese populations - a bioanthropological study*. PhD Dissertation. Carbondare, Southern Illinois University.

Zigler, E. E. 1978. Absorption and retention of lead by infants. *Pediatric Research*, 12: 29-34.

APPENDIX

Trace Element Data

Appendix

ID	Gender	Age	Year	Area dep.	V bone	V enamel	Cr bone	Cr enamel	Mn bone	Mn enamel	Co bone	Co enamel
1/93	m	adult	1993	W	50,3	24,5	8,6	4,36	13,97	7,22	1,91	6,82
1/96	f	adult	1996	E	70,2	7,58	LLD	1,27	12,63	5,11	3,3	1,94
10/96	f	juv	1996	E	72,17	7,23	LLD	0,84	20,23	5,35	2,95	1,49
11(B)	f	adult	1993	W	81,4	LLD	7,3	LLD	3,76	LLD	4,17	LLD
11/96	m	adult	1996	E	46,53	14,07	LLD	0,73	6,01	20,57	2,86	1,61
12/93	f	juv	1993	W	41,83	20,6	25,3	7,45	17,63	12,37	3,22	6,13
12QVIII	m	adult	1996	E	LLD	4,05	LLD	0,85	LLD	5,62	LLD	1,35
13/93	m	adult	1993	W	93,57	14,27	5,7	6,19	14,27	14,53	3,83	3,9
13/96	j	infl	1996	E	79,9	9,9	LLD	0,53	86,33	4,63	3	1,35
14(B)	j	juv	1993	W	29,13	LLD	61,9	LLD	19,4	LLD	5,4	LLD
14/96	f	adult	1996	E	68,17	4,86	LLD	3,43	10,3	3,91	2,69	1,18
15(B)	u	adult	1993	W	45,3	LLD	15,3	LLD	13,23	LLD	2,36	LLD
15/96	u	adult	1996	E	37,8	LLD	LLD	LLD	7,57	LLD	2,41	LLD
16/96	j	infl	1996	E	86,8	6,25	LLD	1,01	40,07	4,39	3,02	1,25
17/93dec	j	infl	1993	W	28,13	24,16	59,6	5,42	277	21,16	8,19	3,79
17/93perm	j	infl	1993	W	28,13	35,63	59,6	8,51	277	1621,33	8,19	6,35
17/96	j	juv	1996	E	97,57	LLD	5,5	LLD	33,7	LLD	2,91	LLD
18/96	m	adult	1996	E	LLD	1,39	LLD	0,69	LLD	1,87	LLD	LLD
18QI	m	adult	1993	W	56,9	15,73	3,3	6,03	50,47	26,1	5,56	3,88
19/96	m	adult	1996	E	77,73	61,43	6,2	0,87	30,73	9,47	2,96	2,85
2/93	m	adult	1993	W	31,67	26,7	6,9	3,22	21	11,23	2	3,67
2/96	f	adult	1996	E	63,1	5,73	LLD	0,94	6,81	5,12	2,5	1,73
20/93	f	adult	1993	W	47,97	9,77	18	3,5	29,93	8,9	2,55	4,53
20/96	u	adult	1996	E	83,3	LLD	LLD	LLD	5,98	LLD	2,41	LLD
21/96	u	adult	1996	E	87,43	24,13	LLD	0,64	12,1	2,6	2,53	1,34
21QIII	u	adult	1993	W	45,03	LLD	19	LLD	19,87	LLD	3,11	LLD
22/96	m	adult	1996	E	73,73	9,49	LLD	0,63	19,37	3,35	3,03	1,33
24/96	j	infl	1996	E	LLD	11,6	LLD	0,71	LLD	3,48	LLD	2,31
25(B)	u	adult	1993	W	58	LLD	LLD	LLD	59,23	LLD	3,28	LLD
25/96	m	adult	1996	E	74,1	24,9	4,5	0,82	15,8	5,45	3,07	1,72
26(B)	u	adult	1993	W	29,23	10,63	18,2	12,51	479,33	47,33	11,9	3,98
26/96	f	adult	1996	E	92,17	14,57	4,6	0,99	7,04	8,29	2,94	1,71
27/93	f	adult	1993	W	42,63	5,78	5,2	34,57	14,87	14	1,51	3,92
28/93	u	adult	1993	W	52,47	LLD	20,4	LLD	15,83	LLD	3,13	LLD
28/96	f	adult	1996	E	61,97	5,77	6	0,93	13,9	11,17	3,25	1,33
29(B)	f	adult	1993	W	35,57	17,3	21,7	8,96	21,8	6,87	2,81	4,09
29/96	f	adult	1996	E	78,03	13,93	6,7	0,96	4,81	4,96	3,69	1,77
2bis	j	infl	1993	W	72,37	14,05	4,2	6,73	492,33	4,48	9,32	4,07
3/96	m	adult	1996	E	75,07	10,6	LLD	0,76	22,4	2,81	2,07	1,31
30/93	m	juv	1993	W	75,87	17,6	5,9	3,48	29,7	4,25	4,48	3,35
31/93	f	adult	1993	W	79,5	11,47	20,4	4,84	34,03	5	3,29	4,25
31/96	u	adult	1996	E	71,3	95,6	3,9	1,18	25,63	48,7	4,06	12,1
33/93	m	adult	1993	W	91,33	8,13	4,7	27,09	42,43	9,31	4,74	4,1
34/93	u	adult	1993	W	83,57	LLD	LLD	LLD	14,5	LLD	3,77	LLD
34/96	m	adult	1996	E	65,97	7,95	5,3	0,59	53,53	2,79	4,69	1,23
35/96	j	juv	1996	E	110,67	5,78	3	0,85	57,57	3,7	4,79	1,36
36/93	u	adult	1993	W	72,87	LLD	LLD	LLD	166	LLD	4,4	LLD
37/93	f	adult	1993	W	33,97	11,7	5,5	69,67	21,83	19,37	1,34	4,02
4(B)	f	adult	1996	E	63,87	21,57	LLD	0,75	6,21	3,57	2,21	1,65
4/93	f	adult	1993	W	42,57	LLD	5,4	LLD	14,23	11,44	1,7	4,61
5/93	f	adult	1993	W	54	8,25	5,8	0,66	5,84	4,81	2,53	1,35
5bis	m	adult	1996	E	74,1	LLD	LLD	LLD	37,2	LLD	4,63	LLD
5n2	j	infl	1996	E	49,73	20,83	5,5	0,77	134,33	21,83	4,69	1,46
6/96	m	adult	1996	E	86,57	19,57	5,9	0,77	3,01	3,61	2,87	1,23
6QI/93	m	adult	1993	W	74,15	LLD	5,7	LLD	16,93	LLD	2,79	LLD
7/93	j	infl	1993	W	101,67	18,43	7,6	4,06	12,9	11,93	4,6	3,76
7/96	u	adult	1996	E	90,97	17,33	LLD	0,69	16,57	3,42	2,28	1,41
8/93	m	adult	1993	W	35,5	18,3	6,7	10,27	18,17	6,95	1,78	4,37
8/96	f	adult	1996	E	71,8	4,42	LLD	0,75	13,9	3,72	2,93	1,41
9/93	u	adult	1993	E	67,33	LLD	LLD	LLD	12,3	LLD	2,76	LLD

Trace element values (in ppm) for bone and enamel samples at Sant'Abbondio. LLD indicates values below the Lower Limit of detection.

Appendix

ID	Gender	Age	Year	Area dep.	Ni enamel	Cu bone	Cu enamel	Zn bone	Zn enamel	As bone	As enamel	Se77 bone
1/93	m	adult	1993	W	26,47	37,73	LLD	439,67	LLD	4,81	LLD	3,5
1/96	f	adult	1996	E	6,37	11,6	17,63	139,9	50,43	16,3	1,88	LLD
10/96	f	juv	1996	E	5,71	LLD	8,56	320,33	60,97	11,33	LLD	LLD
11(B)	f	adult	1993	W	LLD	17,43	LLD	LLD	LLD	18,4	LLD	LLD
11/96	m	adult	1996	E	4	16,93	13,8	225	45,93	11	3,56	LLD
12/93	f	juv	1993	W	92	27,77	LLD	186,33	LLD	4,9	LLD	LLD
12QVIII	m	adult	1996	E	7,28	LLD	3,54	LLD	73	LLD	LLD	LLD
13/93	m	adult	1993	W	30,43	14,83	LLD	LLD	LLD	8,46	LLD	LLD
13/96	j	infl	1996	E	4,85	13,95	4,39	93,57	42	13,9	3,32	LLD
14(B)	j	juv	1993	W	LLD	20,23	LLD	330	LLD	4,23	LLD	LLD
14/96	f	adult	1996	E	4,26	LLD	2,76	-106,47	26,37	15,4	LLD	LLD
15(B)	u	adult	1993	W	LLD	34,27	LLD	55,27	LLD	3,92	LLD	LLD
15/96	u	adult	1996	E	LLD	LLD	LLD	29,53	LLD	10,02	LLD	LLD
16/96	j	infl	1996	E	6,29	16,23	7,34	-4,53	95,93	8,3	LLD	LLD
17/93dec	j	infl	1993	W	18,07	158,67	LLD	117	LLD	6,07	4,36	LLD
17/93perm	j	infl	1993	W	35,2	158,67	LLD	117	LLD	6,07	7,27	LLD
17/96	j	juv	1996	E	LLD	LLD	LLD	LLD	LLD	11,33	LLD	LLD
18/96	m	adult	1996	E	1,17	LLD	LLD	LLD	7,39	LLD	LLD	LLD
18QI	m	adult	1993	W	38,67	30,7	LLD	LLD	LLD	13,43	LLD	LLD
19/96	m	adult	1996	E	7,52	LLD	5,8	LLD	33,13	8,99	3,92	LLD
2/93	m	adult	1993	W	16	45,63	LLD	43,07	LLD	7,48	LLD	LLD
2/96	f	adult	1996	E	10,5	13,13	7,84	460	41,93	9,5	0,92	LLD
20/93	f	adult	1993	W	28,87	34,4	101,67	60,43	LLD	4,8	LLD	LLD
20/96	u	adult	1996	E	LLD	LLD	LLD	LLD	LLD	6,07	LLD	LLD
21/96	u	adult	1996	E	3,74	LLD	24,57	LLD	40,9	8,23	2,28	LLD
21QIII	u	adult	1993	W	LLD	39,9	LLD	58,9	LLD	6,05	LLD	LLD
22/96	m	adult	1996	E	4,18	12,4	0,73	LLD	28,13	13,1	LLD	LLD
24/96	j	infl	1996	E	12,07	LLD	8,14	LLD	28,97	LLD	LLD	LLD
25(B)	u	adult	1993	W	LLD	22,07	LLD	LLD	LLD	9,3	LLD	LLD
25/96	m	adult	1996	E	5,15	LLD	9,87	LLD	42,03	13,27	4,35	LLD
26(B)	u	adult	1993	W	19,87	77,53	1175,33	70,3	LLD	7,83	LLD	LLD
26/96	f	adult	1996	E	6,92	10,9	6,62	LLD	98,7	14,17	1,11	LLD
27/93	f	adult	1993	W	52,53	26,23	LLD	43,43	LLD	4,05	LLD	LLD
28/93	u	adult	1993	W	LLD	36	LLD	69,03	LLD	5,17	LLD	LLD
28/96	f	adult	1996	E	5,36	LLD	8,54	329	105,67	10,05	LLD	LLD
29(B)	f	adult	1993	W	110,33	59,27	LLD	85,83	LLD	6,05	LLD	LLD
29/96	f	adult	1996	E	5,8	LLD	15,9	LLD	59,67	10,69	LLD	LLD
2bis	j	infl	1993	W	105,46	35,23	29,93	LLD	LLD	20,53	LLD	LLD
3/96	m	adult	1996	E	4,58	13,5	3,45	48,67	28,67	9,31	LLD	LLD
30/93	m	juv	1993	W	12,97	27,97	LLD	LLD	LLD	12,07	LLD	LLD
31/93	f	adult	1993	W	315,33	63,93	LLD	106,43	LLD	4,99	LLD	LLD
31/96	u	adult	1996	E	28,77	LLD	19,93	LLD	141,67	9,4	10,47	LLD
33/93	m	adult	1993	W	45,34	50,1	5,71	LLD	LLD	8,11	LLD	LLD
34/93	u	adult	1993	W	LLD	7,92	LLD	LLD	LLD	7,66	LLD	LLD
34/96	m	adult	1996	E	4,33	8,68	4,48	LLD	52,4	6,55	1,47	LLD
35/96	j	juv	1996	E	4,78	LLD	19,47	LLD	71,2	12,63	LLD	LLD
36/93	u	adult	1993	W	LLD	31,6	LLD	LLD	LLD	14,87	LLD	LLD
37/93	f	adult	1993	W	77,37	23,8	30,43	44,07	LLD	5,57	LLD	LLD
4(B)	f	adult	1996	E	3,82	11,22	2,62	94,33	33,03	10,98	1,74	LLD
4/93	f	adult	1993	W	44,28	33	LLD	43,47	LLD	7,84	2,83	LLD
5/93	f	adult	1993	W	5,16	13,2	23,17	390,33	61,47	5,8	1,18	LLD
5bis	m	adult	1996	E	LLD	64,97	LLD	LLD	LLD	11,72	LLD	LLD
5n2	j	infl	1996	E	3,84	76	4,53	774	21,6	13,13	3,71	LLD
6/96	m	adult	1996	E	4,2	14,48	6,48	721	33	10,41	1,21	LLD
6QI/93	m	adult	1993	W	LLD	13,6	LLD	192,7	LLD	8,62	LLD	LLD
7/93	j	infl	1993	W	24,3	8,89	LLD	LLD	LLD	10,47	LLD	LLD
7/96	u	adult	1996	E	4,16	10,01	2,75	-9,1	28,37	8,96	1,93	LLD
8/93	m	adult	1993	W	180	29,83	LLD	42,2	LLD	5,02	LLD	LLD
8/96	f	adult	1996	E	5,16	49,33	10,11	394	51,7	16,47	LLD	LLD
9/93	u	adult	1993	E	LLD	64,53	LLD	373	LLD	7,81	LLD	LLD

Trace element values (in ppm) for bone and enamel samples at Sant'Abbondio. LLD indicates values below the Lower Limit of detection.

Appendix

ID	Gender	Age	Year	Area dep.	Se77 enamel	Se82 bone	Se82 enamel	Rb bone	Rb enamel	Sr bone	Sr enamel	Y bone
1/93	m	adult	1993	W	LLD	LLD	LLD	0,72	1,72	529,33	700,67	0,74
1/96	f	adult	1996	E	LLD	7,07	1,73	1,18	1,95	744,33	189,33	2,35
10/96	f	juv	1996	E	LLD	LLD	LLD	1,09	0,88	926,67	183,67	4,97
11(B)	f	adult	1993	W	LLD	LLD	LLD	1,13	LLD	1111,33	LLD	1,44
11/96	m	adult	1996	E	LLD	6,05	LLD	1,32	0,72	780,67	200	1,91
12/93	f	juv	1993	W	LLD	LLD	LLD	0,5	3,19	451,33	837,33	0,93
12QVIII	m	adult	1996	E	LLD	LLD	LLD	LLD	0,8	LLD	241,33	LLD
13/93	m	adult	1993	W	LLD	LLD	LLD	3,11	1,28	825	409,67	2,72
13/96	j	infl	1996	E	LLD	LLD	LLD	0,91	0,7	853,33	205,33	4,31
14(B)	j	juv	1993	W	LLD	LLD	LLD	0,55	LLD	470,67	LLD	1,98
14/96	f	adult	1996	E	LLD	LLD	LLD	0,53	0,58	712	221,67	3,09
15(B)	u	adult	1993	W	LLD	LLD	LLD	0,55	LLD	344,67	LLD	3,31
15/96	u	adult	1996	E	LLD	LLD	LLD	0,41	LLD	608,33	LLD	1,12
16/96	j	infl	1996	E	LLD	LLD	LLD	0,85	0,7	733,33	176,67	6,72
17/93dec	j	infl	1993	W	LLD	LLD	LLD	1,32	3,07	705,33	569	22,17
17/93perm	j	infl	1993	W	LLD	LLD	LLD	1,32	1,48	705,33	1084,33	22,17
17/96	j	juv	1996	E	LLD	LLD	LLD	0,76	LLD	871,33	LLD	7,55
18/96	m	adult	1996	E	LLD	LLD	LLD	LLD	0,34	LLD	20,6	LLD
18QI	m	adult	1993	W	LLD	LLD	LLD	2,75	1,55	1185	556,33	3,35
19/96	m	adult	1996	E	LLD	LLD	LLD	0,55	1,11	687,67	370	10,02
2/93	m	adult	1993	W	LLD	LLD	LLD	0,91	0,49	453,67	395	1,79
2/96	f	adult	1996	E	1,48	6,65	-0,72	1,15	1,42	956,67	170,33	3,55
20/93	f	adult	1993	W	LLD	LLD	LLD	0,95	1,65	448,33	392	5,23
20/96	u	adult	1996	E	LLD	LLD	LLD	0,31	LLD	513,67	LLD	3,14
21/96	u	adult	1996	E	LLD	LLD	LLD	0,58	0,7	715,33	304,33	6,47
21QIII	u	adult	1993	W	LLD	LLD	LLD	0,75	LLD	551,67	LLD	2
22/96	m	adult	1996	E	LLD	LLD	LLD	1,8	0,98	1132,33	256,33	3,03
24/96	j	infl	1996	E	LLD	LLD	LLD	LLD	0,88	LLD	203,33	LLD
25(B)	u	adult	1993	W	LLD	LLD	LLD	2,42	LLD	968,67	LLD	5,45
25/96	m	adult	1996	E	LLD	LLD	LLD	1,8	1,15	998,67	314	2,29
26(B)	u	adult	1993	W	LLD	LLD	LLD	0,71	0,78	835,33	455,33	5,16
26/96	f	adult	1996	E	LLD	LLD	LLD	1,26	1,01	1253	252,33	5,51
27/93	f	adult	1993	W	LLD	LLD	LLD	0,67	0,85	428,67	220	7,76
28/93	u	adult	1993	W	LLD	LLD	LLD	0,81	LLD	509,67	LLD	2,21
28/96	f	adult	1996	E	LLD	LLD	LLD	1,17	0,93	1171,67	221,33	10,01
29(B)	f	adult	1993	W	LLD	LLD	LLD	0,88	1,41	562,33	283,33	6,06
29/96	f	adult	1996	E	LLD	LLD	LLD	1,78	1,5	1249	280,67	6,06
2bis	j	infl	1993	W	LLD	LLD	LLD	2,27	1,67	1153	291,5	8,6
3/96	m	adult	1996	E	LLD	LLD	LLD	0,85	0,95	722,33	207	1,55
30/93	m	juv	1993	W	LLD	LLD	LLD	2,53	0,96	1095,33	405,33	3,28
31/93	f	adult	1993	W	LLD	LLD	LLD	0,89	1,16	508,67	352,33	1,91
31/96	u	adult	1996	E	LLD	LLD	LLD	3,31	3,49	1085	2164	3,79
33/93	m	adult	1993	W	LLD	LLD	LLD	1,69	1,68	1080,33	506	3,15
34/93	u	adult	1993	W	LLD	LLD	LLD	1,14	LLD	946	LLD	17,13
34/96	m	adult	1996	E	LLD	LLD	LLD	3,6	0,78	1180,67	202,33	4,02
35/96	j	juv	1996	E	LLD	LLD	LLD	2,1	0,84	1031	216,67	10,73
36/93	u	adult	1993	W	LLD	LLD	LLD	2,18	LLD	918,67	LLD	15,9
37/93	f	adult	1993	W	LLD	LLD	LLD	0,58	1,08	556	238	31,27
4(B)	f	adult	1996	E	LLD	3,94	1,85	0,59	1,49	826,67	243	6,02
4/93	f	adult	1993	W	LLD	LLD	LLD	0,88	1,21	351,67	642	0,73
5/93	f	adult	1993	W	LLD	5,22	LLD	0,78	0,78	690,33	132,33	1,66
5bis	m	adult	1996	E	LLD	LLD	LLD	1,41	LLD	912,33	LLD	3,79
5n2	j	infl	1996	E	LLD	7,59	LLD	3,32	0,86	864,67	314,33	31,87
6/96	m	adult	1996	E	LLD	4,84	LLD	0,67	0,76	761,67	234,67	1,92
6QI/93	m	adult	1993	W	LLD	LLD	LLD	2,09	LLD	664,5	LLD	3,61
7/93	j	infl	1993	W	LLD	LLD	LLD	0,82	1,95	1130,33	364	8,73
7/96	u	adult	1996	E	LLD	LLD	LLD	0,92	0,86	635,33	256	5,58
8/93	m	adult	1993	W	LLD	LLD	LLD	0,69	1,48	425,33	416,67	0,55
8/96	f	adult	1996	E	LLD	11,39	LLD	0,87	0,99	738	215,33	2,19
9/93	u	adult	1993	E	LLD	4,47	LLD	0,91	LLD	894,67	LLD	1,7

Trace element values (in ppm) for bone and enamel samples at Sant'Abbondio. LLD indicates values below the Lower Limit of detection.

Appendix

ID	Gender	Age	Year	Area dep.	Y enamel	Zr bone	Zr enamel	Nb bone	Nb enamel	Sn bone	Sn enamel	La bone
1/93	m	adult	1993	W	4,53	53,87	13,83	1,34	0,29	5,72	6,79	0,86
1/96	f	adult	1996	E	21,37	188,33	49	2,28	1,47	1,05	2,11	1,65
10/96	f	juv	1996	E	7,91	132,33	14,1	1,74	0,19	0,74	1,28	5,02
11(B)	f	adult	1993	W	LLD	120,67	LLD	1,47	LLDD	LLD	LLD	0,91
11/96	m	adult	1996	E	0,57	96,67	7,52	1,19	0,69	LLD	0,62	1,79
12/93	f	juv	1993	W	13,27	20,63	38,1	0,66	0,38	19,03	4,12	0,87
12QVIII	m	adult	1996	E	6,1	LLD	23,23	LLD	0,23	LLD	1,24	LLD
13/93	m	adult	1993	W	9,43	302	15,57	2,9	0,24	0,6	2,38	1,82
13/96	j	infl	1996	E	14,43	281,67	49,7	2,71	0,58	LLD	1,04	3,23
14(B)	j	juv	1993	W	LLD	25,67	LLD	0,67	LLD	35,2	LLD	3,3
14/96	f	adult	1996	E	3,56	113,33	11,37	1,14	0,17	LLD	1,26	1,93
15(B)	u	adult	1993	W	LLD	35,33	LLD	0,73	LLD	8,68	LLD	4,95
15/96	u	adult	1996	E	LLD	77,17	LLD	0,78	LLD	LLD	LLD	0,9
16/96	j	infl	1996	E	13,53	218,67	15,13	2,04	0,3	0,51	18,37	6,35
17/93dec	j	infl	1993	W	6,73	23,33	21,93	0,69	0,89	9,95	1,49	38,17
17/93perm	j	infl	1993	W	20,03	23,33	111,33	0,69	1,82	9,95	LLD	38,17
17/96	j	juv	1996	E	LLD	208,33	LLD	2,4	LLD	LLD	LLD	7,05
18/96	m	adult	1996	E	3,21	LLD	2,51	LLD	0,42	LLD	0,34	LLD
18QI	m	adult	1993	W	2,26	182,67	14,47	2,08	0,69	0,62	2,68	2,97
19/96	m	adult	1996	E	35,23	211,67	50,83	2,19	0,59	LLD	1,45	13,83
2/93	m	adult	1993	W	12,73	35,7	26,23	1,18	0,26	1,74	2,92	2,24
2/96	f	adult	1996	E	1,65	182,67	7,1	2,26	0,38	0,81	5,42	3
20/93	f	adult	1993	W	3,61	14,53	10,25	0,38	0,22	16,37	1,76	6,87
20/96	u	adult	1996	E	LLD	171	LLD	1,76	LLD	LLD	LLD	3,19
21/96	u	adult	1996	E	2,84	185	21,23	1,65	0,31	LLD	0,94	6,28
21QIII	u	adult	1993	W	LLD	32,5	LLD	0,63	LLD	9,84	LLD	2,45
22/96	m	adult	1996	E	6,48	123,33	14,23	3,97	0,23	LLD	0,58	3,31
24/96	j	infl	1996	E	1,74	LLD	24,23	LLD	0,58	LLD	3,22	LLD
25(B)	u	adult	1993	W	LLD	136,33	LLD	1,21	LLD	3,04	LLD	5,74
25/96	m	adult	1996	E	5,49	172,67	29,57	3,28	0,82	LLD	1,29	2,8
26(B)	u	adult	1993	W	3,39	22,27	8,08	0,52	0,33	6,59	1,62	2,88
26/96	f	adult	1996	E	12,6	204	50,37	2,33	0,44	LLD	2,05	4,83
27/93	f	adult	1993	W	47,17	37,03	25,2	0,82	0,25	LLD	4,34	11,03
28/93	u	adult	1993	W	LLD	26,17	LLD	1,09	LLD	9,26	LLD	2,28
28/96	f	adult	1996	E	2,83	259,67	6,97	2,74	0,21	LLD	5,24	11,8
29(B)	f	adult	1993	W	16,4	21,77	21,23	0,4	0,75	7,41	75,77	5,84
29/96	f	adult	1996	E	2,45	212,67	14,2	3,55	0,21	0,73	3,49	6,3
2bis	j	infl	1993	W	0,58	201,33	10,69	4,45	0,53	LLD	4,86	10,3
3/96	m	adult	1996	E	1,13	133	4,86	2,1	0,36	LLD	0,61	1,11
30/93	m	juv	1993	W	22,2	110,33	11,13	2,62	0,38	LLD	0,47	3,77
31/93	f	adult	1993	W	3,53	33,33	5,3	0,55	0,13	8,06	8,84	1,38
31/96	u	adult	1996	E	37,57	178,33	213,33	3,46	1,93	LLD	3,26	4,29
33/93	m	adult	1993	W	3,91	187	7,18	2,65	0,17	LLD	4,3	2,51
34/93	u	adult	1993	W	LLD	190,67	LLD	2,61	LLD	LLD	LLD	35,83
34/96	m	adult	1996	E	19,63	164,33	43,53	3,74	0,43	LLD	0,85	5,82
35/96	j	juv	1996	E	8,3	274,67	15,43	2,56	0,14	LLD	1,74	7,75
36/93	u	adult	1993	W	LLD	262	LLD	3,67	LLD	LLD	LLD	29,5
37/93	f	adult	1993	W	111,67	18,57	35,9	0,55	0,57	3,7	2,35	49,67
4(B)	f	adult	1996	E	4,22	196,67	34,4	1,95	0,67	LLD	LLD	5,03
4/93	f	adult	1993	W	14,36	17,8	75,12	0,73	0,77	LLD	3,69	0,95
5/93	f	adult	1993	W	4,37	102,47	9,98	1,37	0,18	0,63	4,73	1,42
5bis	m	adult	1996	E	LLD	221,67	LLD	2,92	LLD	LLD	LLD	2,75
5n2	j	infl	1996	E	2	375	55,97	3,36	1,12	0,77	1,03	56,1
6/96	m	adult	1996	E	34,3	152,67	23,63	1,48	0,3	0,93	0,8	1,32
6QI/93	m	adult	1993	W	LLD	123,74	LLD	1,8	LLD	1,19	LLD	3,75
7/93	j	infl	1993	W	2,19	192	22,67	3,14	0,62	2,36	2,7	7,25
7/96	u	adult	1996	E	15,93	215,33	19,97	1,42	0,3	LLD	0,32	4,05
8/93	m	adult	1993	W	5,19	31,03	26,23	0,56	0,87	3,66	3,87	0,5
8/96	f	adult	1996	E	4,98	142,67	20,57	1,79	0,2	0,48	3,57	1,66
9/93	u	adult	1993	E	LLD	209,33	LLD	2,89	LLD	0,54	LLD	1,7

Trace element values (in ppm) for bone and enamel samples at Sant'Abbondio. LLD indicates values below the Lower Limit of detection.

Appendix

ID	Gender	Age	Year	Area dep.	La enamel	Ce bone	Ce enamel	Pr bone	Pr enamel	Nd bone	Nd enamel	Sm bone	Sm enamel
1/93	m	adult	1993	W	8,55	0,31	1,57	0,14	1,5	0,46	5,35	0,24	0,99
1/96	f	adult	1996	E	48,97	0,52	5,8	0,37	8,69	1,36	30,93	0,31	4,96
10/96	f	juv	1996	E	12,87	1,32	2,05	0,78	2,23	3,69	7,8	0,59	1,46
11(B)	f	adult	1993	W	LLD	0,53	LLD	0,21	LLD	1,1	LLD	LLD	LLD
11/96	m	adult	1996	E	1,08	0,78	0,29	0,29	0,18	1,35	0,71	0,24	0,11
12/93	f	juv	1993	W	20,23	0,59	5,03	0,18	3,63	0,6	12,8	0,56	2,31
12QVIII	m	adult	1996	E	12,77	LLD	2,21	LLD	2,28	LLD	7,8	LLD	1,37
13/93	m	adult	1993	W	18,97	1,02	2,77	0,27	3,21	1,23	11,8	LLD	2,11
13/96	j	infl	1996	E	28,2	0,94	6,7	0,66	4,45	2,36	16,17	0,59	2,56
14(B)	j	juv	1993	W	LLD	0,55	LLD	0,5	LLD	1,82	LLD	1,24	LLLD
14/96	f	adult	1996	E	6,9	0,96	1,26	0,4	1,27	1,64	5,01	0,4	0,8
15(B)	u	adult	1993	W	LLD	0,84	LLD	0,66	LLD	2,23	LLD	0,69	LLD
15/96	u	adult	1996	E	LLD	0,4	LLD	0,17	LLD	0,84	LLD	0,34	LLD
16/96	j	infl	1996	E	22,53	1,11	2,74	0,81	3,94	3,49	14,57	0,79	2,46
17/93dec	j	infl	1993	W	12,61	6,12	3,2	6,21	2,22	21,7	8,25	4,65	1,5
17/93perm	j	infl	1993	W	28,07	6,12	5,49	6,21	4,67	21,7	17,47	4,65	2,89
17/96	j	juv	1996	E	LLD	1,9	LLD	1,12	LLD	5,02	LLD	1,23	LLD
18/96	m	adult	1996	E	5,45	LLD	0,45	LLD	0,91	LLD	3,19	LLD	0,54
18QI	m	adult	1993	W	3,62	1,46	2,06	0,55	0,76	1,96	2,98	0,47	0,65
19/96	m	adult	1996	E	60,5	2,45	6,63	2	9,36	7,73	34,93	1,48	5,62
2/93	m	adult	1993	W	28,23	0,88	2,3	0,36	4,48	1,34	17,17	0,3	2,58
2/96	f	adult	1996	E	2,91	0,61	1,37	0,55	0,5	1,95	1,68	0,56	0,36
20/93	f	adult	1993	W	6,7	1,02	1,71	0,97	1,35	3,53	4,74	0,88	0,91
20/96	u	adult	1996	E	LLD	0,47	LLD	0,46	LLD	1,71	LLD	0,35	LLD
21/96	u	adult	1996	E	6,14	0,7	0,84	0,79	1,08	3,12	3,94	0,53	0,78
21QIII	u	adult	1993	W	LLD	0,67	LLD	0,45	LLD	1,52	LLD	0,49	LLD
22/96	m	adult	1996	E	13,63	1,47	1,13	0,68	2,45	2,66	8,93	0,52	1,55
24/96	j	infl	1996	E	3,14	LLD	0,81	LLD	0,55	LLD	2,08	LLD	0,43
25(B)	u	adult	1993	W	LLD	1,57	LLD	1,17	LLD	5,06	LLD	1,06	LLD
25/96	m	adult	1996	E	11,07	1,51	2,83	0,49	1,8	1,89	6,93	0,43	1,25
26(B)	u	adult	1993	W	6,2	0,82	0,83	0,59	0,97	2,85	3,94	0,77	0,84
26/96	f	adult	1996	E	22,97	1,55	6,59	0,86	4,11	3,69	15,3	0,66	2,56
27/93	f	adult	1993	W	72,63	1,65	5,11	1,6	11,03	5,63	41,4	0,99	6,5
28/93	u	adult	1993	W	LLD	0,37	LLD	0,28	LLD	1,14	LLD	0,48	LLD
28/96	f	adult	1996	E	5,11	1,53	1,28	1,71	0,85	6,89	3,02	1,06	0,57
29(B)	f	adult	1993	W	29,13	0,49	2,73	0,66	4,87	2,31	18,63	0,67	3,04
29/96	f	adult	1996	E	3,59	1,14	1,32	0,99	0,72	3,85	2,73	0,6	0,46
2bis	j	infl	1993	W	1,08	6,46	0,67	1,85	0,21	7,4	0,72	1,19	0,26
3/96	m	adult	1996	E	2,55	0,32	0,49	0,24	0,4	1,26	1,48	0,18	0,23
30/93	m	juv	1993	W	35,2	3,01	1,18	0,71	6,32	2,73	24,37	LLD	4,08
31/93	f	adult	1993	W	5,36	0,38	0,81	0,18	0,94	0,75	3,64	0,36	0,92
31/96	u	adult	1996	E	76,63	2,7	14,7	0,95	12,87	3,74	46,77	0,77	7,24
33/93	m	adult	1993	W	6,09	1,19	2,39	0,39	1,4	1,65	5,2	0,38	0,97
34/93	u	adult	1993	W	LLD	1,43	LLD	4,35	LLD	15,2	LLD	2,38	LLD
34/96	m	adult	1996	E	38,03	5,68	4,46	1,08	6,29	3,74	23,23	0,65	3,68
35/96	j	juv	1996	E	13,33	1,71	2,37	1,31	2,75	5,59	11,03	1,02	1,67
36/93	u	adult	1993	W	LLD	2,83	LLD	4,06	LLD	14,2	LLD	2,36	LLD
37/93	f	adult	1993	W	246,67	2,36	8,62	7,31	40,6	26,87	147	4,25	22,13
4(B)	f	adult	1996	E	9,15	0,77	1,37	0,79	1,71	3,19	6,06	0,72	1
4/93	f	adult	1993	W	24,5	1,11	6	0,2	4,08	0,61	15,8	0,15	2,65
5/93	f	adult	1993	W	9,58	0,45	3,06	0,24	1,69	0,95	6	0,29	0,95
5bis	m	adult	1996	E	LLD	1,06	LLD	0,57	LLD	2,54	LLD	0,5	LLD
5n2	j	infl	1996	E	3,04	12,47	0,79	8,7	0,48	30,07	1,8	5,06	0,33
6/96	m	adult	1996	E	62,27	0,32	3,16	0,24	8,75	1,29	33,23	0,28	5,19
6QI/93	m	adult	1993	W	LLD	2,51	LLD	0,61	LLD	2,18	LLD	0,38	LLD
7/93	j	infl	1993	W	3,45	1,38	2,18	1,12	0,65	4,61	2,5	1,04	0,65
7/96	u	adult	1996	E	32,2	0,92	2,95	0,56	4,82	2,78	16,97	0,68	2,8
8/93	m	adult	1993	W	7,96	0,17	2,23	0,07	1,52	0,29	6,11	0,15	1,01
8/96	f	adult	1996	E	7,73	0,37	2,64	0,27	1,39	1,17	5,27	0,28	0,97
9/93	u	adult	1993	E	LLD	0,68	LLD	0,28	LLD	1,54	LLD	0,31	LLD

Trace element values (in ppm) for bone and enamel samples at Sant'Abbondio. LLD indicates values below the Lower Limit of detection.

Appendix

ID	Gender	Age	Year	Area dep.	Eu151 bone	Eu151 enamel	Eu153 bone	Eu153 enamel	Gd bone	Gd enamel	Tb bone	Tb enamel
1/93	m	adult	1993	W	0,03	0,42	0,04	0,34	0,21	1,02	0,02	0,11
1/96	f	adult	1996	E	0,15	1,31	0,16	1,22	0,44	5,21	0,1	0,87
10/96	f	juv	1996	E	0,25	0,34	0,17	0,36	0,62	1,57	0,13	0,23
11(B)	f	adult	1993	W	LLD	LLD	LLD	LLD	0,24	LLD	0,05	LLD
11/96	m	adult	1996	E	0,09	0,03	0,08	0,06	0,3	0,09	0,04	0,02
12/93	f	juv	1993	W	0,06	0,52	0,07	0,46	0,18	2,39	0,03	0,31
12QVIII	m	adult	1996	E	LLD	0,31	LLD	0,29	LLD	1,12	LLD	0,16
13/93	m	adult	1993	W	0,11	0,39	LLD	0,38	0,37	1,93	0,07	0,25
13/96	j	infl	1996	E	0,17	0,56	0,17	0,53	0,56	2,64	0,09	0,34
14(B)	j	juv	1993	W	0,09	LLD	0,09	LLD	0,43	LLD	0,05	LLD
14/96	f	adult	1996	E	0,14	0,17	0,17	0,17	0,38	0,79	0,05	0,1
15(B)	u	adult	1993	W	0,12	LLD	0,13	LLD	0,62	LLD	0,08	LLD
15/96	u	adult	1996	E	0,09	LLD	0,07	LLD	LLD	LLD	0,04	LLD
16/96	j	infl	1996	E	0,2	0,53	0,26	0,52	0,74	2,6	0,14	0,33
17/93dec	j	infl	1993	W	0,74	0,31	0,71	0,31	3,79	1,29	0,52	0,2
17/93perm	j	infl	1993	W	0,74	0,64	0,71	0,62	3,79	2,43	0,52	0,45
17/96	j	juv	1996	E	0,23	LLD	0,22	LLD	0,99	LLD	0,14	LLD
18/96	m	adult	1996	E	LLD	0,15	LLD	0,18	LLD	0,64	LLD	0,12
18QI	m	adult	1993	W	0,13	0,15	0,15	0,14	0,51	0,67	0,11	0,1
19/96	m	adult	1996	E	0,31	1,14	0,38	1,32	1,2	5,83	0,2	0,82
2/93	m	adult	1993	W	0,09	0,57	0,09	0,49	0,25	2,72	0,06	0,29
2/96	f	adult	1996	E	0,14	0,07	0,17	0,08	0,39	0,27	0,12	0,06
20/93	f	adult	1993	W	0,14	0,21	0,16	0,18	0,81	0,69	0,1	0,15
20/96	u	adult	1996	E	0,2	LLD	0,14	LLD	0,33	LLD	0,05	LLD
21/96	u	adult	1996	E	0,2	0,16	0,16	0,18	0,73	0,73	0,08	0,1
21QIII	u	adult	1993	W	0,08	LLD	0,13	LLD	0,37	LLD	0,05	LLD
22/96	m	adult	1996	E	0,2	0,27	0,22	0,32	0,61	1,42	0,12	0,19
24/96	j	infl	1996	E	LLD	0,09	LLD	0,09	LLD	0,37	LLD	0,07
25(B)	u	adult	1993	W	0,27	LLD	0,18	LLD	0,87	LLD	0,12	LLD
25/96	m	adult	1996	E	0,15	0,22	0,15	0,25	0,41	1,11	0,08	0,16
26(B)	u	adult	1993	W	0,2	0,18	0,24	0,18	0,84	0,56	0,11	0,11
26/96	f	adult	1996	E	0,16	0,55	0,3	0,51	0,82	2,57	0,13	0,37
27/93	f	adult	1993	W	0,23	1,5	0,25	1,59	1,08	7,2	0,15	1,03
28/93	u	adult	1993	W	0,1	LLD	0,12	LLD	0,25	LLD	0,04	LLD
28/96	f	adult	1996	E	0,24	0,14	0,26	0,14	1,11	0,61	0,2	0,11
29(B)	f	adult	1993	W	0,17	0,64	0,17	0,74	0,58	2,78	0,11	0,44
29/96	f	adult	1996	E	0,27	0,11	0,24	0,14	0,96	0,43	0,12	0,06
2bis	j	infl	1993	W	0,31	0,09	0,36	0,08	1,67	0,19	0,17	LLD
3/96	m	adult	1996	E	0,11	0,07	0,1	0,07	0,33	0,19	0,03	0,05
30/93	m	juv	1993	W	0,16	0,82	0,19	0,84	0,61	3,81	0,09	0,47
31/93	f	adult	1993	W	0,04	0,12	0,06	0,12	0,25	0,65	0,03	0,11
31/96	u	adult	1996	E	0,22	1,48	0,2	1,52	0,8	7,49	0,11	0,9
33/93	m	adult	1993	W	0,13	0,18	0,09	0,21	0,35	0,78	0,06	0,17
34/93	u	adult	1993	W	0,54	LLD	0,55	LLD	2,53	LLD	0,26	LLD
34/96	m	adult	1996	E	0,19	0,77	0,24	0,75	0,61	3,47	0,09	0,49
35/96	j	juv	1996	E	0,27	0,41	0,29	0,37	1,04	1,7	0,17	0,25
36/93	u	adult	1993	W	0,51	LLD	0,58	LLD	2,72	LLD	0,32	LLD
37/93	f	adult	1993	W	0,91	4,66	1	4,56	4,65	19,47	0,62	2,55
4(B)	f	adult	1996	E	0,2	0,21	0,2	0,22	0,6	0,88	0,1	0,12
4/93	f	adult	1993	W	0,03	0,54	0,05	0,52	0,14	2,49	0,02	0,35
5/93	f	adult	1993	W	0,1	0,21	0,11	0,22	0,38	0,95	0,04	0,13
5bis	m	adult	1996	E	0,11	LLD	0,15	LLD	0,41	LLD	0,12	LLD
5n2	j	infl	1996	E	0,99	0,08	1,03	0,09	5,34	0,3	0,74	0,05
6/96	m	adult	1996	E	0,09	0,98	0,14	1,02	0,22	5,14	0,05	0,64
6QI/93	m	adult	1993	W	0,11	LLD	0,13	LLD	0,56	LLD	0,08	LLD
7/93	j	infl	1993	W	0,24	0,12	0,25	0,14	1,16	0,33	0,16	0,05
7/96	u	adult	1996	E	0,12	0,57	0,17	0,63	0,78	2,78	0,11	0,42
8/93	m	adult	1993	W	0,04	0,25	0,05	0,26	0,1	1	LLD	0,19
8/96	f	adult	1996	E	0,11	0,21	0,15	0,23	0,29	0,99	0,05	0,15
9/93	u	adult	1993	E	0,12	LLD	0,11	LLD	0,21	LLD	0,05	LLD

Trace element values (in ppm) for bone and enamel samples at Sant'Abbondio. LLD indicates values below the Lower Limit of detection.

ID	Gender	Age	Year	Area dep.	Dy bone	Dy enamel	Ho bone	Ho enamel	Er bone	Er enamel	Tm bone	Tm enamel
1/93	m	adult	1993 W	0,11	0,7	0,04	0,13	0,08	0,44	0,03	0,06
1/96	f	adult	1996 E	0,41	3,35	0,12	0,88	0,36	1,91	0,1	0,53
10/96	f	juv	1996 E	0,63	0,98	0,13	0,3	0,49	0,72	0,11	0,17
11(B)	f	adult	1993 W	0,18	LLD	0,07	LLD	LLD	LLD	LLD	LLD
11/96	m	adult	1996 E	0,22	0,1	0,07	0,03	0,36	0,05	0,04	LLD
12/93	f	juv	1993 W	0,14	1,73	0,04	0,33	0,09	1,16	0,02	0,19
12QVIII	m	adult	1996 E	LLD	0,88	LLD	0,17	LLD	0,46	LLD	0,06
13/93	m	adult	1993 W	0,29	1,16	0,09	0,27	0,23	0,94	LLD	0,13
13/96	j	infl	1996 E	0,48	1,84	0,13	0,36	0,45	1,17	0,08	0,17
14(B)	j	juv	1993 W	0,23	LLD	0,08	LLD	0,19	LLD	0,04	LLD
14/96	f	adult	1996 E	0,43	0,59	0,1	0,09	0,46	0,26	0,1	LLD
15(B)	u	adult	1993 W	0,45	LLD	0,12	LLD	0,29	LLD	0,07	LLD
15/96	u	adult	1996 E	LLD	LLD	0,07	LLD	0,16	LLD	0,05	LLD
16/96	j	infl	1996 E	0,65	1,66	0,18	0,39	0,73	1,1	0,18	0,28
17/93dec	j	infl	1993 W	3,19	0,96	0,67	0,21	1,88	0,56	0,31	0,25
17/93perm	j	infl	1993 W	3,19	2,36	0,67	0,57	1,88	1,6	0,31	0,25
17/96	j	juv	1996 E	0,82	LLD	0,25	LLD	0,8	LLD	0,13	LLD
18/96	m	adult	1996 E	LLD	0,39	LLD	0,12	LLD	0,25	LLD	0,11
18QI	m	adult	1993 W	0,49	0,37	0,11	0,07	0,32	0,28	LLD	LLD
19/96	m	adult	1996 E	1,1	4,6	0,28	0,93	1,02	2,81	0,19	0,41
2/93	m	adult	1993 W	0,24	1,94	0,06	0,35	0,21	0,98	0,04	0,12
2/96	f	adult	1996 E	0,42	0,21	0,12	0,07	0,37	0,1	0,08	0,02
20/93	f	adult	1993 W	0,62	0,58	0,14	0,12	0,4	0,36	0,08	0,09
20/96	u	adult	1996 E	0,4	LLD	0,09	LLD	0,32	LLD	0,09	LLD
21/96	u	adult	1996 E	0,52	0,43	0,2	0,09	0,62	0,24	0,1	0,11
21QIII	u	adult	1993 W	0,33	LLD	0,06	LLD	0,21	LLD	0,04	LLD
22/96	m	adult	1996 E	0,43	0,91	0,13	0,15	0,29	0,53	0,08	0,07
24/96	j	infl	1996 E	LLD	0,18	LLD	0,06	LLD	0,13	LLD	LLD
25(B)	u	adult	1993 W	0,76	LLD	0,16	LLD	0,53	LLD	0,05	LLD
25/96	m	adult	1996 E	0,2	0,76	0,1	0,18	0,22	0,46	LLD	0,08
26(B)	u	adult	1993 W	0,68	0,59	0,17	0,08	0,53	0,29	0,11	0,07
26/96	f	adult	1996 E	0,63	1,74	0,11	0,36	0,48	1,07	0,07	0,2
27/93	f	adult	1993 W	0,88	5,46	0,21	1,18	0,63	3,49	0,11	0,56
28/93	u	adult	1993 W	0,2	LLD	0,07	LLD	0,2	LLD	0,05	LLD
28/96	f	adult	1996 E	1,26	0,39	0,31	0,12	0,86	0,26	0,09	0,17
29(B)	f	adult	1993 W	0,49	2,09	0,11	0,52	0,51	1,35	0,08	0,24
29/96	f	adult	1996 E	0,84	0,37	0,24	0,08	0,65	0,22	0,09	0,05
2bis	j	infl	1993 W	1,25	LLD	0,28	LLD	0,89	LLD	0,13	LLD
3/96	m	adult	1996 E	0,18	0,14	0,09	0,03	0,24	0,1	0,06	LLD
30/93	m	juv	1993 W	0,49	2,62	0,1	0,56	0,23	1,58	LLD	0,21
31/93	f	adult	1993 W	0,19	0,55	0,05	0,09	0,15	0,33	0,03	0,07
31/96	u	adult	1996 E	0,66	4,86	0,14	0,97	0,33	2,6	0,06	0,36
33/93	m	adult	1993 W	0,38	0,89	0,08	0,55	0,25	0,38	LLD	0,1
34/93	u	adult	1993 W	1,51	LLD	0,39	LLD	1,22	LLD	0,15	LLD
34/96	m	adult	1996 E	0,65	2,51	0,12	0,5	0,37	1,52	LLD	0,27
35/96	j	juv	1996 E	1,13	1,17	0,32	0,24	0,91	0,62	0,12	0,12
36/93	u	adult	1993 W	1,83	LLD	0,39	LLD	1,25	LLD	0,14	LLD
37/93	f	adult	1993 W	3,49	13,57	0,74	2,8	2,46	8,01	0,37	1,01
4(B)	f	adult	1996 E	0,61	0,61	0,18	0,14	0,73	0,33	0,12	LLD
4/93	f	adult	1993 W	0,09	1,86	LLD	0,38	0,06	1,07	0,02	0,16
5/93	f	adult	1993 W	0,25	0,76	LLD	0,15	0,21	0,37	0,04	0,06
5bis	m	adult	1996 E	0,64	LLD	0,11	LLD	0,48	LLD	LLD	LLD
5n2	j	infl	1996 E	4,83	0,21	0,96	0,05	2,99	0,17	0,45	LLD
6/96	m	adult	1996 E	0,26	3,75	LLD	0,82	0,25	2,32	0,06	0,34
6QI/93	m	adult	1993 W	0,48	LLD	0,1	LLD	0,3	LLD	0,03	LLD
7/93	j	infl	1993 W	1,05	0,34	0,24	LLD	0,89	0,22	0,13	LLD
7/96	u	adult	1996 E	0,48	2,2	0,17	0,43	0,77	1,26	0,09	0,18
8/93	m	adult	1993 W	0,09	0,9	0,02	0,15	0,06	0,52	0,02	0,13
8/96	f	adult	1996 E	0,31	0,7	0,07	0,13	0,29	0,38	0,08	0,08
9/93	u	adult	1993 E	0,23	LLD	LLD	LLD	0,27	LLD	0,04	LLD

Trace element values (in ppm) for bone and enamel samples at Sant'Abbondio. LLD indicates values below the Lower Limit of detection.

Appendix

ID	Gender	Age	Year	Area dep.	Yb bone	Yb enamel	Lu bone	Lu enamel	Hf bone	Hf enamel	Ta bone	Ta enamel
1/93	m	adult	1993	W	0,12	0,27	0,03	0,08	0,53	0,48	0,61	0,25
1/96	f	adult	1996	E	0,49	1,76	0,13	0,47	2,54	0,64	0,47	0,52
10/96	f	juv	1996	E	0,61	0,69	0,11	0,14	1,8	0,1	0,14	0,05
11(B)	f	adult	1993	W	0,23	LLD	LLD	LLD	0,81	LLD	0,09	LLD
11/96	m	adult	1996	E	0,28	0,08	LLD	0,03	1,44	0,34	0,17	0,12
12/93	f	juv	1993	W	0,18	1,34	0,03	0,14	0,21	0,53	0,09	0,24
12QVIII	m	adult	1996	E	LLD	0,42	LLD	0,06	LLD	0,23	LLD	0,06
13/93	m	adult	1993	W	0,45	0,7	0,06	0,09	1,26	0,17	0,24	0,11
13/96	j	infl	1996	E	0,39	1,11	0,07	0,17	1,46	0,51	0,16	0,1
14(B)	j	juv	1993	W	0,22	LLD	0,04	LLD	0,25	LLD	0,55	LLD
14/96	f	adult	1996	E	0,37	0,26	0,09	0,04	0,81	0,2	0,1	0,06
15(B)	u	adult	1993	W	0,44	LLD	0,08	LLD	0,86	LLD	0,25	LLD
15/96	u	adult	1996	E	0,14	LLD	LLD	LLD	0,48	LLD	0,07	LLD
16/96	j	infl	1996	E	0,87	1	0,16	0,17	3,24	0,17	0,25	0,1
17/93dec	j	infl	1993	W	2,1	0,75	0,31	0,13	0,5	0,3	0,2	0,08
17/93perm	j	infl	1993	W	2,1	2,01	0,31	0,26	0,5	0,92	0,2	0,17
17/96	j	juv	1996	E	0,92	LLD	0,15	LLD	1,56	LLD	0,15	LLD
18/96	m	adult	1996	E	LLD	0,21	LLD	0,06	LLD	0,17	LLD	0,14
18QI	m	adult	1993	W	0,47	0,26	0,09	0,05	2,96	1,1	0,37	0,32
19/96	m	adult	1996	E	0,91	2,66	0,15	0,42	1,29	0,36	0,21	0,09
2/93	m	adult	1993	W	0,25	0,89	0,06	0,14	0,89	0,23	0,32	0,1
2/96	f	adult	1996	E	0,49	0,14	0,09	0,03	1,21	0,16	0,28	0,12
20/93	f	adult	1993	W	0,55	0,28	0,09	0,09	0,14	0,69	0,1	0,24
20/96	u	adult	1996	E	0,4	LLD	0,1	LLD	1,13	LLD	0,1	LLD
21/96	u	adult	1996	E	0,77	0,24	0,11	0,06	1,56	0,22	0,1	0,06
21QIII	u	adult	1993	W	0,27	LLD	0,04	LLD	0,3	LLD	0,1	LLD
22/96	m	adult	1996	E	0,46	0,5	0,08	0,07	2,8	0,17	0,59	0,05
24/96	j	infl	1996	E	LLD	0,2	LLD	0,04	LLD	0,52	LLD	0,14
25(B)	u	adult	1993	W	0,56	LLD	0,09	LLD	0,86	LLD	0,19	LLD
25/96	m	adult	1996	E	0,34	0,46	LLD	0,09	1,81	0,33	0,23	0,08
26(B)	u	adult	1993	W	0,63	0,37	0,14	0,07	0,18	0,21	0,08	0,17
26/96	f	adult	1996	E	0,71	1,2	0,12	0,18	1,6	0,43	0,19	0,08
27/93	f	adult	1993	W	0,68	3,53	0,11	0,52	0,19	0,35	0,13	0,08
28/93	u	adult	1993	W	0,26	LLD	0,07	LLD	1,01	LLD	0,28	LLD
28/96	f	adult	1996	E	0,93	0,19	0,14	0,09	1,15	0,07	0,11	0,06
29(B)	f	adult	1993	W	0,56	1,38	0,1	0,19	0,31	0,74	0,1	0,3
29/96	f	adult	1996	E	0,53	0,23	0,11	0,03	2,87	0,25	0,43	0,07
2bis	j	infl	1993	W	0,84	LLD	0,16	LLD	2,16	1,17	0,18	0,69
3/96	m	adult	1996	E	0,36	0,15	0,07	LLD	1,45	0,07	0,29	0,08
30/93	m	juv	1993	W	0,31	1,31	LLD	0,19	0,67	0,55	0,18	0,11
31/93	f	adult	1993	W	0,23	0,31	0,04	0,06	0,25	0,42	0,11	0,16
31/96	u	adult	1996	E	0,43	2,58	0,07	0,38	1,35	1,03	0,17	0,13
33/93	m	adult	1993	W	0,63	0,55	0,07	0,09	0,92	0,28	0,09	0,45
34/93	u	adult	1993	W	1,35	LLD	0,17	LLD	1,26	LLD	0,11	LLD
34/96	m	adult	1996	E	0,43	1,36	LLD	0,21	0,76	0,26	0,19	0,08
35/96	j	juv	1996	E	1,21	0,62	0,17	0,09	1,58	0,07	0,16	0,05
36/93	u	adult	1993	W	1,18	LLD	0,16	LLD	1,71	LLD	0,1	LLD
37/93	f	adult	1993	W	2,21	6,53	0,35	0,84	0,16	0,92	0,13	0,27
4(B)	f	adult	1996	E	0,81	0,38	0,12	0,05	1,9	0,36	0,21	0,07
4/93	f	adult	1993	W	0,09	1,18	0,02	0,17	0,25	0,7	0,14	0,13
5/93	f	adult	1993	W	0,27	0,41	0,05	0,06	1,05	0,15	0,15	0,08
5bis	m	adult	1996	E	0,55	LLD	0,12	LLD	2,03	LLD	0,26	LLD
5n2	j	infl	1996	E	3,11	0,23	0,45	0,04	4,79	0,71	0,3	0,17
6/96	m	adult	1996	E	0,29	2,15	0,06	0,31	1,98	0,22	0,22	0,09
6QI/93	m	adult	1993	W	0,44	LLD	0,07	LLD	0,85	LLD	0,2	LLD
7/93	j	infl	1993	W	1,04	LLD	0,15	LLD	1,12	0,32	0,09	0,09
7/96	u	adult	1996	E	0,73	1,16	0,11	0,16	1,95	0,18	0,14	0,06
8/93	m	adult	1993	W	0,1	0,6	0,03	0,1	0,27	1,9	0,13	0,5
8/96	f	adult	1996	E	0,33	0,43	0,05	0,06	1,09	0,13	0,14	0,06
9/93	u	adult	1993	E	0,18	LLD	0,05	LLD	1,27	LLD	0,11	LLD

Trace element values (in ppm) for bone and enamel samples at Sant'Abbondio. LLD indicates values below the Lower Limit of detection.

Appendix

ID	Gender	Age	Year	Area dep.	Au bone	Au enamel	Pb bone	Pb enamel	Th bone	Th enamel	U bone	U enamel
1/93	m	adult	1993	W	1,24	LLD	2,39	LLD	0,27	1,02	30,13	5,37
1/96	f	adult	1996	E	2,25	1,3	1,96	3,42	2,33	2,03	34,87	2,03
10/96	f	juv	1996	E	LLD	0,21	3,27	1	1,89	0,51	60,43	0,67
11(B)	f	adult	1993	W	LLD	LLD	LLD	LLD	0,4	LLD	53,63	LLD
11/96	m	adult	1996	E	LLD	0,29	1,84	0,34	0,94	0,99	44,37	18,93
12/93	f	juv	1993	W	LLD	LLD	1,94	5,95	0,16	1,67	28,9	2,89
12QVIII	m	adult	1996	E	LLD	0,18	LLD	0,91	LLD	0,91	LLD	0,62
13/93	m	adult	1993	W	LLD	LLD	2,15	LLD	0,46	1,1	32,33	2,63
13/96	j	infl	1996	E	LLD	0,21	2,72	3,28	0,86	1,88	30,13	2,71
14(B)	j	juv	1993	W	LLD	LLD	4,86	LLD	0,16	LLD	33	LLD
14/96	f	adult	1996	E	LLD	0,18	1,55	1,23	0,56	0,58	28,83	1,54
15(B)	u	adult	1993	W	1,36	LLD	1,13	LLD	1,23	LLD	23,13	LLD
15/96	u	adult	1996	E	LLD	LLD	1,08	LLD	0,21	LLD	29,33	LLD
16/96	j	infl	1996	E	0,41	0,21	2,51	5,94	2,51	0,86	27,8	1,93
17/93dec	j	infl	1993	W	0,36	LLD	6,01	0,66	1,08	1,01	36,6	31,7
17/93perm	j	infl	1993	W	0,36	LLD	6,01	2,2	1,08	2,64	36,6	37,47
17/96	j	juv	1996	E	LLD	LLD	0,74	LLD	0,94	LLD	41,23	LLD
18/96	m	adult	1996	E	LLD	0,24	LLD	0,35	LLD	0,78	LLD	0,35
18QI	m	adult	1993	W	LLD	30,4	1,77	3,52	2,81	3,06	54,5	9,8
19/96	m	adult	1996	E	LLD	0,13	0,8	3,9	1,29	2,28	39,27	8,74
2/93	m	adult	1993	W	1,25	LLD	1,35	2,13	0,93	1,3	21,07	3,42
2/96	f	adult	1996	E	0,5	0,33	2,61	5,39	0,83	0,6	42,5	0,39
20/93	f	adult	1993	W	LLD	LLD	1,2	1,74	0,19	1,5	16,73	1,37
20/96	u	adult	1996	E	LLD	LLD	1,18	LLD	0,42	LLD	41,97	LLD
21/96	u	adult	1996	E	7,02	LLD	2,49	0,55	0,61	0,45	23,3	10,4
21QIII	u	adult	1993	W	LLD	LLD	1,58	LLD	0,19	LLD	32,43	LLD
22/96	m	adult	1996	E	LLD	0,14	1,91	0,47	2,48	0,43	55,9	1,75
24/96	j	infl	1996	E	LLD	0,21	LLD	1,57	LLD	1,46	LLD	2,83
25(B)	u	adult	1993	W	LLD	LLD	LLD	LLD	0,56	LLD	52,5	LLD
25/96	m	adult	1996	E	LLD	0,21	7,17	2,04	1,07	0,95	42,67	8,78
26(B)	u	adult	1993	W	LLD	LLD	1,59	LLD	0,09	0,5	24,03	18,47
26/96	f	adult	1996	E	LLD	0,38	LLD	4	1,01	1,93	54,97	3,14
27/93	f	adult	1993	W	LLD	LLD	1,52	4,34	0,24	2,21	14,43	1,11
28/93	u	adult	1993	W	1,36	LLD	3,63	LLD	1,04	LLD	26	LLD
28/96	f	adult	1996	E	LLD	0,26	0,78	1,89	0,86	0,21	43,2	1,55
29(B)	f	adult	1993	W	0,17	0,65	1,75	13,2	0,16	3,12	28,63	11,13
29/96	f	adult	1996	E	LLD	0,16	0,89	2,18	2,38	0,35	50	2,46
2bis	j	infl	1993	W	LLD	LLD	1,6	3,79	3,72	2,67	56,57	3,62
3/96	m	adult	1996	E	0,29	0,25	1,25	0,57	0,71	0,19	25,67	5,95
30/93	m	juv	1993	W	LLD	LLD	1,44	LLD	0,99	1,81	72,03	16,9
31/93	f	adult	1993	W	LLD	LLD	2,24	LLD	0,1	0,94	26,1	0,56
31/96	u	adult	1996	E	LLD	0,15	2,31	10,83	0,97	1,79	53,03	48,53
33/93	m	adult	1993	W	LLD	LLD	LLD	1,3	0,74	0,72	37,23	1,25
34/93	u	adult	1993	W	LLD	LLD	0,75	LLD	0,99	LLD	59,97	LLD
34/96	m	adult	1996	E	LLD	0,19	3,97	2,11	1,24	0,83	51,77	3,72
35/96	j	juv	1996	E	LLD	0,25	2,11	0,93	1,14	0,49	42,47	0,77
36/93	u	adult	1993	W	LLD	LLD	2,38	LLD	1	LLD	66,07	LLD
37/93	f	adult	1993	W	0,32	0,64	1,65	4,77	0,38	5,04	35,13	2,06
4(B)	f	adult	1996	E	LLD	0,21	2,64	0,95	0,61	0,95	23,17	5,49
4/93	f	adult	1993	W	0,33	LLD	1,09	5,6	0,22	1,98	18,43	11,93
5/93	f	adult	1993	W	0,29	0,14	1,45	6,92	0,46	0,49	45,3	2,27
5bis	m	adult	1996	E	LLD	LLD	1,39	LLD	1,69	LLD	51,93	LLD
5n2	j	infl	1996	E	0,44	0,23	11,67	1,38	4,32	0,98	97	24,63
6/96	m	adult	1996	E	0,7	0,19	12,5	1,42	1,1	1,37	42,87	2,07
6QI/93	m	adult	1993	W	0,68	LLD	2,27	LLD	0,68	LLD	25,51	LLD
7/93	j	infl	1993	W	LLD	LLD	1,83	4,98	1,05	0,73	38,93	5,57
7/96	u	adult	1996	E	LLD	0,13	4,05	0,59	0,94	1,04	17,47	5,6
8/93	m	adult	1993	W	LLD	1,08	1,6	6,1	0,08	4,45	26,57	12,1
8/96	f	adult	1996	E	0,65	0,13	2,09	4,6	0,47	0,58	40,33	0,91
9/93	u	adult	1993	E	LLD	LLD	2,64	LLD	0,54	LLD	29,57	LLD

Trace element values (in ppm) for bone and enamel samples at Sant'Abbondio. LLD indicates values below the Lower Limit of detection.

www.ingramcontent.com/pod-product-compliance
Lightning Source LLC
Chambersburg PA
CBHW061545010526
44113CB00023B/2803

9 781841 718040